Four *in* Thirteen Chambers

Four *in* Thirteen Chambers

V. N. Lewis

ARCHWAY
PUBLISHING

Archway Publishing books may be ordered through booksellers or by contacting:

Archway Publishing
1663 Liberty Drive
Bloomington, IN 47403
www.archwaypublishing.com
1 (888) 242-5904

ISBN: 978-1-4808-5061-3 (sc)
ISBN: 978-1-4808-5062-0 (e)

Library of Congress Control Number: 2017950796

Print information available on the last page.

Archway Publishing rev. date: 8/28/2017

~ Keep our head to the sky and we will have the prize ~
Four in Thirteen Chambers
V. N. Lewis

CONTENTS

HOW TO READ THIS BOOK

It is important that you read this book as an equation. *Four in Thirteen Chambers* is similar to a deck of cards in that 4 multiplied by 13 is 52, just as there are four suits of thirteen cards each in a deck. This book has fifty-two chapters. The depth of *Four in Thirteen Chambers* is shaped like a fish. The beginning of the book is the head and has the most pages, while the very ending chapters are in length as a tailfin and are not long at all. The chapters are in order by four sets. For example, chapter 37 is "Challenge," chapter 38 is "Win," chapter 39 is "Opportunity," and all equals the last chapter in that set: chapter 40, "Success." It is also important for you to keep in mind that the chapters are allegorical to the only four things we need in life, which are companionship, rest, food, and defense mechanisms. We can easily translate the chapters into the necessities of limitless survival categories.

INTRODUCTION

The middle of October marked the one-year anniversary of my resignation and departure from a well-known multibillion-dollar corporation. My former job paid well and provided decent employee benefits. Even though I was working for one of the richest corporations in America, I felt poor, uninspired, and manual. Going to work in a timely manner; punching in at a clock to routinely do the same job tasks as a cashier and pharmacy assistant; and seeing the same people over and over again did not seem to have much purpose. It was after I quit that I felt rich and prosperous; thus, it was not easy at first to adjust. The malicious deeds and negative energy that had circulated in my workplace resulted in a feeling of relief upon my departure. The cries from customers, members, and dopeheads about the urgency of their prescriptions had become humdrum to me all of a sudden. It was as if my foot was on the gas pedal with some insurmountable force guiding the steering wheel as I was blindfolded.

To top it off, my father, Mark Dewaine Lewis, passed on August 29, 2013, because of the side effects of pain management prescriptions while he was battling the complications of diabetes and pancreatic cancer. When I returned to Houston from Fort Worth after I had buried my father, there was no consolation. Rather, I was concerned about getting back to my regular way of working. That time was an excruciatingly intense period for me because of all the circumstances in my hometown. For some reason, I blamed myself for my dad's deteriorating illness, linking it to my move to Houston, even though I clearly knew the status of my father's terminal illness. I had to get away from the feelings of an oppressive trap in cow town. My adventuresome outlook on life and tendency to take chances led me to the armpit city of Houston, Texas. My move back to this North Texas city (Fort Worth) I call home is where my mysterious journey began, and without it I would not be able to write about the many encounters I had that are revealed in these words.

CHAPTER 1

Truth

Love all, trust a few, do wrong to none.
—William Shakespeare, *All's Well That Ends Well*

This first chapter covers the significance of trust because it is the most important value in relationships. In my earlier years, I placed love above trust until I realized how meaningful trust is in our spiritual and earthly connections. Trust in our God-mind will cure any form of illness, disease, and sickness. We can take the life force of believing and having faith in a higher intelligence and transfer that higher energy to a recipient. We literally can move mountains simply because we all operate symbiotically with every form of matter. Every person here on Earth is like a short circuit of energy without separation. This means that a *feeling* can over-take one's subconscious mind and can be transferable to another body. As in physics, *energy in* equals *energy out*, *input* equals *output*, *work in* equals *work out*, and so on.

I have repetitively contemplated the Adam-and-Eve scenario since I was about six, when I had my Bible picture book. God created Adam in the image of himself, and Adam got so lonely that he wanted a partner who complemented him. So God created his opposite, Eve, to be his companion. Then later God told Adam and Eve not to eat a fruit from a specific tree, but Eve broke the rules and enticed Adam to eat the forbidden fruit, with a serpent in the mix. What I am confused about, though, is the shame in nudity and Eve having to go through a painful childbirth because of her having sided with a snake. So the serpent told Eve to eat the apple, fig, or whatever was forbidden in order to defy God. Eve then picked the fruit from the tree and shared it with Adam. Nevertheless, Adam hid the truth after God told him not to eat any fruit from such tree. God found out, cast them out of the Garden of Eden, and made the serpent the lowest of all animals. Both of them had to cover up with leaves and bear fur. At least this is how it was depicted in my children's Bible storybook. Interpreting religious storytelling into spiritual practices simplifies what really happened at the beginning of carnal creation. The significant tree represents genesis itself—genetics, children, descendants, family, spinal cord, and limbs. The fruit, such as an apple, represents technology, telephones, text messaging, telepathy, and all forms of communication. The butting serpent is representative of knowledge, wanting to know, inventions, school, criteria, healing, pharmaceuticals, and

1

man-made objects engineered through the work of the creator. These three objects signal the way to one's power in the universal mind. The excuse of labor being forced upon them when they ate the forbidden fruit is suspect. Now, the tree of life, I feel, is symbolic of fornication as well. Eve and Adam found pain and pleasure in the sex they endured, and before their sexual encounter they didn't care to be naked, for they did not know a body was simply something to ground them. The lust of Adam for Eve and their bad thoughts turned into more ugly thoughts of defilement committed against a woman. The act of sex brought shame to their thoughts, and they felt a certain way for each other. A thought of replacing God with a human body with regard to companionship is what led Adam and Eve out of paradise. Thus, they were ashamed of their bodies when they were caught in the act of fornicating. They felt pain, anguish, and despair in and toward their bodies. At the beginning, each was only a soul, but the fall created the mind-body. Furthermore, Adam and Eve were companions and mates, but they were also adversaries because of their humanistic differences. I'm quite sure with the story of Adam and Eve that Eve had come to the conclusion that she could not trust Adam, because he had kept the forbidden fruit a secret after the lecture from God. In return for her form of disobedience, Eve was the first woman to bear excruciating pain during childbirth. Thus, we have epidurals to take care of that (knowledge). Foremost, speaking about the differences and thoughts regarding Adam and Eve's separation happens over and over again until we become one with our higher selves—and God. Once we realize that a body is just a whole atom of us, a mind is just a part of us, and a soul burns eternally for all of us, then we can become whole (holy) once again—to where we truly want to be. The real mystery is the existence that happened before Eve and Adam's story began.

I want the whole truth and nothing but the truth, so help me God. The search for the absolute truth in matters can be a never-ending journey. As human beings, we can avoid spoken words in order to mask truths. Our vulnerability to one another can leave us blind to the perils that we face. The superego, id, and ego can get in the way of exploring our true self-confidence. True self-confidence improves our livelihood, relationships, and well-being. It is through belief and faith that we can unveil the truth, and everything becomes so much clearer on the reminiscent cloud.

A lot of souls think that being quiet and reserved are forms of weakness. But I say that in being that way, you get to see the advantages of what life has to offer, like how people take advantage of a blind person. You get to see the truth in other individuals. To never let people see that you are coming is a wise decision.

In July 2010, I was contemplating all the troubling obstacles that I had encountered in my life. It was a sad time for me because I could not understand why certain individuals were behaving rudely toward me. Therefore, I went upstairs to my bedroom alone to have a conversation with the Almighty. I got down on my knees near my bed and prayed to Jesus, God, to give me the answers to my shortcomings. I searched deep inside my mind, body, and soul for a solution. I asked what sin I had ever committed to be treated so unfairly by any adversaries. I finally confessed, felt convicted, and repented to my Lord and Savior Jesus Christ. I also asked for forgiveness and that may my adversaries be forgiven as well. Even though my convictions may have been petty at the time, it was the feeling of victimhood that opened an anointing presence on me.

Afterward, I felt as light as a feather and like a weight had been lifted off my shoulders; I could not remember what type of person I had been before then. I went through a rebirthing process, and I was finding it hard to recollect some of my character from before. From then on, without my control, I had to walk, talk, think, eat, and rest differently, like a newborn.

All this time, I had been looking for truth in people, places, and things, and Jesus Christ was always right by me, with the universal God, directing the path. I could even smell the holy presence of anointment as my soul burned with enlightenment after being convicted. I had become more sensitive than ever, possessed by the grace of the Lord. I have been shown miracles, and now I have a better perspective on life. You see, I was never the problem; perhaps there was never a problem at all. It was just a circumstance that led me to breaking down into a portal of serendipity. My soul now burns like a flame. I am definitely not the same person I was before, and to this day I evolve through all processes. I understand that all of us are living either in heaven or in hell. We can make the best of any obstacle and become an evolution of mighty strength with experience.

The world is a paradise. Just look at all the wonders outside. All of creation was formed on Earth with initiations of bacteria, fungi, parasites, and viruses that roamed the globe before any other form of life. It is what you make it. To give love to the world, I imagine a matrix, a bright light of rainbow colors, and I take that light from my heart and picture myself spreading it to the world—or maybe just to a specific person. It really is that easy and simple to give love that way and to shine your light, like many teachers, such as Christ, would spread it abroad to the universe. Seek and you shall find the truth, in Jesus' name. Amen.

It is when we weep, rejoice, or yearn for the Lord that he will appear. Trust makes you determine how many friends you will keep. Trust holds relationships together because of the essence of communicating truthfully and sensibly, allowing people to believe in you. The truth is the foundation of certainty and stability. One way God makes truth valid is through places, people, and things. Scripture says in Joshua 1:9, "Have I not commanded you? Be strong and courageous. Do not be terrified; do not be discouraged for the LORD your God will be with you wherever you go."

CHAPTER 2

Love

Love is patient, love is kind. It does not envy, it does not boast, it is not proud. It does not dishonor others, it is not self-seeking, it is not easily angered, it keeps no record of wrongs. Love does not delight in evil but rejoices with the truth. It always protects, always trusts, always hopes, it always perseveres. Love never fails. But where there are prophecies, they will cease; where there are tongues, they will be stilled; where there is knowledge, it will pass away.
—1 Corinthians 13:4–8

To paraphrase the scripture above, love has no boundaries. A person can love another without trusting him or her, as such love can be blinding. Some people just want the love without the truth. True love is always shared between you and the Lord. The Lord is love and light. Love is patient in a sense that everything is all right. It may be patient, but love does not wait either, for love will transfer somewhere else when taken for granted. Patience is consistent, just like a Ferris wheel at a carnival. If love is taken for granted, it will be patient forever in a lifetime for constant reassurance from other sources. Just as there are reasons to every season, there is a reason for everything. There are no coincidences in this universe. The cause-and-effect theory signifies that for every action, there is a reaction. Our actions (causes), whether communicated through technology, created through inspiration, or gathered by knowledge, always result in a recipient reaction (effect). Therefore, if we are mainly givers, it is assumed that we will receive in abundance. But receiving can be the hardest obstacle for some individuals because of pride and egotism. In order to grasp love, we have to be open to receiving its magnetic energy.

Love is kind. Like the light of the Lord, love does not hurt others. It is pure satisfaction of happiness for others. Love rejoices in the truth, for the truth can set love free from doubt. It does not condone evil tactics to make others jealous. An unconditional love keeps no record of wrongs; it holds no grudges. Love always hopes that the next day will be a better day. It perseveres in moments, lives in the now, doesn't ponder in the past, and has no worries for the future. Love will never die for everybody seeks it, whether through the many aspects of the universal God or through one another. Limiting love between human beings is a sure way to grasp the godly love that is special to every individual. Love is the only religion.

For quite some time, I thought that love was an emotion we experienced just for people. As I got older, I realized that love is in everything, every place, and every person. If we analyze the Fibonacci series, we can configure the very essence of universal love: 0, 1, 1, 2, 3, 5, 8, 13, 21, 34, 55, 89, 144, 233, 377, 610, 987, 1,597, 2,584, and so on. By adding the two numbers 0 and 1, you get the sum of 1. Furthermore, when we add 1 and 1, we get 2; when 1 is added with 2, we get 3. When these numbers are used for measuring distance, the outcome is a perfect spiral circle. The spiral composes the galaxy, a seashell, a flower, a cell, an aura, an atom in all aspects. To show an example, the Fibonacci series is shown on a grid paper with possible x and y axes. You start the first point at (0, 0) to (0, 1) and then move to (1, 1) and (1, 2) until it forms a perfect spiral. Depending on the length of the spiral, you can pinpoint coordinates like (0, 0) (0, 0.1), (0.1, 0.1), (0.1, 0.2), and so on. You can proceed counterclockwise by subtracting the numbers. The numbers are infinite. With this sequence of numbers, centripetal forces are explained and healing takes place within the matrix of sequencing numbers. A matrix can also be grid-like but with an assortment of rainbow colors that is seen with the third eye. Imagining a grid with light, whether it is a white shining light or an array of colors, can open up the third eye. Spreading this grid to the universe is giving out love to a higher connection.

Fanatical replacements of God with humans or with twin flames are said to be complete opposites of each other in similar circumstances. Their DNA is shared, and they are complete replicas and blueprints of karma. I first studied about twin flame relationships when I was twenty-five. One's twin flame is a reflection of oneself. If we were to look at the blueprint of our horoscopes, it is understandable that we would conclude that our twin flames would have opposite placements in most if not all of their ruling houses. For instance, if your ascendant first house is Taurus, then your twin flame's ascendant will be the opposite, Scorpio. Twin flames are here to teach cosmic lessons, but you will not experience anything malefic with a true love, and the real lesson in life is knowing that the God-mind within us is our true love, for it knows what the individual soul desires. If you'll notice, the healing symbols in medicine are two snakes intertwined with each other. That is the significance of twin flame relationships. They meet up when there is a time for spiritual healing. The combustion of auroras in the atmosphere also signifies twin flame relationships.

During a summer morning, I was on my way to work having just gotten back from a mini vacation. It was a very bright, sunny day, and as I was waiting for the warehouse to open, I was talking to one of my coworkers when, all of a sudden, she told me a very saddening piece of information. My ears were in disbelief, and my eyes welled up with tears. When I heard the news, I just kept saying, "Oh, no." The passion inside me overcame my emotions of sadness. I went into the break room of the warehouse trying to conceal my tears as well as my feelings. After I had put my belongings up in my locker, I saw another coworker. I quickly put my head down hoping he would not see me weeping over the mournful news. But he embraced me, and we were within some type of energetic ambiance. I literally felt healed, and the energy compassed around my waist with the initial site of the hug. As soon as the coworker who had initially told me the sad news came to wrap her arms around us, the energetic chain ceased.

Being punctual, I went about my business and proceeded to clock into work. I looked back at my coworker to see if he had felt the same energy, and he had this astonished look on his face while dusting himself off, like he was brushing fairy dust off him. On that day, I fell in love with an electrifying, energetic brace of love and reassurance. To this day, I do not comprehend what type of energy was being transmitted. All I know is that it started out with a feeling.

From then on I could not forget about that energy. I read numerous books on twin flame relationships, matrices, twin souls, ankhs, and anything imaginable that could be studied on higher selves in an effort to find the answer to what had occurred. It is as if I had discovered a wonderful part about myself and experienced the collision of bodies like the big bang.

After the embrace, I was speechless with the coworker, and I believe he was quite fearful of me; he started to treat me with indifference, as if I were not human. Around the middle of November 2010, on a cool day, I was wearing a purple and sherbet-orange long-sleeved blouse with a baby-blue tank top underneath and some blue jeans. The coworker whom I so much adored for hugging me was assisting at the front. Noticing a look of disappointment in his demeanor, I decided to overwhelm myself with a bunch of wonderful feelings. As the sun was about to go down, I looked up in the sky, hoping that my huggable coworker was watching my expressions. I even put my hand under my chin in contemplation, as if I knew what was about to come. The feelings were so real, and as the sun set, the beautiful colors in the sky matched my attire to a T. The sky was filled with baby blue and streams of sherbet orange and purple hues. Many shining stars shone that night. I felt that I had become one with the sky, and I was happy. I experienced true love with the Supreme Being in the absence of a collision of energetic bodies that was astonishing to me. Rather, the thought of togetherness with a human exalted these feelings of oneness or unity. Even though I had the coworker in mind to share the experience, I was one with God by myself. I felt as if I had permeated the sky with just a feeling and opening of a third-eye chakra just as a flower buds and opens its petals to the sun. It is a knowing of certainty and uncertainty at the same time. We can display such higher feelings that can alter states of matter within the universe. Yes, the secret to life does start with a *feeling*.

From then on, all I got from him were stares, and not a word was spoken between us. I had no choice but to ignore his fearfulness. The more fear and suspicion he showed toward me, the more I withdrew from him. The tactic turned me off to his power struggle over me. Foolishly, I wanted to run away due to a feeling of rejection and maltreatment reminiscent of the *X-Men* factor. I would have thought for certain that he would be more intrigued regarding how to tap into different realms than to run and hide away from me. Perhaps he was more concerned about earthly possessions and bodily features in an attempt to match my persona, which seems to be a recurring obstacle in novice situations.

Feelings of new love had me in a frenzy of rejoicing on the night of January 26, 2011. I was usually too shy and timid to dance, but this night I danced like it was the last dance I would ever do. I stayed up dancing to salsa, hip-hop, soft rock, and R&B music. All of a sudden, I was in a trance, and I stood in the middle of the living room moving in a circular, spiral motion. I was experiencing a natural high, and at the time I did not know about the Sufi-whirling dance that is practiced in Turkish cultures. That night I learned how to dance for inspiration and loved it. I quietly went to sleep at around three thirty that next morning. I eagerly woke up at about seven thirty to watch the sun come up from a calling to go outside. I went to sit on the balcony stairs outside with a brown blanket to keep me free from the chill. As the warm, orange sun was rising to the east, the white crescent moon and a bright shining star appeared behind it. In deep prayer, I gazed at the picturesque image in the powder blue sky. I must have been gazed at the sky for almost thirty minutes; I turned to my right arm and saw speckles of gray matter within my sight. Then there appeared to be sparkles of light floating on my right side close to my arm. Afterward, I felt an amazing rush of lightness just from star gazing.

It is graceful to have faith that we are surrounded by this wonderful light energy that is invisible to us through the naked eye but that becomes apparent when we open the third-eye chakra. One of the best early sci-fi examples of the third eye is in *The Twilight Zone* episode called "Will the Real Martian Please Stand Up?" In it, a Venusian reveals his third eye to a Martian with six limbs. The Martian represents a man from Mars, war, chaos, destruction, and everything evil. The Venusian, on the other hand, represents peace, love, music, passion, and everything good. Both of the aliens have the intention to conquer and colonize planet Earth. There is a balance between good and evil where there is technology, knowledge, and experience. We all live in a world of Venusian and Martian energy powered by the Sun with an intellectual communication through Mercury because these planets are nearest to the Earth and their influences are felt more readily.

You have to believe that the Lord your God is in everything perceived in the five senses and beyond. The sixth sense can be identified as the perfect sense within imperfections. Observing the world through a sixth sense taps into a dimension of random déjà vu. Our stimuli answer our five senses (hear, taste, see, touch, and smell), and the sixth sense is a feeling. Composing all of these senses together consecutively will form a pattern of the everlasting presence that is shared in the kingdom of heaven by observing the food we taste, the sounds we hear, the people and things we touch, and the aroma of everything by which we are surrounded. When you taste food, chew it slowly and patiently, enjoy the smell of it and the sight of the colors that it has, partake in the texture of your meal, and delight in the sounds that it makes while cooking, and also appreciate how that particular meal or recipe makes you feel. Does it bring back childhood memories? Does it remind you of a place? How about a person? Yes, indeed, you can make love to your food just by using all of your senses. For love always hopes that the meal will turn out delicious by preparing and patiently cooking the food without rushing it. Love listens and looks at the food to determine whether it is ready. If something doesn't go according to plan for the recipe, love easily finds a replacement for the food, spice, or herb. And after everything is all set and done, love rejoices in the delightfulness of the meal or harvest.

In the Teachings of Rumi in Book 3, translated by E. H. Whinfield, Story VI goes,

> A lover was once admitted to the presence of his mistress, but, instead of embracing her, he pulled out a paper of sonnets and read them to her, describing her perfections and charms and his own love toward her at length. His mistress said to him, "You are now in my presence, and these lover's sighs and invocations are a waste of time. It is not the part of a true lover to waste his time in this way. It shows that I am not the real object of your affection, but that what

you really love is your own effusions and ecstatic raptures. I see, as it were, the water which I have longed for before me, and yet you withhold it. I am, as it were, in Bulgaria, and the object of your love is in Cathay. One who is really loved is the single object of her lover, the Alpha and Omega of his desires. As for you, you are wrapped up in your own amorous raptures, depending on the varying states of your own feelings, instead of being wrapped up in me.

The true mystic must not stop at mere subjective religious emotions but seek absolute union with God.

Whoso is restricted to religious raptures is but a man;

Sometimes his rapture is excessive, sometimes deficient.

The Sufi is, as it were, the "son of the season,"

But the pure (*Safi*) is exalted above season and state.

Religious raptures depend on feelings and will,

But the pure one is regenerated by the breath of Jesus.

You are a lover of your own raptures, not of me;

You turn to me only in hope of experiencing raptures.

Whoso is now defective, now perfect,

Is not adored by Abraham; he is "one that sets."

Because the stars set, and are now up, now down,

He loved them not; "I love not them that set."

Whoso is now pleasing and now unpleasing

Is at one time water, at another fire.

He may be the house of the moon, but not the true moon;

Or as the picture of a mistress, but not the living one.

The mere Sufi is the "child of the season;"

He clings to the seasons as to a father,

But the pure one is drowned in overwhelming love.

A child of any is never free from season and state.

The pure one is drowned in the light "that is not begotten,"

"What begets not and is not begotten," is God.

Go! Seek such love as this, if you are alive;

If not you are enslaved by varying seasons.

Gaze not on your own pictures, fair or ugly,

Gaze on your love and the object of your desire.

Gaze not at the sight of your own weakness or vileness,

Gaze at object of your desire, O exalted one.

In more ways than one we can experience God's loving presence through the love we have for one another. When love dwindles for a human being, it can be temporary. It is not rare that a mystic will want to experience rush of raptures often. Euphoric escapades, hallucinogenic images, and light spells are a contagious continuance. You will want it all the time, and if you can achieve that natural high on demand, you will have to get better at living a purposeful, prosperous, happy life.

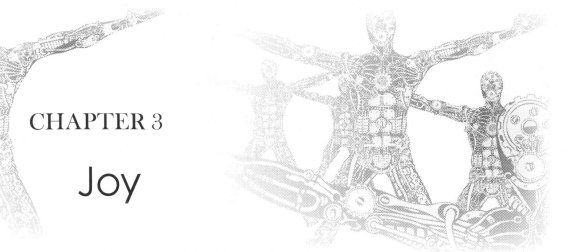

CHAPTER 3

Joy

To be at peace within is quite blissful. In order to have peace, you must have virtue in understanding that the universe and God are positively working with you on success. Peaceful people focus on what is working for them and are grateful for the things and people that they presently have in their lives that also focus on positive feelings. Through many challenges come great opportunities; thus, it is wise to be optimistic in your journeys and undertakings. One way to be at peace with yourself is to be able to trust in the Lord and God that everything is planned and created for your higher good. Finding laughter in the most terrible of circumstances defeats unnaturalness, for everything happens for a reason. The joy that is found in your heart is of a child's heart and is as bright as the sun. Life is full of games, and we are all children at play. This is how life shall be taken—as if you are playing. We are not to ignore responsibilities but to be in the know that everything is so. There was a reason for my waking up today. The past troubles, tribulations, shortcomings, and victories were all forthcoming for my purpose in the future. I will let no one or nothing steal my joy and peace on Earth. And if one is tempted to do so, I will gloriously smile with the rewards to come.

Positive thinking causes you to ascend. Whenever a negative thought creeps into your brain, immediately throw it out of your perception for your problems are already taken care of through the grace of God. You have to believe and have faith in planned circumstances while also staying active. Operating the subconscious and the conscious mind together is like bringing two magnetic poles into unity; this is how you draw positivism to yourself. Acting is the form of playing and using creative visualization as if everything is set and done on your behalf. Imagine a grid with the x-axis being the subconscious and the y-axis being the conscious. Inactive negative x- and y-axes are the result of pain, anguish, and despair in the subconscious and conscious mind, bringing malevolent situations and circumstances. Active positive x- and y-axes are the result of happiness, peace, and joy in both the subconscious and the conscious mind, bringing forth better circumstances and living situations. For a positive result, the subconscious and conscious mind have to be activated for the higher self. Deactivation is represented by the negative coordinates. Semiactivation results from a negative and a positive coordinate, whether it is in the subconscious area or the conscious area. A positive subconscious and a negative conscious mind equal a person who is interested in material gain and less in spiritual awareness; an example would be a person of financial success but with marital and family troubles. A positive conscious and negative subconscious mind is a result of high spiritual awareness but lack of or difficult connection to share their force with other individuals; an example of this person would be someone who is admitted into an asylum.

Stability, protection, security—we feel that we "need" these things at all times. We buy guns to protect ourselves, and we install security systems for our cars, houses, and luxuries. We make money to stabilize our lives. But I tell you that we do not need these three for God protects, stabilizes, and secures us. When I was working at a warehouse one day, I was having a very good day. I was rejoicing in the Lord's name and enjoying the daily atmosphere of the sun. In the middle of that day, my car was broken into at work. My car stereo was yanked out, and my car was left a mess from the sloppiness of the intrusion. My children's car seats were in the back of my car, so the thief knew I had children to take care of. After finding out that my window was busted, I was in an even better good mood. I did not mind the thief's ways because I felt as if he may have needed the equipment more than I. This was the third time a car of mine had been broken into. I just hoped that the man used this luxury to support his family or for some other good deed, instead of for alcohol, drugs, or sex. Love thy neighbor more than yourself and be happy for what you have. I should have been more careful about where I parked and hidden my belongings. That day, I defeated negativism by shrugging off the obstacle.

A positive attitude is like a stream or a river; there are rocks, marshes, and rapids, but the water always streams along through every rough area. Once you internalize that every situation is within your ability to be accomplished without fear, then you are able to experience the true bliss of not knowing what is to come in the near future. Embracing the precious time of today by also keeping active will bring forth many opportunities.

Positive thinking is quantum leaping. When you have two positive charges, they can only infinitely increase in order. Whatever will be will be, but you have to remain active and always act on new ways, new ideas, and new thoughts. At times it is wise to listen to the mind regarding when to be still in contemplation. By being positive, your mind is susceptible to powers of universal intelligence, also known as extrasensory perception (ESP). Your conscious mind is always receiving inspirational vibrational waves about what is necessary for you to do in life. When the subconscious and conscious mind energize together, then they can telepathically lead you to your true higher purpose and thus your true happiness. Deep meditation in yourself can make you more aware of your destination and success. Forget the past, forgive the present, and come forth into the future.

A positive mental attitude welcomes challenges and is even in competition with itself because of the ego. The difference between an amateur and a professional is that an amateur can be turned down by many people and be negatively defeated, while a professional can be turned down just as much and still optimistically proceed with his or her agenda. Having faith in yourself also is conveys the assurance of having faith in your God-mind.

The feelings of joy and excitement come from the first love feelings—the first time you were in love, the first time a child was born unto you, the first time you ride a bike, the first time you got that job that you wanted. Shoot! As of October 27, 2014, I found out that I was a great aunt for the first time. Joy is not temporary but recurring. For every moment and event that true happiness was experienced is remembered, whereas a dull moment is hardly ever recognizable. A temporary circumstance is better than permanent damage.

When I was working for a corporation, I was very thankful for the job that I had. Even though I wanted to quit the first day I started working there, I remained loyal because of the compensation and the benefits. One of my former supervisors told me on my first day there that this corporation was looking for a particular employee who can relate to its members, meaning that well-to-do members were more comfortable seeing faces that appeared to be similar to theirs. During all of my work history at this warehouse location, I joyfully pushed carts and reluctantly lifted and transferred heavy items into member's carts. Although the job was physically demanding, I liked getting paid. There was continuous tension resulting from the micromanagement and low morale that had settled within the work atmosphere of the warehouse.

Every day was the same: get out of bed, maybe eat some breakfast, go to work, come back home to the family, and then do it all over again the next day. I was usually way too tired to enjoy activities on my off days; I just wanted to rest and enjoy my leisure. I was making money but not enjoying it. Then again, even when I did have extra money, something or someone else was the recipient of it. I was passed up on positions that were to my liking. When my interview skills were good, my attendance was shabby. But when my attendance was punctual, my interviewing skills were undermined. I was not the only employee who went through discrimination at that corporation. I simply had to adopt an attitude that would not be taken advantage of. Now, we can say that the managers probably wanted me to be placed in a supervisory or upper-level management for my own good, but I knew there was more to life than titles and higher wages or salaries.

Nevertheless, I did not see the benefits of babysitting grown adults at a management level. I was told one day by a male upper-level manager that I should smile more. Actually, I have been told that all my life. So when I abruptly experienced this huge amount of inspirational laughter, I could not help but smile as much as possible. Then, one day, that same manager had the audacity to tell me and others that when people smile very often while they are working, they are showing that they are not serious about their jobs. I was quite baffled by the hypocrisy in his comment. Many people are satisfied with routine, nonpurposeful work. There were temporary moments when I had been at peace in the past, but now since all my faith is given to the Lord and God, with an active creative mind, I am complete in not worrying about financial obligations, which brings a permanent peace of mind since finances coincide with my health.

As contained in my realist of "dreams," the beginning is just like the ending—everlasting tunnel visions of laughter with a Supreme Figure. My life flashes before me, and I am reminiscent of all of the special events and moments that were beside me. A sort of feeling of "the joke is truly on you" encompasses me, and I am breathlessly happy once again.

CHAPTER 4
Eternity

Eternal Truth, Eternal Love, Eternal Joy
In the beginning was the Word, and the Word was with God, and the Word was God
—John 1:1

My dad was a God-loving man. After he passed away, I bought a snow globe with an engraving of the John 1:1 verse above. Dad loved that verse, and he would mention it to me quite often. Inside the snow globe was an embroidered heart that read, "The Light of God surrounds me. The Love of God enfolds me. The Power of God protects me. The Presence of God watches over me. Wherever I am, God is and all is well. Amen."

Eternal truth is within the world of God, from the depths of the sea to the breadth of the sky. The Earth is here to stay, with a record of existence 4.5 billion years old. The daily replication of life's existence is a mundane, routine operation. Evolutionists have on many occasions proclaimed that the big bang theory explains life's existence, that at the beginning there was complete darkness, and then all of a sudden a big clash of dust particles made light, stars, planets, and the universe. The Earth formed from these particles of dust, and then there was water, prokaryotes, eukaryotes, plants, animals, and then people. Evolutionary science has thus far had trouble keeping up with the metaphysics of the beginning, such as what are the reasons for life's existence? Who is God, and why did he create all this existence? These are the questions that some disciplines in science cannot demonstratively answer. Albert Einstein created the equation $E = mc^2$, where E is energy, m is mass, and c is the speed of light. I believe that the meaning of these variables can be replaced, with E being feelings, m being mass of emotions, and c being speed of thoughts, where there is hardly any thinking at all based upon the fairness of air. The feelings bring out auras, while the emotions bring out senses, and the invisible speed of light brings out rapid thoughts.

Furthermore, to go back to the book of Genesis, the Bible portrays that the Earth is about six thousand years old in existence. But if we examine the Earth through geoscience, it is proven through the Earth's crust and layers that the evolutionary approach to the birthday of the Earth is more accurate. So about 4.5 billion years ago, an infinite-matter substance intelligently designed the whole universe to form things, places, and people. The sound of light eroded out of this atmosphere and formed clusters of energy among stars, galaxies, the sun, and the moon. In comparing Earth to the other planets in our solar system, Earth is the only planet that has greenery upon it. All the other planets are composed of mainly rock or gases and vapors. Plants provide energy, oxygen, and hydrogen to other living organisms. Thus, humans and animals were strategically placed and meant to exist on planet Earth in accordance to having every essential necessity and natural resource to sustain the soil and ground. Within the "now" of circumstances, the earth is solely meant for experimenting because our celestial bodies expire.

When death rushes over one's body, it is like a clash of nonexistence to the Earth but within another dimension. Eternal truth is found in all living and nonliving things. Everything that has matter actually matters in a fluorescent structure with different rays of invisible color. The body becomes the infinite after death and the invisible (transparent) after life. In between the infinite and the invisible, or rather the Alpha and the Omega, is this substance called gray matter. In mixing the colors of white and black, you get gray. And that is how the here and now is personified by the color gray, which represents gray matter—everything in between life and death. Upon meditation, we individuals can experience this gray-matter effect upon awareness while still not knowing, just as black is infinite and white is invisible. That's the gray-matter effect, the eye between your two eyes. When you start to notice the gray matter effect, you will start to feel the middle of your forehead open up, as if your two physical eyes are separating from each other to make room for your ever-seeing third eye. A lot of people have the perception that they have not meditated before because their agenda and intention is not on meditating. But most of the time, meditation can happen without will.

For instance, I was visiting a former friend at his apartment a couple of streets down from my townhome on August 10, 2013. That day, he wanted to take my three daughters and me to the zoo. My plans were disrupted, though, when the father of my kids was wondering where I would be going with our daughters without him. Afterward, back at the apartment, I was feeling quite tired from the workweek and just wanted some peace and rest.

As I lie down on this friend's futon in my pink, white, and black sundress, I realized in humiliation that "Aunt Flo" had visited me while I was there. I quickly got up and headed to the corner store to purchase some sanitary napkins. I went back to his place and became rather baffled at what the day had brought. On his Pandora music jukebox, he was playing a rap song that had the word "bitch" in it about forty-seven times. As I was staring at his curtains, he seemed to telepathically open them so I could get a good view of the environment. I egotistically did not pay any attention to his vulgar music, for I was enjoying the amazing view of the sky as I lay upon his sofa. I was enjoying the blissfulness of being able to just relax. As I looked out of his window at the rays of the sunshine and powdered clouds, I could not help but notice that I was peacefully alone with the world and the truth, which is with God. I drifted on aspirations of the goodness of God and the Earth. The aloneness became oneness, and as I breathed out air methodically in anticipation of some sort of unknowing surprise, there was this beautiful sunset with colors of pink, white, and orange hues that matched me. It was definitely a revelation of belief to me and I am sure to my host as well.

All things are created through manifestations of creative visualization. We are all made unto the image of God; thus, our creations are manifested from the mind of our intelligent designer and implanted into us for creation. Our image is perceived as dualistic—two arms, two eyes, two hands, two feet, and so on. But we have to understand that God is three-dimensional, and through all of God we are three-dimensional as well with bi-dualistic physical features. This means that our celestial bodies operate on two planes of the Earth but our souls operate in the three-dimensional realm of the universe.

An eternal love is everlasting. For without love there is nothing; there is no light. Eternal love is said to be the greatest power that has ever existed. It is constant and does not end. This is the type of love that Jesus Christ has for everybody and the reason he was crucified upon his Passover. His amazing power of love made him into a recognizable force to be shared with everyone. The son of God performed miraculous wonders in the world, and for his demonstrations he was of course hated for having a personal relationship with God. People who demonstrate everlasting love cannot ever be hateful to anybody because pure mortals know that they are mere reflections of other people. If they were to hurt another, they would be hurting themselves as well.

Eternal love sees a wrong action done to them and most times just keeps silent. People with everlasting love do not have to fight with words, physical objects, and grudge tactics. They simply persevere the moment of love being as light as a feather. It is easier to love people than to hate them. Love is an exponentially more positive energy that cannot inadvertently be reverted to negativity. White light is invisible, and so can love be as well. Love can be blind or blinding because of its massive and augmentative energy source.

Thus, eternal joy is an abundance of goodness and rejuvenation. When you are joyful and jolly, nothing matters in the world. There are no worries with the initial period of joyfulness. With joy, you can be in a state of completion or nirvana. The cells in your body are refreshed because of the newfound energy. The feeling makes cells replicate moderately or more efficiently. Joyfulness causes better cell reproduction, regeneration, and repair. Being encompassed with eternal joy means experiencing eternal growth. For every learning *eureka* moment, there is room for growth. The gratification of rejoicing for all good takes you to experience an amazing grace. That grace can easily come from just being grateful.

In referring back to $E = mc^2$ we can interchangeably convert the equation to E standing for joy, m standing for truth, and c standing for love. Mass can be converted to energy, just like energy can be converted to mass. Thus, joy and truth can be exchanged. Since we are unable to see the speed of light with the naked eye, love—which can also be invisible because of its lightness—is relevant to the speed of light. The velocity of that light is calculated, and a small piece of matter can produce a big amount of energy. Contrarily, humans are able to provide a high abundance of energy that is invisible and hidden from public view. But if we were to use Einstein's physical mathematical equation, we can get a glimpse of how this phenomenal energy works.

CHAPTER 5

The SELF (Self-Evolution Lasting Forever)

As I sit here at my computer desk, I cannot help but notice that this chapter has to be the most time consuming so far. Reflecting on my true self right now is quite a challenge as I have to dig deep into this phenomenon. The self is what makes every individual unique. Every person has a different blueprint of his or her self, unless he or she is an identical twin and therefore shares genetic DNA with another. Still, twins more than likely have different personalities that distinguish them. So no two people are completely the same. Pretty much, the self is a witness of you, and the ego tells the self that you are better than you. Digging deep into oneself can be a tumultuous process because the ego does not want to accept the self. Therefore, the ego can bury the true self underneath the surface of the skin. Gaining true self-confidence means not having any fear of humiliation, defeat, or turmoil and taking life day by day, moment by moment, minute by minute—living in the present now.

I want you to imagine that you are the only person in existence. You can picture yourself in a dream or in a private room. You are with the creator, and you are picturing all the obstacles that you went through in your previous life and how you quickly overcame those obstacles within a decent amount of time. You may even laugh at the trials, lessons, tribulations, and victories of that time. So when you are experiencing this backtrack of persona and look at all the important people in your life, just witnessing yourself, you are filled with relief. As you gather all the people you want in your life, you start to manifest their existence, just like the replication of a cell. The manifestation of the self is in the center, and the others are outliers and points around the circumference of you. This is how the SELF recognizes everything—through projected perceived stimuli. The SELF makes other individuals, places, and things manifest around them. We have a free will to choose whom we want in our lives in the beginning and thereafter. Every single one of us is manifested as well as our thoughts.

The ego is what tells the SELF that you can be better in the beginning of life and the hereafter. The ego fools the SELF into darkness, into detachment and illusions. Things matter with the ego and its perfection of personality. We can admit that most of us are our own enemies and that we constantly try too hard to fix things that were never broken or in need of fixing. I like the phrase "I am as richer than I will ever be; and I am poorer than I will ever be." A lot of people like to play with the delusion unknowingly and unconsciously to play a game with the self. Games are considered trivial and nontrivial. Playing a board game is trivial. Listening to a play is nontrivial. The self plays like a curious child in the world. The SELF is never serious. It is concurrent with events, places, people, and things. Make believe in duality. The SELF is two-sided like a coin. The self tends to forget about the true self and comes up behind it and scares the self when there are games to be played (challenges, problems, and issues), like seeing yourself in the mirror for the first time. The renewal process of these games gets you back closer to your true self. As long as there is uncertainty in the playing field, life is great. There is competition within everybody, including with oneself. Human beings cannot get better because they want to keep playing this game of delusion with themselves. There would be no life if there were no game. There would be no faith if there were not perceptions of destruction and self-destruction.

The unconscious self, which was thoroughly explained by Carl Jung, is the most rigid part of the self, the most gratifying when there is a perception of selflessness. Great artists have come in contact with the dark side of the self and different experiences in order to create masterpieces. The creation of their work offers liberation because of the lesser degree of condemnation. The worse and darkness of the self has to be accepted in order to be qualified. Finding one's true self is a golden opportunity. The path to finding your true self is realizing where you came from, where you are right now in life, and performing great feats of faith to get where you are going in the future. With all the guidance like cosmos and astrology in the world, discovering the true self is enjoyable to the superego.

In the West, dramatic play is pictured seriously compared to the Eastern counterpart. The United States, being a capitalistic country, can merely focus more on calculations and business rather than deeper meaning. Observing that a moon is half full has far more meaning than the calculation of its circumference for comparison. The West makes observations and situations less simply and less easily than the East. We can say that this concept is a duality within the two hemispheres. The East is less concerned with material gains and more in tune with spiritual wealth. As you can tell, the East is less focused on the newest trends, skinny physiques, and mechanical transportation. The East is more primitive than the West and thus is centrally grounded into higher meanings than material earthly aspects. A lot of speculators blame the capitalist approach for the destruction and chaos in the Middle East due to scarce resources and the capital gain for draining the sustainability and competition of natural resources. For example, the continuing issue of borrowing oil has abruptly caused a developed nation to become dependent on the supply of Eastern resources. The East and other ancient civilizations have known and been practicing the secrets to the self for quite some time. To share this expertise is only comical because the teaching of the true self is of a true essence.

The abundance of fast-food chains and the overstimulation of java shops programs those in the West to believe that the self is put here to be a slave forever. You are to go to school, pay for college, and hopefully find a good career to support you and possibly a growing family. Then after so many years of working, you retire when your body is meager and susceptible to illnesses. Everything is to be done in a specific order of what others tell you to do in a chaotic perfection with limited resources. Since I am female, I identify with the HER (Human Evolving Rapidly) phase. I can identify with this phase because of my adaptive nature to the Earth's changes. And even though my genetic makeup consists of two X chromosomes, I am still chemically androgynous. Acceptance of both female and male traits has made it easier for me to identify with both sexes.

To better explain the SELF stage, I would like to first introduce myself and give you a glimpse of my past, present, and future life by starting out with my astrological chart.

Name: Valerie Nicole Lewis

Date of Birth: May 06, 1985

Birthplace: Fort Worth, TX

Time of Birth: 11:40 a.m. (CST)

Sun sign: Taurus in 10th house

Moon: Sagittarius in 4th house

Mercury: Aries in 9th house

Venus: Aries in 8th house

Mars: Gemini in 10th house

Jupiter: Aquarius in 6th house

Saturn: Scorpio in 4th house

Uranus: Sagittarius in 4th house

Neptune: Capricorn in 5th house

Pluto: Scorpio in 3rd house

Vertex: Capricorn

East Point: Leo

Houses

Ascendant: Cancer/Leo; Second house: Leo/Virgo; Third house: Virgo/Libra; Fourth house: Libra/Scorpio; Fifth house: Scorpio/Sagittarius; Sixth house:

Sagittarius/Capricorn; Seventh house: Capricorn/Aquarius; Eighth house: Aquarius/Pisces; Ninth house: Pisces/Aries; Tenth house: Aries/Taurus; Eleventh house: Taurus/Gemini; and Twelfth house: Gemini/Cancer.

This is a short detail of my natal chart without the focus on the aspect placements.

I was born in Fort Worth, Texas, on May 6, 1985, at 11:40 a.m. On that day, the sun was in Taurus with the north node of ascendant Leo, and at night the moon was in Sagittarius. I have always been a quiet, reserved, and placid person, which is detailed with the Taurus sun sign influence. As I got older, I gradually ascended into Leo around the age of twenty-five. My character went from pushover to someone who demanded respect. I was a tomboy growing up, and the first handful of friends I made were males. I really did not care for dolls and dress-up materials because I found them boring. I rather played sports and preferred rigorous activities. I also liked to play alone, especially riding my bike or climbing trees. When faced with challenges, I would quietly face whatever came my way. My childhood consisted of many experiences. I was a quiet and reserved child but a leader as well. I even organized a small little clique of friends into a harmonious gang relationship. The gang was constructed straight out of boredom. My friend and I were writing down lyrics to songs during the summertime, and we came up with an idea to initiate a gang. Even though our gang consisted of a whole bunch of fifth-graders, we portrayed ourselves as Crips and decided on the name Southside Killaz. The group provided a great learning experience. I learned some leadership skills as far as how organizations operate. The group gave us a sense of belonging because we were more than just friends to one another. We looked out for everyone in the group, like brothers and sisters do. We did not get into much trouble; we really just wanted the childish respect that we could not get inside our households. A lot of the gang members were in and out of juvenile delinquency, while some moved away to other parts of the state. We all looked out for one another and practiced true selfhood, and the affiliation gave us confidence.

If I look back on my childhood, I cannot imagine it being any different. I understand that some things happen for a reason. The experiences impressed on me what to look out for in people and to not be naive. I'm sure the obstacles made me into a person who is fully aware of other people's motives and demonstrated to me how easily people are influenced by substances and peers. Each day I tell myself to not look to the past because there is nothing there, but at times I cannot keep myself from fantasizing about the past, restructuring *could have*s. I try to allow my relationships to not be affected with the tribulations of yesterdays. I have to live in the present and not even bother about thinking about the future. Just let it go and let it be for the time being.

I questioned my existence for so many years, like most people wondering what the true meaning to life is and why we are all placed here. Cosmology has helped me to understand a bigger picture regarding the perceptions of selfhood. I like to incorporate these unique natal birth charts in answering and telling the ways of the individual. I like to play with the cosmos and I AMs to gain a clear view of the friend in myself. For instance, since my ascendant starts with Cancer/Leo, I picture a short synopsis of my story saying that, out of pure nothingness, there was a feeling since Cancer identifies itself with "I Feel with God," creating all there is.

During the night there had to be light that came from the moon, and then when the feeling was surmised came the will; and God's will was done when the aspects of the sun were born. Daylight from the sun overtook the night, which made dualities. During the season of Virgo, there was detail analyzing and critiquing that which corresponds to the data of numbers and replication of DNA and matter; and this is when the first living creatures, such as viruses, bacteria, and symbiotes, became part of the creation to start a mass of healing mechanisms since Virgo is a medical sign. Balance was achieved during the season of Libra, and it is daunting for me to contemplate that God was quite alienated and wanted to form communication that made the universe home. The fourth house ruling Scorpio was a time of transformations through death that created insects, arthropods, and mollusk kingdoms. But yet God was still lonely and knew that there were other creations to be made that would result in more happiness. So God created an image of the self in the season of Sagittarius, a half-human half-animal creation that would aim at the stars and wander among the Earth perceiving good luck. After that came the Capricorn, the Sea Goat, and during this season there was an understanding that the half-human half-animal creature was capable of overcoming the high mountaintop obstacles of survival. The needs of living things were tolerated and resources from the Earth were used. Aquarius gave abundance by providing water for nourishment. Relationships helped us to get to know God through one another, recognizing the small images of God. Pisces helped us to believe in a higher being, and once the creators believed, then our existence was in the being of God-mind-spirit. Aries is the first sign of the Western zodiac, and it is explained that Aries was the fire combustion, whereas Taurus is the formation of Earth, Gemini is the communicator through air, and it goes back again to Cancer forming water on Earth and being the depths of feeling. I cannot help but mention that DNA and cosmology have an interesting role together that will tell us about ourselves. Now, according to my natal chart, I like to contemplate that Aries is the coming together of philosophy, and even though a person can be a strong believer from Pisces, there are still questions to which philosophy can answer for existence. Taurus allows me to help obtain the resources on Earth through the planned careers in caring for the places, things, and people in the world. Gemini is where I connect with talkative people who are always thinking to learn. At the end of this time is Cancer, and since this sign covers the early childhood (six- to seven-years-old age range), it is understandable to renew myself at this time; at that age is when I started to identify myself and to still question my existence in a worldly game of playing self-identity. So there you have it—a whole explanation to the start of my being that renews itself season after season sequentially. With the formation of birth natal charts, people can rediscover the self in planning and playing a game when they are at a loss for words and in between worlds. Cosmic influence is the way to knowing God and the self, and in my story I started out with the initiation of feelings forming a will. Therefore, everyone has a story to tell through his or her own birth natal chart, and this connection helps us to better know the self.

CHAPTER 6

Jesus Christ Consciousness

Being Christ conscious is being aware of the lightness in you. To be filled with light is to be in the cosmic consciousness. Jesus was cosmic conscious in his teachings. A Christ consciousness entails the belief that the entire universe is working for us and that we are a part of every energy source that is perceivable and imperceptible to us. Stars, the sun, the moon, the sky, and the Earth are all a part of our neurons and neurotransmitters. When we use our five senses, messages are sent to our nerve endings that signal the neurons for stimulation. The neurotransmitters not only signal our bodies from within, but they also signal externally as well. And it is when we are in awareness that we can affect all around us that we perceive and our senses can become a source of predicate. Holistically speaking, you have to be complete and whole. One way to be whole and to work within the holy, spiritual realm is to be in the light, alone with the lightness just as Jesus was. The Lord showed no fear in strife and also performed miracles to demonstrate that God runs through him. But most importantly, Christ demonstrated magnificent hope that other people would find the lightness in themselves as well.

Hitherto, cosmic consciousness is just the perception, awareness, and realization that we are all connected with the universe. The community of the universe is expressed through vibrational waves, including radio, ultraviolet, visible light, invisible light, and micro waves. The UV rays from the sun in the atmosphere affect the health of people, the trees, and ecosystems. Radio waves affect the stimuli of neurons in the entire body and vibrational frequencies. If we are affected by other forms of light and vibrations, then it can be hypothesized that we also affect different parts of the universe by using the light within us, neurotransmitters. This light within us is amplified when we generate a heightened sense of feeling—the feeling of completion and wholeness when we are perhaps emptying the body of negativism. Neutrons are neutral, protons are positive, and electrons are negative. Neutrons weigh the most, and protons weigh more than electrons. Specifically, protons weigh 1.672623×10^{-24} g, neutrons weigh $1.6749286 \times 10^{-24}$ g, and electrons weigh 9.109389×10^{-28} g. The electrons literally involve themselves with other electrons and are very small in size, making them seem invisible.

Turning this invisibility into invisible light and emitting that from within is a sure way of becoming Christ like and cosmic conscious. To think and feel positively and not to be bothered by negativism and pessimistic circumstances will increase the lightness. That is why we must treat these negatively charged electrons as opportunities to feel light. This act will purify the cells and atom by focusing on the nucleus of the matter and is an action of centeredness.

Once in a trance, you will feel a sense of euphoria, nirvana, or ecstasy. The blood flow of your brain will electrically rush to the parietals of your skull to the center of your head. You may even feel some sensation throughout your entire body as you are hosting the Holy Spirit. This is a meditation of being in the light. It is not rare that you will see individuals who are Christ-conscious being more sensitive when it comes to sunlight and touching trees and sedimentary things like rocks. These individuals have a heightened realization of the energy fields of matter and their circuits are more centered because they have become one with matter. The relation of positivity can be better felt while your shoes are off because negativism excretes through the feet. You want to feel as free as possible with your body without trapping or attracting any negative energy to you.

If you look at further technology advancement, it includes telecommunications, such as cell phones, texting, computers, and other gadgets to keep us being in communion with ourselves and everyone else. Wires in communication with people through social media and television can have us out of tune with reality. A lot of us might as well consider being robots with little feeling, being in touch with just the technological waves of telecommunications, broadcasting, and radio. But if we tap into a deeper realm that is noninfluential, then we can connect with the entire galaxy just by using our vibrational forces of light.

The world definitely becomes a different place when you are in Christ consciousness. All of a sudden you want to live differently than you have before. That includes changing your nutrition habits, exercising, giving up old habits, feeling carefree, and not being too enthusiastic about media manipulation. If you do not make these changes, the universe will make them for you. For instance, after I was enlightened at twenty-five, I started to have stomach and intestinal problems. I would get really sick, especially around the holidays. I went to the doctor to see if I had acquired some form of disease, but to my surprise the tests revealed that I was in good health. Never wanting to feel the excruciating pain again, I tried to adjust my eating habits. I do not know what triggered my stomach upsets, but it had me in a frenzy to prepare and cook my own foods and continue a routine of moderate exercise throughout the week. Even though my stubborn behavior almost detoured me from a healthy eating regimen, I had to force myself to be kinder to my body and eat lightly, giving up the greasy fast food that I am drawn to.

Highly conscious spiritual people do not need to see a physician for they can heal their bodies themselves. The emptying out of negativism is a result of spiritual healing to oneself and others. When feeling ill, a Jesus conscious–minded person can grab energy from higher intelligence—God, the Creator—and transfer it to another body, another soul. It is the faith and belief of God's essence that the receiver gathers and exchanges with the taker. The three forces of light—God, Jesus, and you—are performing the healing regimen. As long as the reciprocation of belief and faith are nominal, then phenomenal feats can be accomplished.

Illnesses, sickness, and disease will be cured and made whole. Now, pharmaceutical medicine can be used to alleviate pain, but ridding the body of illness with them is not probable. People of a higher consciousness rather use therapeutic remedies and meditational methods to restore and repair cell damage.

Christ-minded people do not care for any returns on their good deeds and helpfulness. They do not have any hidden agendas or use manipulative tactics when sharing their love with others. They recognize the space in between the mind and the heart. They are givers and are not comfortable with taking for the majority. Establishing compassion and love for one another augments the light where there once was darkness. Gaining authority over the universe is Christ consciousness, and alleviating the body to become less dense is illuminating.

One day, I experienced anointment by Jesus. I was in my room, and I could feel the presence of light and smell an odor of lightness; my faith was insurmountable. My heart and mind connected with each other in the communion of higher consciousness, higher thinking, and higher learning. There is nothing wrong with giving and taking, but it does have to be reciprocated or there will be consequences for both parties. The giver and taker will feel the consequences of chained hearts, enjoying the essence and value of what that person has to offer to the relationship should be the main focus. These are the reasons a lot of individuals arc loners—they hate for other people to make them feel alone in a relationship. Then, once again, through the strife of feeling emotionally vulnerable, the individual weeps to the Lord to be anointed and sustained again after the heartbreak of an intoxicating chained communion with another being. The cosmos and higher intelligence have no choice but to divide the two until either one or both of them are able to reconnect with Christ consciousness.

This practice of consciousness is always good news. It seems as if consciousness is a new phenomenon to many people and that technology and science are old news. Furthermore, the trends of today will be old news tomorrow. But even though Christ consciousness is an ancient practice, it never gets old and is falsely hidden from the public view to comprehend. Jesus Christ consciousness is a preparation for becoming God-conscious-minded. To get to God, you have to go through the Lord of the land.

CHAPTER 7

God Consciousness

Being God-minded is being aware of the self. The world is separated into duality, but consciousness is a three-dimensional fabric. As stated before, we have gray matter that pulls the duality together into a trilogy. Black and white makes gray, and that is how we must see our own consciousness. Where there are two magnetic poles on opposite ends of each other, this centripetal force brings them together for moderate flow. If you look at the solar system, the sun leads the other planets as they orbit around the sun. All planets in our solar system are affected by the sun no matter the distance. The formation of the solar system occurred centripetally around the sun like a record player. The sun is joyous, warm, burning, aflame. When you are God-minded, you become like the sun by being in the center of everything. You realize who you are, what you are, and how you are deep down inside your soul. You start to burn and rekindle like a flame. The ego is subliminal, and you become more sensitive to your surroundings. Getting into that gray matter, that gap of consciousness, the absence of judgment, the silence, or the void helps you to regain the power of the source.

The ego will always try to interfere with what it is realizing. For example, dreaming is unconsciously perceiving messages from your higher consciousness; the ego is the culprit that wants this information to be hidden from you. Then when your soul realizes what your mind is doing, the dream can be completely forgotten or placed in the back of your consciousness. This is why a lot of mystics recommend that you record your dreams for further interpretations.

From earlier scriptures and interpretations, it is assumed that from the beginning we had separated from the main source in terms of duality. We became good/evil, peace/war, love/hate, knowing/unknowing, certainty/uncertainty, male/female, two hands, two legs, and so forth. But when we get out of this duality of thinking and experience, then spiritual God is the surprise that manifests in between the two sides of this duality. To take away the negative duality, we can achieve oneness and harmony with a high spiritual source. The ego loves for us to believe that we are all separated from one another and that we are separated from God as well.

Everything is in circular motion, whether it be cells, objects, matter, or people. When you sit at a red light, in traffic, or in line, if you pay little or no attention to your surroundings, you can slip yourself into consciousness. When one person radiates and meditates, the energy is spread to other people because of the energy field forces. People are more calm and relaxed because the serotonin is increased in the brain upon meditation. Serotonin is the hormone that keeps us from being depressed and decreases anxiety. Judgment of the self in competing with other people is just the surface of fulfillment. The thoughts of having to have a better car, house, job, and family are a result of the ego separating the true self. But when you become aware of the inner voice with God consciousness, these things that separate us become less apparent. The material will always leave you empty and in separation of the true self. When we question things and get angry, depressed, anxious, and sad with not only ourselves but with other people as well, we are having difficulties with God. We use the unnatural emotions to give us lower energy, and it puts us in fear.

CHAPTER 8

Realization

God consciousness can be referred to as quantum consciousness. Contrarily, Christ consciousness is specific in the cosmos, and God consciousness is specific in quantum physics. God made men and women in the image of himself. I don't believe that God is male or has human qualities but I want to make it easy to refer to the deity. This type of consciousness is microscopic and small scale, the size of an atom. Scientists try to do basic calculations with quantum computers by observing entangled subatomic particles to explain cause–effect relationships of how one object can be in two places at the same time. The conclusion is quantum enigma—you get only microscopic waves when not looking at the object. But when you are looking at the object, you can observe the vibrational sequences of the electrons of an object forming a circular motion. Therefore, we have an influence on the way things are projected when using our stimuli and senses. Quantum tunneling proves that an object's electron can pierce through another dimension or possibly another universe.

Dark matter is still a science that has not been thoroughly discovered. Dark matter is felt but not discovered because it exists in another place. The smallest subatomic particles, like atoms, neutrons, protons, neutrinos, and electrons, create vibrations. In order to see how these vibrations work, scientists are trying to invent a tool that uses more energy to go beyond the microscopic vision of atoms. Understanding the concepts of time and space will help us figure out how quantum physics works. The accumulation of human behaviors can have a significant influence on this matter. This emphasizes why twin flame relationships are so popular; the actions of one twin equal a reaction from the other with mostly no recognition. For instance, one twin may be thinking of his or her twin, and in response to that telepathic communication, the other twin will call or think about him or her as well. The manifestation and occupying thoughts result in a reaction or, further, in another action. Action plus reaction equals actualization and realization. When you come into realization, you feel a sense of fulfillment and appreciation for life as if you have achieved a milestone of consciousness. To gain this realization, most individuals go through what I would call a cleansing and reunion of the actualization that God is real. And to understand the realness of God, you have to go through Christ by repenting and convicting your sins and wrongdoings, as well as the sins and wrongdoing of others.

Realizing that you have only four necessities to survive is primal. The four necessities of life are rest, food, companionship or sex, and a right to defend. People who are experiencing realness will not be as interested in material resources because they know that those resources will not satisfy them. The soul yearns for completion and wholeness of the SELF, Christ-mindedness, and God-mindedness. Fascination in and inspiration from this concept are quite difficult to explain and understand. God-realization is the highest state of consciousness, where the soul is separated from the ego. To dig further into consciousness, imagine a universe with several planes on a Ferris wheel. These planes consist of separate universes from past, present, and future realms. Once a person has evolved to be sustained from God consciousness, he or she goes through another plane level of awareness. The soul reincarnates itself to reach this acknowledgement of creation—that God is the ultimate Creator of everything and that the designer created us also in an image of itself. Therefore, all beings can be procreators like the main source, which is God; and self-realization is God-realization.

Growing up, I was always told and encouraged to do well in school, go to college, and fortunately, seek out a good career based on my education. The years I spent in college studying about all different disciplines have helped me to understand how every subject relates to one another. After I had graduated from college with my bachelor's degree in interdisciplinary studies, I gained a sense of fulfillment and completion. The obstacles that I encountered afterward pulled me through the dimension of realization. My soul wanted a purpose in life, and I was clueless at the time of realization about how to obtain that purpose. Eventually, the cosmos and my soul's higher purpose have led me to write this book and try to demonstrate the power of this realization.

The most important concept of self-realization is in believing in the self. The mind is a steady flow of thoughts, and when you steer yourself into a deeper channel (concentration), you can become one with the object of meditation (a deep trance). You become like a flame that is radiant and blissful. In order to achieve realization, you do not have to be focused on a specific meditation regimen. We meditate sometimes without knowing. For instance, when you are in traffic, your mind can sometimes veer off into a trance of meditation. Yoga and other meditation experiences will increase your encounter of realization, but attaining realization is just experimenting with the self.

CHAPTER 9

Salvation

Can you whisper in my ear sweet nothings that will not disappear? Tell me I am beautiful for all to hear. Remind me of how we fell in love forevermore. Console me at my weakest moments. Cherish me with weekly awards. Yes, you do this and so much more, my Lord. My will is to serve and be merry with you, thy savior in Christ. And that is the ultimate price.

—Valerie

I carry my helmet, armor, shield and swords before the Lord. It was the tenth of July as I set forth before the Lord in a room by myself to ask for clarity regarding the circumstances in my life. As I wept at the foot of my bed configuring my boggled thoughts and praising the Lord for forgiveness of any sin and wrongdoing, I lifted. Everything became clear to me that all was right. My heart was not heavy anymore, and my head was clear. I could not have cared less about my circumstance. From that day on, a new world has been and continues to be presented. Yesterday is the past and no longer here, and the future of tomorrow has not yet begun. But now, I live for today in the here and now, caring less for predictions but fond of creations. Deliverance was granted upon me because of my profound confession and the depth of my soul to pure faith in the Lord. I felt that I would no longer feel the fear of another day and that my wishes were protected and manifested.

Salvation is the conjugation with Christ and God or some other higher intelligence in the universe that delivers you from instability. A lot of individuals seek salvation through the need of security (defense) from the outside environment. All living things and people need four things for survival in life: food, rest, defense mechanisms, and companionship. Just like the plants need the sun for energy, water for growth, insects for defense, and other plants for pollination, people and animals need the same. With salvation the need for defense in the general population is guaranteed. There is no need for material artillery weapons for protection of material goods nor security systems for homes, vehicles, and jewels. Your faith and ever-knowing of the Word (world), which is granted from our savior, protects you. It delivers us from evil.

About two years before my Earth father passed away in 2011, he explained to me the protection verse, in which we carry every day what we need when we proceed through the world.

… in addition to all, taking up the shield of faith with which you will be able to extinguish all the flaming arrows of the evil one. And take *the helmet of salvation*, and the sword of the Spirit, which is the word of God. (Eph. 6:16–17, emphasis added)

Now, like I said before, to discover salvation you do not have to go through a traumatic experience. You can obtain salvation through any means or event that instills faith and dedication in serving higher intelligence for a higher purpose. You finally get a piece of mind regarding how words (world) come together as a whole. I correlate *word* and *world* together because God's Word is the world. You literally have the whole world within your hands. Your faith is exchanged with the world, and it's yours. During the completion of salvation, you will feel as if you have no enemies, especially if you have prayed for your adversaries; there is favor in man and with God as well. So there are no worries in the time being. Of course, a human or even sentient being will still go through tests, trials, and tribulations because of the life we live. We are here to experience as much as we can in this lifetime so that we can be better in our future decision-making. I will tell you that the whole mind, body, and soul have to be connected at the initiation of being saved. If those three—mind, body, and soul—are disconnected from one another, then salvation is unachievable. If you have never experienced this moment and you wish to, then ask for it. Pray for you to be able to "see" the truth of your being and the purpose of your life. Explore yourself for the deeper meaning of your existence.

Furthermore, defeating the enemy or adversaries, we shall say, is an easy task. Obtaining perseverance against anyone who has wronged you is a great defense mechanism. Remaining silent through tough times is a sure way to halt a difficult situation because it does not swarm in the universal atmosphere. If it is out of sight and out of mind, then the situation will become stagnant. Contrarily, if your situation seems worse due to upward mobility, take accurate, calm precautions and ask the Lord, God, angels, Buddha, Jesus Christ, Mother Mary, or whomever of a higher realm to give you strategic guidance for this force. Establish your outlook to take every obstacle as a journey to betterment. So if an idea feels good to pursue, then by all means, just go ahead—take action now and ask questions last.

So I did not lose my head (helmet) when embarking upon salvation. I prayed for myself, for all of my adversaries, and for everyone who was going through the same circumstances that I was going through. I forgave them and myself for any past wrongdoing that led me to go through that traumatic experience. I thanked my adversaries ultimately. I was treated with a lot more respect after taking action on what I felt was not right in my head, and I became ever so lighthearted by not letting it bother me again. The Lord's salvation became my emotional, physical, intellectual, spiritual, and material strength evermore; I was officially a renowned warrior.

CHAPTER 10

Redemption

The poor long for riches, the rich long for heaven, but the wise long for tranquility.
—Swami Rama

After salvation (which entails a surrender, the confession of sins, and asking for forgiveness; it can be a breakdown or realization of newborn life), there comes redemption. Redemption is a state of rest. Just as salvation protects us, redemption leads us into rest and rejuvenation, a peaceful status of blissful existence. The body, mind, and soul require rest in the same way that a car requires maintenance. *Sleep* and *rest* are two different words and two different things. When you sleep, you are unconsciously aware for a certain amount of time. Rest is limitless; you can rest when the body is inactive or active. A person can be at rest anytime of the day or night. Some people do not understand why they can sleep for seven or eight hours and still feel fatigued; it is because their bodies received an abundance of sleep but did not get an adequate amount of rest.

After the salvation stage, the soul yearns for peacefulness in its being. It is through the realization of survival completion that the body can rest, through understanding that past and present circumstances are nothing but illusions. When a person starts to live in the *now* (the moment of living existence), he or she has no worries. The individual still may suffer in the future, but the soul knows that everything happens for a reason and that the universe guides us into positive situations through temporary circumstances.

To redeem oneself is to gain a ticket to prosperity because the spirituality of one's essence is augmentative with faith. Redemption can come in all forms of repentance that the being knows that there is a higher intelligence orchestrating our lives around us. The feeling of knowing that we are never alone is a form of redemption. It's like having a ticket to access creation and all that God has created and recognizing that the Divine is everywhere. We are engineers of success with little or no need for the material world. Now, having no use for the material things can lead into a state of depression because we realize that we will never be satisfied with material things. They are nice to look at, smell, touch, hear, and possibly taste, but we will always want more meaning in our lives. And with redemption, we have traded that wanting for a need. Upon the realization that the five senses are just perceptions, we begin to enter what is sensual to us. Self-actualization and self-love occur within the redemption phase through self-sacrifice, a sacrifice of worldly possessions. Also with the exchange of not desiring worldly goods, you receive the Word. You do not have to read the entire Bible, Koran, or some self-help book to know the power of the Word. It is given to you because you searched for it and wanted to know deeply about the phenomenal truths of this world with redemption.

Furthermore, redemption feels as if you are trying to buy back your freedom. Whatever your family members, teachers, and peers have taught you in the past can be of little relevance. Those concepts have no use to a people who have experienced redemption in their own way of life. In Christianity, the death of Jesus Christ paid a ransom for all sins and death so that we could be reborn and reincarnated again and again—and so that we can go through the higher realms of existence of God-mindedness and be free of slave bondage. I guess we can subsequently confirm that we are used as magnificent seeing tools that are deemed to spread the Word to the whole and to make other people aware of their God-mindedness as well.

Until you become more creative in sharing God's request, which is expressing the truth, you may go through numerous types of redemption. Our intention is not to waver off the righteous path, but sometimes we can get distracted and tempted back into that world of possessions. We may be distracted by the company we keep, the job we still hold, and the neurotic pattern of thinking we may have. But be reminded that those experiences are to help us accomplish our higher good and purpose to come. Working at a job that you hate going to everyday makes you a slave. Working against your will is mental slavery. Adopting the ideas and trends of others is mental slavery. Listening to music that promotes hate, violence, sexual exploitation, and so on is another form of mental slavery. Some of the modern hip-hop music is filled with negativism and separates the sexes through female degradation. Music is a great influence, and a lot of souls follow it and astoundingly try to become its Neptune illusion. Dwelling in money, cars, sexual partners, drugs, and underworld is downgrading and valueless (mental slavery); when you do, you disallow yourself from knowing the truth of living. In the West, materialism is big business and is a facade to keep you from turning inward into yourself and realizing what you truly need in order to be truly happy. On television, all the commercials have one thing in common: they are all trying to sell something to you in exchange of a want, whether it is for your health, your place of residence, for show, for your body, and so on. Most of these things are for your wealth or natural good. Spiritual people do not need a doctor or pharmaceutical drug when they can heal themselves, cars when they can walk, or fast food when they can cook. Redeeming oneself is reversing ourselves with actualization of worthiness. During the process of redemption, the redeemer is Christ himself.

CHAPTER 11

Liberation

Just let it be

In late November 2013, I was suffering from bondage resulting from not letting go. Even though the resignation of my job was alleviating, the loss of a paycheck every two weeks had me feeling insecure. When I quit my job, my boss gave me a resigning bonus of about $2,600, and I also had saved up about $17,000 in my 401(k), which I was reluctant to withdraw that following year. By then, I was happy again and moving along with my plans. Knowing that I had a great support system and that I could do anything that I put my mind to was liberating. Contrarily, at this moment, I have no worries about my financial status even with all of my monetary resources being exhausted. For some reason, I feel free and that I am on a journey back to true happiness.

We can compare liberation to food, even though *liberation* means "to breathe." Rather, I believe that we are breathed upon by Jesus Christ when we go through liberation. The ingestion of food liberates us from hunger, and the digestion and excretion of food through our waste liberates us from toxins. Liberation is a support system that allows individuals to create without unnatural emotions getting in the way. Whether that support comes from family, government, or friends, it is what liberates and keeps networks together. It is necessary for women and overly feminine men to have support from people, even if they do not want it. Constant catering to female needs through support systems makes sure that families are well taken care of.

Western countries have castrated women to make them inferior to men. Listening to the lyrics of the music that influences youth and younger adults makes it clear that women are devalued. Television and other media portray women as sex symbols and that is about it. Sex has taken over the meaning and value of a woman. The word *woman* means "to come out of," like a womb. I can only speculate from the book of Genesis that Eve came out of Adam because of his yearning for companionship. Adam needed Eve for survival, but Eve did not need Adam. The world can procreate without a man but not without a woman. The fall of Adam and Eve began with the deception of Adam, when he chose not to tell or reveal the Word (world) to her. He did not mention her worth to him in all her work. Eve was blindsided and made ashamed of the essence of her body. They were cast out of Eden for not being able to live in the present, which was Eden. Eden was the place for everything to dwell upon. The Garden of Eden provided all species with the survival necessities of the earth as of a cornucopia of abundant resources. The separation of females and males is interpreted to mean that men and women are of another species. We are all androgynous simply because we each have a mother and a father. One gender chromosome comes from each of the parents, whether it is an XY or XX formulation. Some individuals have mutations of XXY or just one X chromosome, but they are still a part of the human species.

During the liberation movement in the 1970s, women were taking a stand on the inequality of women, birth control topics, and empowerment of women. The awareness of men regarding conceptions about women were simply based upon the notion that most females lack the physical strength of males, thus making them inferior to men. But whether we believe it or not, a person does not have to be physically strong to compete. Emotional, intellectual, spiritual, and mental strength can be more rewarding than a body of physical mass.

During the months of April and May 2014, I encountered the kundalini awakening. How it came about is something I do not comprehend. Maybe I was stressed during that period in my life and was not submissive to letting go of some of the toxins I had. Anyway, I had trouble releasing the energy from my body. It was hard to turn my neck and difficult to breathe, and I felt fluid in the back of my neck by my medulla oblongata, which controls breathing. Euphoria would overcome me because of the limited amount of breathing and possibly from the excretion of serotonin in my body. But the pain was so unbearable that I even filed for disability on my birthday, May 6, when it was at its worse. The culprit could have also been the pressure of a jailbird wanting me to come see him in the rehabilitation center after a heated argument that we had in letters we exchanged with each other. The kundalini energy may have been a sign for me to not proceed to see the jerk since the pain quickly went away after I failed to show up to visit him in rehab. Beforehand, as the pain in my neck got worse, my body was forming on its own some breathing patterns, and I could not help but to utter ohms under my breath as in an ancient chant while I was in a resting, meditative mode. The language gave some relief to my ailment. If you ever get time to observe Shakti and Shiva in Indian kundalini, you will notice that there are dual energies of equality—one being female and one being male—that are evenly exchanged upon the completion of becoming one person instead of two. The kundalini features a woman with six or eight arms with weapons, and a man is beneath her feet as a snake. She issues defeat through her mental, spiritual, and feminine strength. So henceforth, women should be treated with the highest respect for they have the heavens beneath their feet. Liberation is a state of release in the viewpoints and intentions of other individuals.

CHAPTER 12

Unity

In the beginning, God created the heavens and the Earth. Now the
Earth was formless and empty, darkness was over the surface of the
deep, and the Spirit of God was hovering over the waters.
—Genesis 1:2

Before you were born—or rather, when you were asleep—you were having tunnel visions. In the cloudiness of your surroundings came upon you this voice of childlike humor. You felt alone but yet noticed a presence behind and beside you. It was you and only you in this world, in this universe, and on this earth. Everything that you sense is a panorama of thought and stimuli. What you perceive is a mere correlation of what you hear, see, feel, touch, and taste. In the beginning, it was only you in this darkness, just like a fetus within the womb. Then this circle of cloudy light came from you to lead the way to the life you had planned for all along. Your emotions separated you from the union you had with God just so that you could experience the power of believing transforming into the power of knowing. We came from the water of emotion when we were born out of our earthly mothers' wombs. The world was formless before life claimed it, filled with just water and darkness. Our perceptions that we have of ourselves and of all forms are just a game of illusions. All things, people, and places that we sense are not real; they are simply a custom of our imagination that we see with our apparent two (snake) eyes. But in the orbital of your third eye lies the secrets to your union with God and the bountiful connection with the universe through earthly resonance.

I have to say that this chapter is the hardest to write because it can be so vague yet is of so much of importance. As we become conscious-minded, the awareness of time and paper money are profound illusions. Since I asked the Lord to use me for higher purposes, I have to stay focused on creative works that are independent upon me, no matter what anybody thinks. The struggle of trying to please people has left my progress stagnant in creating the occupation and career that I am most passionate about to this day: writing.

Nonetheless, there seems to be this big competition among family members and other people trying to outdo one another. Family and friends will talk about you behind your back, and they will nag you about obstacles that you do not have any control over. They may be there for you for moral and financial support but will request something in return. By observing others' situations, most family members will tend to act forgetful about the giving from others in the past and expect praise in the present, as in, "What have you done for me lately?" Yes, family members can be a jealous lot of folks that can tear you down more quickly than a fleeting stranger.

The disheartening violence and lack of self-acceptance and self-love have torn people apart but have also mended them closer to God for answers. Once we experience discrimination or racism, then we can relate and grieve with the victims of violence. We can mirror each other's emotions and feelings and become one with our brethren, something that we long for within our souls for so long. When some individuals feel that the world is against them, the cores in their bodies yearn for oneness. And from within that yearning of dark thoughts, feelings, and emotions comes forth a burning light of soul that is willing to soar above and below the cosmic realm. For there is first darkness, and then there is a speck of light that opens all doors to serenity and union with the wholeness of all-knowing. The compassion and seeking of unity is demonstrated through other people's strife and is related back to one's own strife as well, no matter what color you are. What goes around comes back around through the godly hands of the self. We are all different shades of color, and that is reflected through the colors of the galaxy, planets, sun, moon, stars, sky, cosmos—you name it. We are all a part of and connected with the atmospheric aspects of everything in existence. The separation and division of communities is bringing forth the acceptance and love for one another. What is done for one (the self) can be done for everyone. For if you keep your business beneficial within yourself while keeping others in mind, you are thus doing and returning beneficial minding of business to others. It is our godly duty to know what we are here to do while we are living on this earth, whether it is to serve, teach, create for ourselves and others, or something else. We all have a godly duty to fulfill on earth that which is our business.

When I was attending the University of Texas at Arlington, one of my anthropology teachers made us watch a very informative and thoughtful documentary that explained genetics and the first discovery of man. The film was called *The Journey of Man* and was hosted by Dr. Spencer Wells, a geneticist and anthropologist. It explains the first *Homo sapiens* of southern Africa through genetic recombination and historic anthropology. Dr. Wells states that upon discovering and colonizing different parts of the earth, the tribe that originated from the Bushmen community decided to separate themselves from the rest of the tribe by traveling north. Some of the few went way up north where the climate was very cold, and they lived in caves instead of huts and tepees. The long duration that they remained in caves and in the darkness of the cold weather without much sunlight resulted in the skin color of the northern tribe turning to a lighter complexion. The continual mating of this tribe made them lighter in color as generations procreated, and they gained a recessive gene by evolution that causes the pigment of the skin to be of a lighter hue—Caucasian white. In this cold climate, there were many diseases, viruses, and bacteria. Thus, the people of the North became susceptible and used to the famine that had killed many generations of people who were not accustomed to the coldness and abundance of prokaryotic cousins. This tribe lost the knowledge of how to cook for themselves. They were eating raw meat and acting in the most barbaric, violent way, banging wood clubs against their own heads and those of others. The lack of sunshine can do that to people, making them feel depressed and anxious. Their ancestors had passed down the knowledge and discovery of how to create a fire, which kept them warm and empowered them to remain stubborn about not seeking help from the original, primary tribe. Henceforth, the recurrence of violence stemmed from the caveman era and started upon the separation of community tribes from Africa.

A PBS documentary I watched about legendary singer Marvin Gaye addressed his career, love life, and family issues. Gaye struggled with egotism in his career, failed marriages that caused him to be in debt, and confusion within his household as his father was a churchgoing man as well as a cross-dresser. It was not until Gaye had moved to Paris, I believe, and left behind his memories in the United States that he was alone and truly happy for once in his lifetime. Then and there, he had found a peaceful serenity and union with nature. He ran almost every day, and his well-being was healthy. He did not consume any drugs or alcohol. He was mainly focused on himself and his connectedness with God. When he went back to the United States, he had to live with his parents because of his debt. He became miserable and saw a way out of his misery—he got into an argument with his father, and Gaye struck his father hoping that his father would murder him. Growing up in a strict religious household, suicide was not an option. Thus, a lot of people find tranquility and happiness in being one with themselves and just observing everything around them. I can imagine that when Gaye went to a foreign country, he felt like an alien, not having a care in the world. And that is where God wants you to be. The God within you wants you to be like an alien, a part of this world and yet being of it. God wants you to be disgusted with the violence, hatred, and ignorance of this world so that you can "see" the hypocrisies, joy, and everlasting love of what God has to offer you by just being alone. One with God is true love without conditions.

A comedy special put on by Dave Chappelle on *The Dave Chappelle Show* included a skit about a situation that happened in real life to Charlie Murphy and Rick James. Murphy had been invited to one of James's parties, and back then—in the seventies or eighties—James was pretty out there with the influence of drugs and all that. So on the night of the party, James wore a ring that spelled *unity*. Murphy explained that James punched him in the forehead and called him "Darkness." Afterward, the word *unity* was impressed on his forehead from the engraving of the ring. In the skit, James laughingly, jokingly, and repetitively calls Murphy "Darkness" and waves his ring finger and hand to Murphy, saying "Unity." I just thought that skit was so funny and relative to this about unity and meeting our maker inside the womb when we are fetuses in pure darkness. Last but not least to this chapter, we can get a better understanding of what perception and illusion are in *The Twilight Zone* episode "Will the Real Martian Please Stand Up?" The Martian from Mars is an alien who comes to populate and colonize Earth with Martians of his tribe who value war, structure, and patriarchy. The alien from Venus (Venusian) wants to colonize Earth with aliens from Venus and spread peace, love, music, and other good things. The Martian could be in two places at one time and had six arms and hands. The Venusian had a third eye that was covered up by a chef's hat for the entire duration of the episode to disguise him as a human. Anyway, the Martian explained to the Venusian that everything was an illusion, including the music playing from the jukebox and the telephone that rings. It was all made up by perceptions of our brains and minds. But of course, through the power of love, the Venusian heroically exclaimed to the Martian that the Venusians were taking over Earth and that they were here to stay; intercepting the powerful dynamics of the agenda of the Martians; and destroying the Earth with hate, war, and corruption. This notion holds truth to this day among the people of God who play with weapons for fuel in war and who have hidden agendas to increase crime. But then there are people who spread the exponentially powerful effects of the appreciation of love through beauty, music, and art. And their appreciation to sustain this beauty on earth is in competition with darker forces. We always have to balance out these two dualities in real time on Earth.

CHAPTER 13

Live

One of the most untrue notions is YOLO, or "You only live once." You have to live at least twice. I do understand that you have only one life in this lifetime, but we are reincarnated time after time on earth. Reincarnation brings maturity and well-being to our essence throughout the different life cycles we experience in various lifetimes. A lot of people have the perception that in order to truly live, you have to be rich, and others may think that in order to truly live, you have to be young. The art of living, though, is not in being rich in money or young in age but in being primal and enjoying the little things about nature. A person who is truly living enjoys the company of real people, real plants and flowers, real talk, and so on.

Therefore, to be alive is to be real. As mentioned before, everything and everyone that is living needs four things to survive: food, rest, defense mechanisms, and companionship. A human being can suffer a great amount of stress if one of these necessities is missing for even a short amount of time. Nevertheless, individuals who fast often or quite a bit may not need to be as dependent on food as others. Some people practice minimal amounts of rest, secluding themselves from outside obligations, and can live as a sort of hermit so that they can feel the joy of being without and alone with nature. Constant focus and meditation can train the body to be minimal or not needy. As we surrender to the fact that we are all just children at play in this universe, what becomes prevalent is the conclusion that we are all losing to win.

During triumphant obstacles, circumstances, situations, problems, and negativism, we have to play our lives like a game. Whether that game is Life, chess, Monopoly, a card game, or something else, this is plainly how we must see our lives. Out of the negative energy of opposition always comes positive opportunity. Many people spend their lives wondering and pondering why certain aspects of their lives did not quite go their way. But if knowing the self and being true to the self are recognizable to a person, then a great understanding of karma loops and growth is undertaken while in a perceived negative circumstance. Some may ask, "Why does God create obstacles?" God does not create obstacles, nor does your true self. We are given a road map of our highest good from the time of existence, and it is up to us to make the drive. For one, God wants you to believe in the power of faith through knowing what is unknown. If obstacles were not created, then our duality would not exist. With that being said, everybody would be one-sided and living would just be boring. As a matter of fact, living would be so boring and unadventurous that there would not be any fate to foretell. People might as well not have two eyes, two ears, two lips, two nostrils, two hands, two feet, two limbs, and so on. You are truly not living if the dualities are not being expressively experienced. Within the living experiences is a lot of growth and reincarnation. The reincarnation of your thoughts, emotions, and feelings allows you to evolve to the whims of the earth and enjoy it even more for everlasting truth.

Have you ever noticed that any circumstance you experience always gets better with time? The time is always right for other opportunities to come your way while you surrender and sacrifice to turmoil and anguish. Can you see that there is really no such thing as time? Of course we have to tolerate time for earthly business and pleasures, but when it comes to infinite circumstances, time is really not relevant. You simply go with the flow of living and wing it. We are rewarded greatly when we can persevere and be patient with our everyday doings. God gave us the world to live in, and the world is ours. It is up to us to play in it and decide to live our livelihoods how they are planned to be. You see, we planned our whole entire lives before we were even brought into this world. We decided what family members we wanted, and we chose our friends and occupations—all of that. In a glimpse, though, it can be forgotten like a dream, but it is our everyday duty to remember why we were placed on this earth and what we came here to do so that evolution and higher intelligence can take place. There is reality beyond matter that we call perceptions. Light always comes out of the dark matter, forming a magnetism of perfected opposites. The attraction of negative energy catalyzing into positive energy formulates perfection in an imperfect matter. Nothing lasts forever but the soul and spirit. Neither the body nor the mind is kept the same. They both change. But the soul or spirit is always whole and complete with the one and holiness of the light.

Now, you either live more than once or you do not live at all. Some people claim that they feel they are living twice or have an old soul and lived on earth numerous times through past reincarnations. A person who has never lived obviously never learned from their previous reincarnations; he or she is just a walking vehicle in the world that he or she did not serve in, teach, demonstrate, share, or present further knowledge to. Nonlively people do not have loving intentions for themselves or anybody else. They can be very pessimistic, complaining, inactive individuals who turn out to be the bitter fruits of the atmosphere. But as said before, it is never too late to convert a person to live while in a negative status. Sometimes the problem has to bring us out of an old way of thinking to recall and recollect a livelier living style.

Living is not about having the best clothes, trendy material possessions, or fast cars but rather is about good food, some good rest, a nice companion, and the ability to be safe, which is acquired wealth. The finer things in life are within the fitness of the person in the form of survival tactics. Thus, when you can rid yourself of these necessities from time to time, all at once, then you can feel how it is to live with nothing. And how wonderful a feeling it is to be living in a world independently of acquiring pure opportunities out of nothingness. Doors continue to be opened, always originating from a door or chapter that had to be closed. For instance, I installed a program on my computer that is causing my computer to run very slowly. Instead of getting angry with myself and slacking into a depression, I am using my time wisely by continuing to write this book. Maybe if I attended to this work of mine more often than I did, then maybe I would not have acquired the problem of a slow motherboard on my laptop from fiddling with a destructive program for my leisurely pleasure. The absence of earthly fathers and mothers in a child's life can be a blessing in disguise. Who knows if it would be a great idea to spend time with a deadbeat father or mother. Monitoring time keeps people in bondage with a constant everyday hassle of punctuality. I try to go about my days without knowing what the actual time is. I am able to do this mainly on the weekends, when my children do not have to attend school. When I get fatigued or exhausted, I rest; when I want to wake up, it is up to me, not an alarm clock, to wake me up. I eat when I am hungry, and at best I still remain active within my leisure. The real time exists without my notice of time. The Old Testament in the King James Version states that the observation of times, seasons, and holidays should be avoided. But to this day, most of us celebrate traditions. We promote business relations by shopping for different occasions and even I, myself, get caught up in cosmology. The most celebrated US holidays are New Year's Eve, New Year's Day, Valentine's Day, St. Patrick's Day, Easter, Mother's Day, Memorial Day, the Fourth of July, Halloween, Thanksgiving Day, and last but not least Christmas Eve and Christmas. Traditional holidays do bring family and friends together for festivities, but then again a lot of people go through depression and despair during these times because of their lack of friends and relatives. Nevertheless, holidays promote constant business, especially for grocery stores, mall centers, and clothing stores. Christmas Day is a Jewish pagan holiday that actually celebrates the twenty-fifth of every month. Much analysis and research has proven that Jesus Christ was not born on the twenty-fifth of December during the winter solstice; rather, his birthday was during the month of March or April. The only reasons Christmas is celebrated are to give people a reason to spend money on family and friends and to gorge on food during these days at the end of the fiscal year. Holidays are also a reason to look forward to some days. Just imagine if we did not celebrate these festivities around the world. You can say that living would be boring because of the lack of get-togethers we would experience as a whole. But then imagine if we did not celebrate the holidays. Quite frankly, there is not much of a difference in the day. We are just not present and the exchanging of gifts or sharing of food is not apparent. Since there is this constant focus on money accumulation, people are getting more tired of celebrating these bank-breaking holidays. We really just celebrate them for the children and elderly. We adults couldn't care less about the exchange of gifts and sharing of food with one another, unless we are very hospitable. Now, these holidays do lead people to give from the goodness of their hearts, but what is more precious is to share your time without any exchanges. That is true giving. True giving is the willingness to communicate with the people we love often, instead of for some phony-pony show-off holiday. Let's face it—most of us are relieved after the stress and time consumption of gathering gifts for holidays.

Let us take a look at the observed holidays for a brief moment, starting with New Year's Day. New Year's Day is a celebration of new things to come in the following year, whether it is new wealth, health, money, love, or some everyday regimen, we want to make sure we make the right start for the New Year. Nevertheless, resolutions should not be limited to just once a year. Our whole life is a constant, continuous cycle of the same goals in different scenarios. In addition, Valentine's Day is the day of Cupid, love, and professing your love to somebody, usually showing it through gifts. The purchases of candy, stuffed animals, flowers, jewelry, greeting cards, and paper stock are abundant during this saintly holiday. But just imagine how lovely we would feel if love was celebrated equally every day among our loved ones. St. Patrick's Day is pretty much an indulgence day for alcohol, so the price of and demand for liquor is affected around this festive occasion. Good luck and fortune are represented by the green apparel of the Irish leprechaun that is the holiday's mascot. Easter is the day we acknowledge Passover and resurrection of Jesus Christ, yet we celebrate with spring-colored eggs and holiday Easter candy. I'm guessing the colored eggs are representative of rebirth. A lot of families go to an early church sermon for Easter to honor the resurrection of Christ and gain an understanding of reincarnation. We can celebrate this holiday during the cycle of our manifestations that coexist with life, death, reincarnation, and revolution. In May, Mother's Day is celebrated around the second week. Cards, flowers, candy, and anything lovely and motherly are advertised around this time to help us show our appreciation for all of the caretaking mothers in our lives. Memorial Day is at the end of May and is celebrated for the remembering of loved ones, especially those who have passed away while or after serving the country in the military. Contrarily, the underappreciated holiday is Father's Day. The lack of recognition for the holiday emphasizes that many women are the saviors on this planet, while many men are still reinventing themselves through trial and error. It shows that women have evolved in the hardest circumstances. Usually, tools and manual merchandise like watches are purchased for dads to help them understand the essence of timeliness and punctuality that Mother Nature and this earth have to offer. The Fourth of July is the day that the United States of America declared its independence from Great Britain's rule. A day with such patriotism and comradeship calls for very festive events. Correlated with fireworks, barbecue, and alcoholic beverages; this holiday too is a great business driver for grocery stores and convenient stores. In school I was taught that Thanksgiving Day was about the Native Americans and Anglo-Saxon Pilgrims coming together for a feast in honor of their friendship and gratitude. The trading of food goods with others was evidence of the brotherhood and friendships among the people. Thanksgiving is still celebrated like that to this day. Now, Christmas Day is greatly hyped from August on. Stores get people into the buying mode for Christmas to promote profits and sales. We all live on a time schedule in this capsule of recycled holidays and traditions that routinely happen over and over again in our lives. The continuing revolution promotes insanity because it recurs every year. There is nothing new, eccentric, and unpredictable about how to celebrate these gift-exchanging festive holidays. You will get a gift, and it will be consumed, die, or lose its value unless it is of sentimental value. We give because we want to give and we get what is given. And if we do not appreciate what our loved ones have given us over the years, then ideally it can be given away at the right time.

CHAPTER 14

Laugh

The most endearing feeling is laughter. Laughing excites the hormones in our bodies to react to a positive feeling, such as something that is funny, silly, or happy. Can you remember the last time you had a good old-fashioned laugh? If you can recall, in the moments you have laughed until you cried, you may have lost some calories from the energy it exerts from your heart and subsides in your stomach. The moments of laughter can cure ailments like depression, sadness, grief, guilt, or any type of negative emotion there is. A simple laugh overtakes a lot of obstacles.

Through every unpleasing problem, issue, or situation, there is an exchange of opportunity. Thus, when one obstacle gets in our way, we gradually have to become satisfied with it for the time being because no one thing lasts forever. All things are ever changing, ever moving, and ever loving in order to feel the embrace and godly presence that we are meant to feel. We live in a world of ups and downs, but those ups and downs are still circular, as demonstrated on an *x-y* axis graph. There is order to madness and chaos, and that order lies in the center orbital of all matter.

Nevertheless, all that matters to you regarding what you desire and seek will not be of as much importance after you accomplish or obtain it. For example, you get a nice car for transportation and are satisfied with it. After some years or maybe even months, you are going to want another vehicle. Some people, after getting married, are dissatisfied within their union because of the loss of adventure and the realization that the thrill of dating is pretty much over. So some people want a marriage that is more adventurous and fulfilling, or maybe they want more of a challenge for some type of stimulation.

Dissatisfaction is no different than being addicted to drugs and alcohol. You get drunk or high, and eventually you sober up or come off that high. But there is a recurrence of events that rotates 360 degrees; the same feelings and emotions are felt time and time again. The condition labeled bipolar disorder has four phases: manic, depressive, real-self, and higher-self. It is my understanding that in bipolar conditions, the individual will go through all four of these phases within a month's time. I thought that these phases were quite normal because we are all different and all have to interact with the world. Thus, through these connections, we are going to experience a mirror effect of other people's emotions and feelings. Picture an analog clock. Between 12:00 p.m. to 3:00 p.m., a person begins the manic phase, but the depressive phase may last a bit longer, from 3:01 p.m. to 7:00 p.m. The real self will come back from 7:01 p.m. to 10:00 p.m. Then all of a sudden, the person is in a higher state of mind from 10:01 p.m. to 11:59 p.m., and then the process starts over. You may feel this way every workweek. It is the same with a Ferris wheel. At the very top, you are high with excitement, but going down, you become manic. At the very bottom, depression sinks in, and then as you go back up from depression, you return to your real self and the process repeats over and over again. Abroad, feelings and emotions are modified with medication. Physical pain can be modified with pain management medicine in incremental, measurable amounts. But the utmost high in healing is through God consciousness with the self.

These days, everybody tries to find a way to not become angry, depressed, or sad. A lot of us capitalize our well-being on drugs, alcohol, sex, and other devious things to submerge the negativism that our feelings and emotions bring upon us. Why try to fix something that is not broken? Laughter cures all negative emotions and feelings. Being aware that opposition is just temporary will make us understand and feel our real and higher selves, the way God wants us to feel. You automatically have to play with life; therefore, just laugh at everything. Laughter is the God-presence and grace that we all want and yearn to be with. We love God more when we look back at the past and may think, *Why was I ever upset in the first place with all that happened?* The difficulties of yesterday will lead you into better days. It really takes practice over the years of processing these fragrant energies of prosperity. We cannot alleviate our problems with temporary resources and substances. The permanent, ever-lasting resource is God and God consciousness, and in my case it was through prayer with Holy Spirit that I was able to experience this.

Laughter increases serotonin, dopamine, endorphins, and metabolism. All of these can beat any psychotherapy drug. Alcohol just depresses the system even more by the agitation of thought processes in past-tense observation. Substances that we take into our bodies are excreted as waste through the liver, kidneys, and digestive systems. Therefore, these man-made substances are harmful to the organs based upon their side effects and take more energy to excrete because the energy is wasted throughout the body. Contrarily, the medicine of laughter does no harm to the physical body. The hormones that are excited from laughter are distributed from our neurotransmitters, and like a flower sprinkling pollen, laughter shakes the feel-good hormones throughout our total essence.

Smiling creates the same feeling as laughter but within. When we smile at one another, we are reflecting the manifested connection that we have with others. Smiling generates a feeling of oneness. We connect our smiles by mirroring the symbiotic initiation of happy feelings with others. If you ever genuinely tried smiling out of the goodness of your heart, you would recognize a positive adjustment about yourself. Now, when you smile to others, that adjustment is amplified because there is more than one person being smiled upon.

If we take the ups and downs of life with a grain of salt, then laughing will come easy to us. If we let every obstacle, Tom, Dick, and Harry get in our way, then we will be more susceptible to health issues and unhappiness. As you smile, you will come upon frowns. Some individuals will be unable to connect with you because they are on different planes from you at the moment. Disallowing other people's downs to resonate with your energy is a standard. All of us have to comprehend that even though downs are present, we can still experience the ups simultaneously. If we look at a simple, four-square x-y axis coordinate graph, we'll see that there are four positions and the center, $(0, 0)$, where a point can be. First, $(1, 1)$ is located in the top right corner of the graph, at the corner of what we label the first quadrant; $(1, -1)$ is located in the bottom right corner of the graph, marking the fourth quadrant; $(-1, -1)$ is located in the bottom left corner of the graph, in the corner of the third quadrant; and $(-1, 1)$ is located in the top left corner of the graph, marking the second quadrant). The point at $(0, 0)$ is the center force. Since we are all connected with one another, it is easy to assume that all of the planets, the sun, the moon, and the universe affect us all. It shows in our astrological natal birth charts that we house planets, and depending upon the positioning of the stars, it falls under a zodiac sign as well. So there is more influence that the universe offers us celestially with the ornament of uniqueness among us all.

As mentioned before, as reincarnation circulates back again, whether it is after an actual death, a trauma, or inspiration, laughter is reestablished after the incident. That feeling is the God-conscious presence of our soul cleansing, as if in a washing machine. Such whirlpools are experienced through our spinning, rotating chakras so that we become our higher selves in the seventh spiritual chakra, at the forefront of the center of our heads, which stems from the back of our heads where our breathing is controlled. Thus, this realization of some sort of completion or victory allows us to become whole by manifesting a uniqueness in faith of the everlasting love that God has for us and that we have for ourselves.

Now, the ways people perceive others is a laughable matter. Since we all have brains that use and experience thoughts, feelings, emotions, and what we have learned from family and peers, we are all judgmental of one another. This notion sets us apart from one another. Even animals have a sense and perception of judgment from one species to the next. As we learn and relearn things throughout our lives, we have to distinguish which information is true and which is false. Most of the untruths are surface-level fallacies that lack depth and dexterity.

For example, the cannabis plant has been the impetus behind overflowing jail and prison cells. People use this herbal plant recreationally by inhaling its substances and residues, and the effects increase their laughter and feelings of ease. Many legal pharmaceutical drugs have tremendously adverse effects on the body and brain. I believe that whatever makes people happy and in good spirits, without costly side effects, is good for them. Thus, the hypocrisy surrounding the illegality of marijuana consumption and possession perpetuates a false truth about the medicine we have to offer to people. Some people exploit the notion that marijuana detours ambition, but marijuana simply keeps people relaxed and less anxious. As with most things, heavy consumption of marijuana can make people a bit lethargic and sometimes can lower blood pressure, causing a person to get dizzy and faint. However, it is known to help with the excruciatingly painful illness Crohn's disease, and some cancer patients are prescribed medical marijuana along with leukemia treatments. Overall, marijuana keeps people's minds off their concerns.

Many individuals who smile, laugh, tell jokes, and keep other people laughing are actually the most depressed people. They tend to hide their depression with drugs and alcohol or through their good humor. Some people who commit suicide are perceived as generally happy people, such as the popular actor and comedian Robin Williams. So then again, another step to assuring our happiness is to be aware of the people we choose to be committed to and to realize that our true happiness may be found in being alone and away from the troubles that the people we love have caused in our lives. Now, some folks have to have others around them to feel a sense of being and realness. These people may not have lived many previous lives on earth in which to separate themselves from other humans. I'm not saying that you have to be an introvert, but there comes a time when even extroverts want to be alone. Having the company of other entities can simply make us happier as well. But people who have old souls and are ready to experience higher realms of God consciousness are solely concerned with experiencing God's presence and with teaching that awareness to all individuals. Robin Williams said, "I used to think that the worst thing in life was to end up all alone. It's not. The worst thing in life is ending up with people who make you feel alone." The company that we keep can destroy us. We really have to realize that we mirror one another. Therefore, the mirror effect is the simultaneous connection with others, and we mimic each other through laughter.

CHAPTER 15

Pray

One of my former coworkers told me that she needed a favor. She needed many prayers because it appeared that her stepdaughter's illness had taken a turn for the worst. She messaged me saying that it was too early to say and that she just needed many prayers for her family. I replied, "I'm sorry to hear that and that I will be sure to keep your stepdaughter in my prayers."

We all need prayer at some point of our lifetimes. I don't care if you are a born atheist or a die-hard evolutionist, there comes a time when you have to surrender to the power of prayer. When we pray for others' well-being, we are also praying for our own well-being. When we pray for those who have dissed us in terms of discouragement, discrimination, discourse, disability, or disappointment, then we love and pray harder. It is not our place to take other people's external actions or verbal stances into a personal matter to the point that we become dysfunctional adults. So, pray for everyone, pray for the world—you never know; you just might get it. Don't pray for money. Pray on how you can obtain more of it; then you will be killing two birds with one stone—career and money.

Now, there is a certain way to go about praying. In the Christian faith, when we pray, we are to say at the end, "In Jesus' name, amen." That has worked for me thus far, and apparently all of my prayers have been answered formally. Prayer brings a familial state of faith in our belief systems. It is satisfaction to our hunger or weariness. It gives us hope during pessimistic circumstances and peace of mind. Many religious and spiritual groups incorporate meditation into their daily prayers. Daily meditation combined with prayer gives better situational insight. Prayer is all the security, protection, and safety that we need.

I can remember that when I was a freshman in high school, a daily morning prayer was said before the flag was raised. Now, prayer is absent, and people are criticized for even speaking of it. I bet that if we were to bring prayer back into our school systems, there would be less violence among classmates. If meditation was allowed daily in school, it could dramatically increase peacefulness and improve studies. For some reason, we do not adopt these daily practices for our youth, which could profoundly increase concentration as well. Prayer and meditation represent reality and a reason for existence. Therefore, praying before school starts would enhance students' confidence and their ability to create solutions rooted in God's essence.

When making our affirmations to God, we have to be serious with our intentions. Now, we can be jovial in a prayer, but our *intentions* have to be for good. It is not much about what we say in prayer but the feeling and intent of what we want that prayer to produce. And just as we should be careful what we wish for, we should also be cautious about what we pray for. If we pray for God to find us a mate, then we cannot complain if we end up in the same merry-go-round that we were in fifteen years earlier with our first loves. We also have to watch what we pray for because it can surpass us. We can be given the answer, clues, and intuition to our every question if we choose not to be blindsided. That is why we should also meditate when we pray—so that our chakra energy force will operate properly and our third eye will be open to give us better clarity on any situation.

The relationship that we have with the universe is communicated through praying. Even though we may pray in private, we are still connecting with the whole world because what we pray for ourselves, we also pray for one another. It is best to keep in mind the connectedness of every energy entity. People can live just off a prayer due to a sense of pride in achievement. For instance, we can be more relaxed and go about our business when we say a prayer over something or somebody and let Jesus fix it with our faith.

What happens when we pray for something but do not obtain it? Well, there must be a good reason for us not receiving what we want. There could be something better as a replacement or something else that will be just as good for us. When I do not get what I prayed for exactly, I try to set up a cause-effect relationship in terms of my affirmations and agenda on things. I thank the Lord for answering me anyway. If you want protection for whatever reason, it would be wise to pray to God and the proper angel that will protect you. If you want strength, pray for God to give you strength. If you are lonely, pray for Jesus to walk with you. For sickness, pray for a healthy body and understanding of how to make your body sustainable.

We cannot act on prayer alone; we always have to be active in our daily lives in order to not pass up opportunities. The more active we are, the more options we have to choose from. Furthermore, it does not help to worry about any circumstance after our conversation with God. I know that sometimes, it is difficult to keep our minds off certain obstacles, but if we stay active, then most of our problems will not affect us as much. A frenzy of problems can be subdued within a length of time. If we ever get lost or fall from our paths, there are always friends in higher places, such as angels and spiritual guides, who will find and catch us time after time. When we look for answers, we will find them because it is the God-presence that wants the resolution.

Some of us foolishly pray for the perfect relationship. So then, when we get in a relationship with someone who is heartless and uncaring, we are startled and confused about it. A karmic relationship can be a perfect relationship because it involves yin and yang, the opposites. We keep on taking this person who we want to be perfect and to be in tune with unrequited love. A lot of us get into relationships with people who can be the scum of the earth and nothing but childlike takers. And yet we ask to have the perfect relationship with another human being who is just the mirror image of ourselves. All relationships, whether karmic, business, or personal, are meant for our own good. The perfect relationship is with God, and you will experience less-than-ideal relationships with other people so that you can realize that the only real relationship is with Jesus Christ and God. People will fail you every time and disappoint you to humility and despair because, in your eyes, you are the perfect one. God will never disappoint you and will never forsake you. Thus, when you ask for a perfect man or woman to enter your life, keep in mind that God will always show up.

Furthermore, you should be careful about what you pray for because prayer is powerful. For example, I have always been cautious about my weight. I have been teased and bullied about my weight ever since I was in the third or fourth grade, and my parents constantly told me to watch my weight. Right after I turned twenty-five, I prayed desperately to God that I would lose weight, as if my life depended on it. From then on, around every major holiday, I would get very ill for three to four days. The illness would start with my burping a sulfur taste, which was unbearable, and follow with heartburn. Afterward, my stomach would feel bubbly, and I would excrete a lot of waste (diarrhea). I would also vomit continuously. I couldn't go to work because I was in the bathroom defecating and vomiting at the same time. I could not even observe the holidays, much less get paid for them, because I simply could not work on those days. I was tested for Crohn's disease, parasites, and irritable bowel syndrome, and all the tests were negative. Doctors told me to just watch what I eat. In the back of my noggin, I thought that my body was just aging, but I then came to realize the power of prayer. Every time I would get "bubble guts," I would lose about five pounds during the ordeal. Over time, I lost a lot of weight, and my coworkers were worried about my rapid weight loss. I even think that I was more attractive to people before I lost the weight. You see, I never really had bad eating habits other than eating fast food. The excruciating pain that I experienced made me appreciate the best foods in life. I incorporated exercise regimens at least three times a week to make my body feel better. I literally had to learn how to eat and take better care of my body from the fear of feeling sick to the pits. Instead of praying to lose weight, I should have prayed for a healthier body and an understanding of how to be fit.

When we pray in congregation, meaning with two or more people, the power of prayer is maximized. I remember once when I went to church and it was time for prayer and congregation. It was my first time at the church, and my neighbor who had invited me to attend the Church at the Cross suggested that I pray with two of the ministers. So I decided to do so, and a man and a woman prayed with me. The gentleman asked me, "What do you want to pray for?" I replied hesitatingly, "The world." So we prayed, and I got vibes from them and the Holy Spirit. He proclaimed to me after the prayer that I should receive more. From then on, I became more receptible and driven to open myself up to receiving. However, still to this day I have difficulties in receiving due to false pride.

Prosperity is formed through prayer because it sets a standard of knowing that there is higher entity above and within us all. The absence of prayer in schools derives from policy-making lawmakers, constituting disruption of religion and spiritual values in learning. Our country is heavily influenced by the sensitivity of cultural backgrounds, versatile origins, and trends of scientology. Teaching students the existence of God through prayer would enhance morality and good character. The ban of prayer in schools since 1962 disallows public schools to have freedom of expression and speech. The inclusion of prayer could improve our school systems tremendously by helping students understand the universe. I believe the problem lies in between how the existence of God will be taught since students of many different religions attend public schools. But if we only incorporate a daily prayer into morning or afternoon announcements, then other religions will not be excluded. The term *God* can be easily replaced with *higher intelligence,* which is the same as Allah, Buddha, the Virgin Mary, and other religious higher beings. It is as if we don't mind the children in public schools growing up to be egocentric heathens. If we can speak of men who discovered and colonized land on this earth and speak of the ones who set the standard of hypocrisy on this land, then we can surely set the value of existence with prayer in our public education facilities. We idolize and express ourselves through clothes, shoes, cars, and other material aspects but fail to recognize the existence of an entity higher than ourselves.

CHAPTER 16

Prosperity

Prosperity is about learning to observe the presence of God by removing the self-ego and surrendering to God's will. You will know when you are in God's presence from the anxiety of hitting rock bottom or from knowing your true potential. When you hit rock bottom, you basically have no choice but to surrender to your virtue. Under certain circumstances, there is a natural force that will push you to do better than what you are doing now. By grasping the God-presence within you, you will be led to do godly works, thus progressing your livelihood. Also, knowing your true potential improves your understanding of what is expected from you. When you tap into the higher realms of God's presence, you are forming a relationship with your natural good that is endearing to the whole universe.

Prosperity has little to do with money and achievement but more with certainty and consistency. As we observe the gears on a clock, a Ferris wheel at a fair, or the spiral in DNA nucleotides, we can see that they are the catalyst to our drive. We either find thought processes that will detour us from this godly presence, or we get stronger and unleash the godly presence within us. God is so great that he wants to be a part of us in every which way he sees fit. The more belief we have in ourselves, the more that God wants to be a part of us, for believing in ourselves is believing in God. It is pleasing to the universe to overcome fear and doubt because it is limitless.

Now, being certain of something takes dedication to daily rituals. Certainty has no limits on any circumstance and protects humankind. It progresses the world and keeps the wheels turning in life for fortunate gains. Remember, everything is mobile, even the matter inside a rock. All concepts, places, people, and things are energy circuits that form energy whirlpools. Whirlpools are mainly observed in water, resulting from vibrations and waves. Water is emotional and carries a lot of strength within it. We are mainly composed of water; thus, we can produce energy from it. Depending on how big the whirlpool is, it can be independent of the emotion that is on top of it. For instance, let's say you want to sell a product to consumers, and you are sure of its potential. Your emotion of certainty around the product will affect how it sells and how you make your profit. The more sure and confident that you are about yourself and the product, the more active your whirlpool of emotion will become at the idea of it. In other words, as you focus on a certain thing, more whirlpool emotional energy will surround on it. This amplifies your results due to your consistent focus on the energy. Let me clarify that it is about focus and not about thinking; the difference between thinking and staying focused is doubt. Thinking is one-dimensional and mainly uses just the brain. Anybody can think. But to stay focused is the ability to set out your will without succumbing to fearful thoughts like rejection. No matter how many rejections or fails you encounter, you always gravitate away from dissipation when you stay focused.

The same goes for relationships. When you put your time, energy, and effort into a relationship, you form a whirlpool between yourself and that person. So what happens when you put a lot of focus on a human and do not get anything in return? You start to lose confidence in that relationship, and that whirlpool can cause a sense of insanity because you are forming the same habits in that partnership and not seeing any progression. When this happens, you feel that it is rather out of your control to salvage the relationship, and you must step away to gain clarification for your higher purpose. Letting go of the person or business partnership will open and lead to certainty. The relationship will not prosper without the feeling of prosperity, which is euphoric, ecstatic, and erotic.

Money is just a paper form of energy. A homeless person may feel prosperous because he does not have to answer to anybody or follow somebody else's rules. Being prosperous also has a lot to do with experiencing freedom—freedom to do, go, say, be, and feel as you please, not being subjugated to others' opinions and rules. Therefore, a prosperous individual has to be somewhat of a rebel who makes up his or her own rules to form a positive behavior. We cannot depend on other people's rules and behaviors to become our own. By making our own rules, we make ourselves unique and offer our own special blueprint that is marked on this earth. With the thoughts of certainty in a ritualistic demeanor, we can do great things that we would might think are impossible to accomplish. We are limitless like the sky and are rewarded the gifts from the universe, which are here on earth. As an old saying goes, if we keep our heads to the sky, we will have the prize.

Practice makes perfect. Mentally practicing your dedication and continuance of being faithful to your godly work will make you prosperous. Practicing the feelings of gain is appreciation for the more fine and pleasing things in life. Having the confidence that you gain assets and rewards requires your faith in the God-presence that will someday become your present. Therefore, looking in magazines at merchandise, imagining it is yours, and even telling people what you will get in the future optimizes prosperity.

It is important to note that the company we keep affects our prosperity as well. Everybody and everything here on this planet has a job to do. Whether it is to fulfill a divine order or to defame idolatry, we all have a job to partake in. We must take the good with the bad. Good works are done to help others and not to harm others. If we have surrounded ourselves with people who still have old concepts about life and are not progressing, then we must leave that partnership or relationship because the lack of movement has become unbearable and miserable. We must surround ourselves with people who support us, protect us, and give to us. We must distance ourselves from common fads and trends that make us less than human, from the music that we listen to, and from the words that come out of our mouths. I have come to find that the more I distance myself from toxic relationships that are not fulfilling and pleasing, the more at peace I am with myself. We cannot please everyone we encounter. Being in the bliss of loneliness makes us rejoice because we know that we are never alone.

Do not surround yourself with individuals who give up on love because of false, dehumanizing relationships. Love does not have anything to do with how people behave in a partnership. Love has everything to do with God and the light of Jesus being shone throughout it. I see memes on social media time after time advising people to forget about love because it's all about the money. But without love, you have nothing. People mistake sex for love and commitment to somebody and lose the very essence of their beings, the essence of what God wants us to be, which is a love light. So those individuals will continue to face hardships, struggles, and detrimental circumstances all due to their ignorant beliefs about what love is. By forming an intimate relationship with God through Jesus, we can experience how it feels to be prosperous. We gain solitude and peacefulness by having an intimate relationship with God, whether we talk to God and Jesus or simply think about them. And through this intimacy, we do what God wants us to do and become godlike. The way a jump shooter scores multiple three-pointers on a basketball court or flies in midair to dunk a basket are examples of our godly-presence expression. It is all in the form of what we do that makes us have the grace of God. You can only be lifted higher when you have the awareness of the everlasting presence of God within you.

You may ask why some people are prosperous when they do unlawful or evil acts and deeds. The unlawfulness of a person depends totally on his or her intentions. As long as fellow brethren or neighbors are not harmed, then the law is inclusive. The evildoers will always be exposed for their perverted ways. Their time is short in the paradise on earth. They will not experience the kingdom of heaven. If they have a guilty conscience about anything that they are doing, then they will be persecuted and judged for they were warned through their conscience. If an act harms another, then it will be adjusted accordingly. Thus, let's not focus on or be obsessed with the punishment of evildoers but be more focused and compulsive about the works of the righteous.

Now, globalization has taken the blame for people being in poverty. Many politicians, economists, anthropologists, and scientists want to place the fault for all of the nonprosperous aspects of this world on globalization. The outsourcing of jobs, the stagnant wages in America, and the number of people below the poverty line are all due to this one thing. But if we look at the details on how world trade began and follow its history, we will come to understand that poverty comes from one source. The banking systems among us have capitalized on borrowing, loaning, and charging interest to the commonwealth and practically every person on this earth who is born into a developed or developing country. Due to the initiation of banks, there has been a siege of disgusting conspiracy theories behind each continent's debt that are deeply stimulated through the act and play of war.

We are all slaves or servants, and we all have a part to play in this universe. Furthermore, we can choose to be slaves to devil idolatry, or we can choose to be servants of the Lord. Prosperity is not determined by how much money we make, what liquid assets we have, or where our investments are. Better yet, prosperity does not have anything to do with outside forces but rather is achieved on an individual basis that is taken care of by the universe. No man or woman is greater than God but is of like to God. We still have to be aware of our surroundings and dealings with others. We have to work smarter and not harder in order to beat the triumph of poverty. Therefore, globalization has formed a mobilizing effort to compete, monopolize, and increase trade in global markets.

The American dream is supposedly composed of having a home; nice cars; a healthy family; and memberships to the finest golfing, dining, and entertainment attractions. Much of material wealth is hyped up to make us feel a sense of gratitude and connectedness to other like-minded people who follow trends. Thus, most Americans are stuck with occupations that do not pay all of their major bills and that take up most of their time, which is stolen from their families. As businesses try to "race to the bottom" by outsourcing jobs to third world and underdeveloped countries, a generous number of Americans are focused on self-made, self-owned businesses. In order to be a success in entrepreneurship, you do not have to borrow and take out loans from banks. You can be sponsored.

Some people believe that their prosperity was constricted through just one family—the Rothschild family, which started and created cultural globalization, political globalization, and economic globalization. According to Jay Adrianna in her article "5 Lesser Known Facts about the Rothschild Family," the family still possesses US$350 billion in assets throughout the world and maybe even more. The dilution of the Rothschild heirs includes financiers. The history of the Rothschild family reveals that they literally helped financed wars between rivals and only stepped in when they perceived their fortune to be at stake. The five sons of Mayer Amschel Rothschild were noblemen who conquered the interests of kings and monarchs during the 1800s. During the Napoleonic Wars, Nathan Rothschild, who had established his empire in London, helped to finance the war against France and was given the title Baron Rothschild by the United Kingdom in 1885. He intervened because the war was a threat to his business practices. Nathan did not care about the act and game of war; he only cared about his empire and tyranny to rule the finances of the United Kingdom. Therefore, the Napoleonic Wars had to be waged. Nathan financed the British allies with US$10 million in the year 1815. During the British War with Napoleon, the five Rothschild brothers had begun networks that were used for shipping, courier services, and agents that orchestrated the war. Nathan played with the stock market during the opportune moment of the war by selling his stock to the London Stock Exchange and sold all of his government bonds to send market prices into a crash. Afterward, as the prices for these bonds gravitated upward, Nathan bought all the stock bonds back at a lower price to gain profit for the Rothschild family.

The members of the Rothschild dynasty had their hands pretty much all the way in the cookie jar. The Suez Canal in Egypt that connects the Red Sea with the Mediterranean Sea was used for trade between Europe and Asia, and the family members were the main shareholders of the construction project. When Brazil wanted to gain independence from Portugal, Nathan financed Brazil two million in sterling to pay to Portugal as part of their agreement. Brazil also had to take on the debt of the Portuguese government. The interest charged on the loans kept the Nathan Rothschild family in profit and in power for a long period of time. Let me remind you that the five original sons of Rothschild had dealings in France, Germany, Austria, Italy, and England. These countries are the main contributors to big business and world wars.

Thus, to keep the money flow abundant within the families, wars were fought for illegitimate reasons and more interest was added to loans.

The United States of America did not want anything to do with any major war after the Civil War. Even that war—also called the War between the States—was financed by the Rothschild dynasty. The conspiracy to sink the British ship *Lusitania* (which was smuggling arms to British efforts) with a German torpedo launched from submarines in 1915, killing 114 Americans, lured the USA to stupidly play a hand in World War I. Thus, American public opinion was the propaganda for entering World War I with our British allies. Within two years, America declared war and therefore borrowed monies from Rothschild, making the manageable US debt of $1 million skyrocket to the billions. The act and play in war opened the major countries that participated in the game to form the General Agreement on Tariffs and Trade (GATT), signed in 1947 after World War II. Later, in 1994, it was renamed the World Trade Organization (WTO). This plan has no protections for economic policy. It is as if nobody can come up with a plan that will benefit everyone involved in trading. Imports are at a 3 percent tariff, and exports are at 8 percent.

The International Monetary Fund (IMF) was established after the Great Depression in the 1930s. Whereas the WTO deals with trade, the IMF deals with exchange. This organization oversees the transactions of each trade partner. Its mission is to maintain stability within international monetary systems. It is a preventive measure to make all policies fair to all countries. The IMF gives access to loans and lending through the Monetary Fund and World Bank. IMF offers technical assistance on its policies, regulations, management, and legislative law. Accountability is dependent on the governments of its member countries.

In the past, the Intergovernmental Organization (IGO) was created by a treaty involving two or more nations to work in good faith on issues of common interest. The G7 consists of France, Germany, Italy, Japan, the United Kingdom, the United States of America, and Canada. The IGO composed of G8 heads of government, G8 ministers, G7 finance ministers, and G8 environment ministers. Both France and United Kingdom want to expand this group of leading countries to include five developing countries, known as Outreach 5 or the Plus Five: Brazil, the Republic of China, India, Mexico, and South Africa. The countries or states that are not included have citizens who exhibit overtly violent behavior or do not have as many resourceful goods for common interest. Rather, they rely on purchases and vendors from among their own citizenry and may export goods with help from other countries that have cargo access. Contrarily, it is not a surprise that the seven out the eight G8 organizations were heavily involved in the orchestra of modern war. As of right now the G8 no longer exists. Still, prosperity goes deeper than people playing with violent toys during manufactured rivalries.

CHAPTER 17

Play

The game of life brings us equal probabilities of winning and losing. In order to win, you have to lose. With losing comes sacrifice, and with winning comes surrender. Most people wonder why they don't have the career they desire or why it takes a struggle to obtain money. The main reason would probably be that they fear success. If they did what they were passionate about, then there would be no questions regarding what they lack. Maybe some people do not know how to use their resources as being limitless. We are constantly told to have good behavior and to go to college, to make our dreams come true. By all means, if you are a school person, take the opportunity to complete your education and get a degree or two. However, some people know that even having a master's degree in some discipline is limiting and that titles have nothing to do with fulfillment. Going after what you want is the essence of playing the game of life. True gamblers play with thoughts of losing so that they can calculate every move they make in life or against an opponent.

Now, for many years I have not had a real opponent. I don't associate with a lot of friends, so my circle is very small. What I have noticed, though, is that best friends make for good enemies. And this is the very reason I keep to myself—so that I can avoid spreading treacherous feelings and unnecessary words against a person I love. I like to think of myself as a generous, nice, friendly person, and I have been told by several people that I am—until I feel provoked, which is natural. My persona attracts heartless, egocentric, selfish people. My partner relationships have been turbulent, lesson-learning experiences. The only person to blame for putting up with those relationships is me for staying in them. I am a very loyal, stubborn, respectable person (at least I feel that way), which has not gotten me very far in relationships. The main focus in these unfulfilled relationships was sex, friendship, and some communication. My problem with relationships is that, in my mind, they are built on commitment, but the other party wavers. So I have to ask myself what I am doing wrong to make my mates disloyal, unreliable, and disrespectful toward me. The only explanation I can comprehend is that I am mimicking what I want from my partners through my mind and body, which is male and female, excluding the first party (the soul), which is holy, as not being present. Now, I could have talked about spirituality and God consciousness till I was blue in the face and my partner still would not have heard me. When it comes to lovers, the man is blind to spiritual evolution; thus, it takes a woman to show him the way to spiritual freedom and the godly presence. I was not talking to my partners but rather at them, as if I was trying to ram it down their throats. I am glad for every relationship I have encountered because each one has helped to shape the person that I am today. You can say that I am the type of person who likes to stay on edge without even recognizing my procrastination. I can have all the time in the world to do something but will wait till the last minute to actually do it. The rush of getting something done, like an assignment, with minimal time is invigorating. It just would not seem right if I turned in assignments before the deadline. I am fascinated with the contemplation and planning of how to present it. I am rarely late to work or for assignments when I want to be on time. Living life on the edge is the only way to truly live.

A player, whether male or female, is not defined by having multiple active sex partners. That is a whore. Players, though, are always up for game. It does not matter what card is dealt to them. Players will always play the game to lose so they can be surprised by winning. Players laugh at defeat and ponder on sweet victory no matter how long the game is, for patience is within the triumph. When there are adversaries, players use them as pawns to fulfill destiny. Players use everything and everyone to their advantage for a purpose. Players know that they do not owe anybody anything, and they also know that nobody owes anything to them either. Players do not have to woo people to their side or give much attention to their environment because people are drawn to them automatically. Players love themselves very deeply for they are playing for the rewards from God's Word (world). Many are rebellious because there is a yearning of oneness and unity within oneself with God and only God, a communion of fond serenity with the belonging to oneself of truth. Players love and are not hateful. They congratulate other people's success but shy away from attention to their own successes for their work is never done. We play with our thoughts, eyes, and hands. When you go to work, you use your hands, brain, and eyes for efficiency.

We all should be having fun like children no matter how bogged down our lives get. I like the quote by Bob Basso: "If it's not fun, you're not doing it right." We are children of God, so we should rejoice on the playground. Having fun includes being in the now and in the moment; learning something new every day; not being afraid of leaving your comfort zone to try something different; performing playful acts while doing something rigorous like chores; and smiling to make you a joyous, playful person. Recognizing nature, like watching the clouds move in the sky, and climbing mountains and trees can help you appreciate elevated heights and cleaner air. Embracing your flaws will make you fall in love with yourself all over again, no matter what people say. The use of the imagination can help you manifest and accomplish simple tasks that previously seemed impossible to do. Being a person full of surprise by changing your routines can make you more open and knowledgeable. Being a cheerful person in your environment will make life playful and less boring, and it will make you a breath of fresh air to others. Being creative by taking up hobbies, especially with your hands, will teach you the playful aspects of God's power of turning a perception into something you and others can experience, such as writing, drawing, building, painting, playing a musical instrument, and cooking. Not being afraid to get dirty like a kid makes for the greater experiences, and finally, breaking the rules—as long as it is not harmful—is relieving and can lead to better and more innovative ideas.

Now I feel that in order to get the gist of the word *play*, it is relevant to examine the tarot card deck and meanings. I learned to play cards with my father at a very young age. My mother gave me my first card game, which was Uno, and she taught me how to play spades and tonk. While visiting my dad on the weekends, we would play card games such as gin rummy. You can even play cards by yourself with the many versions of solitaire. To bide time at school, my classmates and I would play war with a deck of cards. Now, I just started getting into the apprehensions and meanings of tarot; my father shunned it for being devilish, and my mom does not know much about it. Thus, tarot card and horoscope readings can be addictive for a person like me who was an introvert turned extravert.

Tarot Card Meanings

When looking at tarot cards, it is wise to observe the colors and scenery of the cards and what the major figures are doing to gain an understanding of a situation. The major arcana cards correspond to our human consciousness, which teaches us about life lessons. When examining tarot card readings, we should take the negative teachings as a clue to turn it into a positive. A lot of folks actually try to ignore the unfortunate readings and hold to the belief that they are the ones who shape their own futures. But so that we can learn the concept of play, it is important to explain the cards in their upright positions. We also can interpret readings very positively if we listen to what tarot readers call "spirit." I will cover only the major arcana cards since there are seventy-eight cards in an entire deck.

The fool is at zero, and he or she represents freedom and God's presence without consideration of others' opinions. The fool has a lone companion, a dog, which reminds him or her that nature has to be nurtured. With the dog's primitive and animal nature, it can sense a better direction for the fool. The fool is so much in the air with delight and carefree that he appears to be stepping off a cliff. The fool has no fear and is not even worried about the potential end of his life considering how close the cliff is. The fool's friend, the dog, is trying to warn the fool about the direction to take on the journey. The fool's nose is not at level to the ground but is rather elevated in an airheaded manner. You can compare the fool to a homeless person who is for the first time experiencing the pure bliss of being alone with nature and feeling uplifted by the knowledge that he can go as he pleases with his few possessions on his shoulders, which is all he needs. There is a sense of material loss and knowledge gain. The fool does not have obligations and can feel free take the easy road. The fool is satisfied with nothing. In the background, the sun is bright with the cautionary color of yellow, and the fool is happy with the nice, fresh air in the atmosphere, but there is some type of baby-blue frozen mountain cascade in the background of the old tarot decks. So we can conclude that the fool is blind in a significant way, not noticing or enjoying the countryside or high plains as he seeks to become successful in the world. "Look before you leap" comes to mind. And the journey may be a rocky one. The fool teaches us that at some point in time, we have to be unafraid of losing control to fully trust ourselves.

The magician raises his right arm in the air to cast a spell of opportunities that surrounded him. The number 1 designates the magician because he has the power to turn nothing, which is zero, into something, which can be contradictory to some people. Contrarily, the card is prompted for creation with the divine will to transform substance into matter. Substance can be as simple as a thought. Matter is different from substance because it is perceivable and establishes purpose creating dual outcomes. Any form of creativity or artistry is seen with the magician. He uses the resources and materials that are provided from the Divine to accomplish its goal. When you get this card reading, it represents higher powers and confidence in your skills. The tarot card shows that limitless power is depicted with the figure 8 or infinity symbol above the magician's head. In the background, the color yellow represents caution to his experiments. Even without all the materials and resources, the magician still has a will, which can make him very powerful. This is a card all about doing once methods are established on what to do and how to do it. It is quite simple for the magician to actually set a motion to do and see his work manifest and become true while he sits back and watches it work. There is also red, which represents fire, or ambition. Where the fool had yellow and blue, representing calm, cool, and cautious, the magician has the colors yellow and red, which represent caution, ambition, and willpower. One pentagram is on the table, representing the start of a new enterprise, and a sword on the table signifies protection. A full gold cup represents positivity, and a gold cane or musical instrument indicates creativity. The right hand raises a flamed wand for casting spells, and the left hand is by the magician's side to stay grounded on earth. It is such a divine picture because it reminds me of Sufi whirling, with one arm in the air reaching for the divine while the other arm is downward for balance. Flowers are also in the scenery, so this is about spring and moving forward, getting out of hibernation mode, and performing actions to transform and bloom from the negative. This card is harvested mainly from divine inspiration of making something out of nothing at all costs.

The high priestess can be a confusing feature. The card is mainly filled with hues of blue, representing water and air, which are mysteries. She is our inner voice and conscience. She represents intuition and dwells in the unconscious mind. She gives the magician higher thinking for the best ideas. Where the magician uses resources and materials outside of himself, the high priestess uses her resources and matter that is from within. Emotion and a bit of ephemeral thoughts are represented. She is clothed in a nun habit that is light blue and white. The magician is on the positive side of the spectrum, and the high priestess is on the negative side. You can use the negativity to your advantage, though, by searching for balance from within yourself. It will always be there and is just the opposite of how you portray yourself to others. The true self, which can be covered, is the dualistic theme of the high priestess. By sitting on the throne appearing to wait patiently, she reminds us that being inactive and pondering on our thoughts can help us as well. The two pillars beside her that are black and white represent negative and positive forces. The Gemini symbol is above her crown and throne. She wears a cross and carries a scroll in her lap for she is very informative, but she draws from within. She is the perfect balance of emotion and thought, and she lets feelings surface in her atmosphere. Regarding the colors, the high priestess has a perfect balance of coloration from the fool and magician cards.

The empress, quite frankly, does not correlate with the first three major arcana cards in the tarot. She represents the physical body and the material world for nature and nurture. She is accompanied by Mother Earth, Mother Nature, and fertility. She is seen in all of nature and is very becoming by just being. She also represents unconditional love as she loves everyone equally; thus, she can be vulnerable to being taken advantage of. She does not complain and is not demanding of others; she just goes about her way, being the bearer of protection for all humankind. This card reminds us to take breaks from our routines of work, thought, and obstacles. We can just stare at nature and be at peace whenever we want to, especially on a vacation. Bits of yellow, red, orange, green, blue, black, and white are all about the finer things in life that are materialized and shown throughout nature. We can probably include that the empress is correlated with motherhood as well. The roman numeral III is above her head, which signifies omnipresence. If we examine nature closely enough, we will start to see that everything is God's creation and a collaboration of mind, body, and soul.

The emperor separates the heart from the brain and is accompanied by the empress. He gets his spirituality and understanding of the natural law of God through her. The empress actually guides the emperor to spiritual healing and divinity. He is ruled by Mars and is an Aries tarot card, representing warrior, fire, and leadership; there are four rams on his stone throne. He has years of wisdom, indicated by his long, white beard and cold, side-eye expression. He carries an Egyptian ankh in his right hand for ancient religion and a gold globe in his left to represent domination. He is the ruler of the world and is a great listener for his empire. The emperor is an authority figure and is masculine. The number IV is representative of stability and the strength of four seasons, four corners, and four elements. He can represent some obstacles we have to overcome, like the superego since he can be quite egotistical. He is clothed with armor that protects himself from bodily harm in war. The red sky and gold mountains compose his scenery, which correlates with stability, steadiness, and sure-footedness.

The hierophant replaced the pope in the arcana cards as the great teacher and holy man. The hierophant holds esoteric knowledge focusing on religion and spirituality. This card has a lot to do with institutions and the people within them. The ability to control and persuade is key in this tarot. Churches, rebirths, a high priest, and marriage are present here because it's all about communion without the negative and positive duality; it's about a reunion of traditions. This card focuses on the good for the majority rather than the minority. But when something is empirically proven to be wrong, then change is made for the betterment of the whole. There is a strong acknowledgment of one's beliefs, but a true teacher exchanges those beliefs with old ideas. The Roman number V is above the hierophant's head to signify testimony with his right hand. Two people at the bottom are listening to the teacher, so this is definitely for more than just one figure; it is about the group.

The lovers card is about what was mentioned before as far as the mind, body, and soul. Romance can involve unrequited love when three members are involved in a love triangle. The general meaning of the lovers card is union with female, male, and God in the center of it all. This is a card about duality and is ruled by Gemini. The conclusion of this card can be unrequited love, which can result in separation of this union that was divinely brought together. The card has both a negative and a positive meaning in that one choice must be made over another. The man in the card is looking at the woman's body, and she is looking at God or an archangel, meaning that it is up to the woman to guide the man to spirituality. He cannot do it alone and thus risks losing the right to enter the kingdom of heaven due to straying elsewhere. He must trust the woman to see the angels, spirits, God, and any divine figures throughout life. The female has access to these higher realms of consciousness and powers, therefore enabling communication between the physical and spiritual planes. One lover is lost, and the other is found. One thinks with the mind, and one talks. One is optimistic, and one is pessimistic. This card can help remind us about the Adam and Eve Bible story where God is in the center of their union, but other outside forces tear them apart, such as superficial aspects like the body. Through the power of love, we can experience heaven right here on earth. When this card comes about, you must make the choice of listening to your intuition and inner voice that is fulfilling for you, and you must stick with that choice no matter what.

The chariot is heavily into the emotions of push and pull. Ruled by Cancer, the sweet chariot knows that emotions can be used for their greater benefit. The expression of emotion can create inspiration while amounting to a masterpiece of work. The chariot is not scared nor fearful of the depths of emotion. This card is about forcefulness and control. The two sphinxes on either side of the chariot are negative and positive. The chariot is able to pull both of these forces together for a remarkable creation. Most artists find that dwelling in negative emotions and finding a positive outlet for them works in their favor by maintaining balance. If you observe how a crab moves, you can see that it moves left, right, forward, and backward at dramatic speed. With a chariot, if the horses are not attended to, they will just run wild. Thus, the chariot pulls these forces together to gain equilibrium and moves forward with their power. This is a battlefield card, and people in battle or war can put all of their emotions into use during a fight. You can easily depict the martial arts in this card; as Bruce Lee says, "Become one as like water, my friend." Defeating your inner fears is the lesson so that you can defeat others. You must believe in your willpower and the ability to control anything that comes your way.

After the chariot comes the strength. This is all forms of strength, whether it be physical, emotional, intellectual, spiritual, financial, or any other kind. Ruled by Leo, it transcends from the chariot and blossoms into taming our emotions so we can rise above them. There is no emotion in this card, just determination and patience, which lead to will and action. This card reminds me of the movie *The Life of Pi*, which told the story of a young man who had to be patient in waiting for the tiger to tire so that he could make his move to tame the tiger and befriend it. The woman in the card is shown as having control of the lion after she has control over herself. The strength lies in the quietness of victory to demolish defeat. Strength is a process, and once we have overcome our deepest emotions and our most profound fears, then we are able to attain our desires. Your rejections and fears are going to be what mobilize your drive so that you can accomplish your goals.

Even though the hermit has a reputation for sulking and being isolated, this card actually is good for transitions and transformations. When we want to be at peace and search for deeper meaning within, we will come across the hermit. He shines his artificial light from the outside and his real light from the inside. We are guided into true wisdom and soul searching. The darkness is helping us to return to the light but without the confusion of emotions and desires. After the hermit reemerges into reality, he does not teach about his experience because every person will have to find that wisdom within him- or herself as well. We have to sort out our fears and our own unique higher purpose, and we can do that by just observing ourselves for a moment. Sometimes this may take longer than expected, and the hermit may represent a person who will guide us back to the lightness of the real world.

The wheel of fortune teaches that what goes up must come down and that what is down can proceed upward. The wheel is a cycle of events that claims our destiny and fate. Whether we believe in destiny or fate, the wheel of fortune has no limits in a constant chain of events. Knowing your fate or destiny before it happens is the fortune in this wheel. When situations turn for the worse, just know that they soon will turn for the better. And if you have been enjoying the high life, be prepared for a downfall. You literally have to take life as it is handed to you. The wheel of fortune can get quite boring as you discover its predictability of push and pull, let go and grab. After that, then you can accept the emotions of despair during treacherous times. Big wheels keep on turning, so just roll with the punches and enjoy the mystery.

Justice is the arcana card that rarely has to do with judgment from peers and authority but rather deals with justice from the universe. What you reap is what you sow. If your intentions are ill in any manner, just remember that the universe is watching you. The cause-effect theory is expressed in this card, as well as with karma. What goes around comes back around to us. That is why, if there are any earthly confrontations, we must do our part within our control to resolve the issue with good intentions and let bygones be bygones, because the universe will handle it for us on its own. If you give good things, you get back good things. If you do bad things, bad things will be done to you. This card teaches us about righteousness and being satisfied with what we deserve. Humility is the best lesson to learn from this card when it is time to judge ourselves without the blindfold.

The hanged man represents sacrifices made to gain a new viewpoint on worldly things. He is suspended in the air upside down, going nowhere. The hanged man can swing back and forth or side to side but will not be released through these movements. This is a confusing card because we have to figure out what it is we need to turn upside down so that we can experience freedom. This card deals with lessons that we have learned and gathering knowledge from our experience so that we can move on to our next task. This arcana card does not express much emotion but does express contentment with a current situation. Sometimes hanging ourselves can rush us through circumstances so that we are set upright once again. Sacrificing time for money, career for family, one hobby over the other can be a difficult decision for some of us. Doing just plain nothing can be the solution that reveals the answers. Letting things unfold as we stay still and observe is articulated in the hanged man card. When the brain says act, the body tells us to stay still and clear the mind for an uplifted soul.

Next is the death card, one of the major cards in the tarot decks. Death can be unexpected and unknown, so some people will fear it when it creeps up. But death is also important for our growth and acceptance. This is truly a card for transformations. If we kill off or get rid of the obstacles that hinder us, then we can move on to the next steps to progress because it required forceful action and acceptance within us. Changing our environments and the people with whom we associate can ultimately change our lives for the better. Death is like relieving the body of useless garbage, and perhaps we are in dire need of a spring cleaning. Never put up a fight with death for there is nothing that you can do about it. Death does not discriminate; it occurs for all of us, leading us to regenerate our attitudes, beliefs, standards, and values. We must let our doubts and fears go or death will come around and rip them out for us.

After death comes temperance, the recovery period that follows transformation. We can either be in awe of the circumstance or move on with an attitude of relief. Acceptance in negativism and your shadow side is of utmost relevance to the temperance card. Integrating both your positive and negative sides is the only way you will accept moderation and go with the flow. Maintaining a balance in relationships and partnerships will mostly be the issue when temperance comes up in a reading. Before you can balance a relationship with somebody else, you must balance the relationship within yourself by making peace. When you have become peaceful with anything that is perceived as negativism or positivism, then you will be able to feel the godly presence that you are meant to experience and feel. It is all about keeping calm in the storm and being blissful in the peacefulness, not just being content but being fulfilled with happiness.

One of the most confusing cards and my preference of the evolving cards is the devil card. A lot of people establish this card as negative because the devil does not have a good reputation with God. But restrictions, limitations, and fears are all a part of what the devil will take us through. The devil mocks the hierophant or pope, and the lovers are also seen in the card, but they are loosely shackled with chains around their wrists and necks. The card is ruled by Capricorn and is a representation of pleasure and materialistic possessions. The rule of the card is that the two humans are being voluntarily used as puppets. They have all the power to get loose of the devil but are satisfied with the downfalls of being either submissive or controlling. Instead of the lovers' being equal, they are practicing superiority and inferiority situations. This card is not at all negative—you may be getting a cash or material reward from the universe when this card comes up in your reading. Denying your negative side will give the devil full power over you, and allowing the negative side to take over you will eventually demolish you as well. We all have this notion that we would not mind if positive forces were second nature to us, getting out of the grasp of our devilish ways by taking action to step away from people, places, or things that are unhealthy for us. If we observe the mountain sea-goat (Capricorn), we will notice that the goat always loves to be on top of things, and more millionaires and billionaires are born under Capricorn than any other sign. Upon the mountaintop is this spectacular view that reveals all the heavens and the world. Below the goat, down the mountain, is the underground world that is very tempting to the goat because there are more options down there, but they do not amount to much of anything compared to the mountaintop. So paradoxically, the sea-goat, which is an emotional sea creature, will investigate what is below the mountaintop just to see what he is missing from below, and that mist will symbolically trample all over his dream while he is doing so because the mountain goat always likes to be on top and cannot stand anybody ruling or being above him. Thus, this is the significance of the devil within us being our own worst enemy. You can release yourself from ignorance and pessimistic viewpoints when you can let go of control. You can make your dreams come true when you submit to your higher powers of abiding to righteous, angelical works. The devil loves defeat and exposing your fears, and you are either overly submissive or controlling when the devil is dealt to you.

The tower is an indication that what we build may one day have to be demolished and rebuilt because of evolution. Nothing is ever at a standstill, and we must keep on learning new and innovative ways of going about things. Adjustments have to be made, and sometimes we have to tear down all the walls that took so long to build up. Therefore, if we tear down all of our destructive and outdated buildings, then it just might take less time to rebuild them than before. By having the perseverance of true wisdom, the reconstruction of self will emerge once again. This card is like a fire that has started in a tower and burns all the negative factors that built the tower in the first place. The tower burns all the way to the ground to leave us levelheaded and with a clear, practical conscience on the way life is to be lived. Egos can be revealed in this tarot that people tend to hide from. The tower will force us to reveal our true selves, and we cannot hide from any due change no matter how stable, secure, or protected the old self seems.

The star leads us to the right path of destruction and reconstruction that took place with the tower. The star is warm, loving, and pleasant compared to the turbulence that takes place with the tower. The star will lead you to the path that is suitable for you to evolve from. The woman in the picture is naked, depicting new beginnings, and she is pouring water out of a container for healing which represents what is necessary and simple from the Divine. Keeping and establishing a new faith in life is indicated in the star card. An air of lightness is the feeling in the card with the ability to obtain the necessities of the spiritual realm. This is the beginning of any solution, and it is a rejuvenating arcana card. You can feel a sense of relief and comfort when the star pops up. You are inspired by the natural way of doing things and have hope to carry out your true works.

The moon is illuminating and illusive, and under the influence of the moon you can pro-long to delusions. We do not want to reveal something when the moon is in play, whether it be our emotions or something expectant. The moon is very feminine and can also be a representation of our moon sign. The subconscious is the influence over the conscious mind and can deceive us from the truth. This journey of the moon is done alone, and we must travel without sunlight under the influences of the moon so that we can rely on our own inner light, which will guide us to our true higher purpose. Some things may not seem as bad as they appear in this reading since it can be hard to see in the darkness. Let your inner voice and intuition guide you by listening to your conscious mind.

The sun is our return to a happy, childlike state and is shown when we have overcome the path of darkness. The rays of the sun beam down on us once again to show us that we still rise just like the sun does every morning. We have emerged from the depths of despair, and the power of the sun has made us overcome negativism and turn to positivism. The warm, cozy temperature of the sun is our reward for enduring the hard times and stepping into the light of opportunities, taking our negatives and reinforcing them to work for us. The sun is a sign of completion of tasks and being successful at them for the present and future. The creativity that you underwent during the moon phase is now gaining the spotlight. You can enjoy this feeling for a while before another process takes hold and the true path is revealed for better understanding. Everything starts to unfold, and you can ride the rays of the sunlight.

When all is well in the spirit and the individual has succumbed to integrating the self, judgment arrives. When we can accept the negative and positive traits of our duties in spirit, then we can enjoy the material and spiritual world together. The child within us and the combination of mind-body consciousness, represented by the man, and the renewal of the subconscious, represented by the woman, is the reconciliation of our journey. We are definitely wiser and more loving to ourselves and others due to where we have been and what we have learned from our paths. In the card, the angel is blowing a musical instrument onto the man, woman, and child to signify change and inspiration from spiritual sources. Nothing can really hold you back unless you are still resistant to change; you must move forward. This is a calling.

Last but not least, we come upon the world tarot, where eternity is the true lesson of all that is learned. The everlasting circle of trial and error, positivism with negativism, loving what we fear, and being who we truly are is what rounds up our entire life. The nakedness of the woman wrapped in a divine ribbon and carrying a wand in each hand is pure ecstasy to the person living in both the material and spiritual realms with lots of energy for every matter within the limits of time in space in every plane. During the beginning, we are foolhardy and can only see a cliff to step off and a new journey to approach. At the ending, we can become that cliff, risen up to all that is behind us. Though the cycle is never ending and the slopes may take us longer than expected to surmount, we are always reaching higher expectations of ourselves every day.

To give you an example of the tarot cards I will explain to you my experiences in a poem, starting with the fool.

> Through repeated rejections and aspirations of freedom I chose to move from Fort Worth to Houston; leaving behind a confused mind so I can see and enjoy the true me. I traveled away foolishly. As I sent my transfer request to the southern city of Houston, I cast a spell just like a magician in jail. Quite frankly my request was accepted, and I was shocked but not surprised for the High Priestess I taught told me lies. She combined my emotions and my conscious thoughts and turned them into my will in the pharmacy part where I was taught. At first I was nurtured because my true nature had not yet been revealed. The Universe was kind and showed me much love through the Empress, but I knew I was left behind an earthly true love. I conquered my fears with the few tears from the war I had won with many battles under the sun. The Emperor knew I had to rule and do things my way. Now being first is all I know, and I understand that I make the commands so righteously so. The Hierophant taught me to work as a team in a group of sheep and followers of trend and status. H-town is a city that is fast, but the people are laid-back handlers wanting something to take but rarely give. I came upon a new fondness to love again and through it all I still win. The lovers quarrel and then they stay together for the girls. But the chariot was so hot that every which way was moving like rot. To gain

control over all the blows I dwell in networks for some Strength I suppose. And on those networks I found friends from former work and school perk flirts. I came on strong when my intuition told me to leave it alone. Like the Hermit with his dim light I rest on new opportunity. But temptation was calling me to start something new steadfastly. Everything was going my way and that is the way I like it. The Wheel of Fortune definitely had me psyched; I felt like I had a brand new bike. Justice was definitely calling my name for the fun bondage times I had with a crude man. I am sure I hanged myself time and time again with a person who was just way too fast for love from the beginning. Death had come to my earth father, and I began transforming into an emotional wreck who became vulnerable to submit to thoughts of regret. Temperance may have been the solution but was conventionally ignored. My expressions were vague, thus leading me to a downpour, taking into account that losing control was the way to go. I loved playing with the Devil; it was something different for sure. Not being in control was my ultimate submission. I lost light to my true self and did not care for pleasing someone else's ambition. That was the test, when it was confessed that my body was stretched and my skin was not cleansed. The tower came down; I rebelled like I knew how and told that Devil it is your time now. But through all the rubble and the constant struggle I quit my job out of pure purpose. After all the hell in a commenced jail of isolation was a Star for rejuvenation. She had her cups from all my works and continued to pour her inspiration of hope and faith. The Moon was much of a delusion because I was on a path of not knowing how the darkness would lead me into prosperity. The Sun now gleams and I have a mind-body-spirit of a child. My thought process has matured and what I feared is much more than what I endure. I only judge myself and I like what I see, a person of growth further loving me. For I love the day of Judgment will prove I love thee. The World and all that surrounds it is my universal company. I know this is not the beginning and not the ending but a continuance of foreplay reaching for true eternal framing to get to the heavenly gate with an unlocking key.

Wordplay can be an addictive game in conversations. If you have ever taken the SAT (Scholastic Aptitude Test), you know how analogies correlate with each other. You can take a prefix or suffix of a word and basically narrow it down to its proposed meaning. Take, for instance, the word *fascinating;* it has the first three letters of the word *fast.* The definition of *fascinating* is "arousing great interest or intense interest or attraction." That sounds fast and fiery, and like a fire, attraction can flicker and burn out if it is not tended to. Here are some words to check out to see how they correspond with one another:

- false, faith, fame, fan, fade, fake, fail, fall, far
- bless, bliss, bleed, bleep, blotch
- cat, catch, catalyze, cap, car, catsup

- apple, apply, application, apparently, appease, appear
- red, read, ready, real, reap, reach, reef
- dis, discord, discriminate, disappoint, discourage, disability, dismantle
- egg, ego, egocentric, eagle, egg on
- far, farmer, fart, farther
- her, hereditary, herd
- leap, leak, leech, leave, leaf, lean, leer, left

Take into account that most of these words have the same first two letters. Play with it.

I have always been fond of board games because they do save me from boredom every now and then. I think that it is important to see your opponents as pawns in your own little game. Whether the pawn is an annoying lover, unreliable friend, or way-too-nosy neighbor, he or she is a part of your life in an endless game. At first you can be the main character who is pulling the strings, so to speak. You are constantly on the inside looking out and steadily pulling the strings of all the players. When you come to the point of ending the game, you discover and adhere to your true power. You pull away from your opponent so that you can be the one who is on the outside looking in, fooling your adversaries. All of a sudden, you will come to realize that you do not want to play the game anymore and withdraw yourself from it to end it because you are the main component to the game's existence in the first place. This can astonish the other players or haters and cause them to make fools of themselves. It can be a sad game, but everybody wants to come out a winner. You have complete control over the game when you can just pull away, pull out all the stops, and say, "Hey, game over." You will shame and surprise the actors in that circle and just get to be who you truly are without the disruption of undertakers.

When it comes to relationships, the main problem is trying to balance our feminine and masculine energies. If a woman's natal chart is mostly masculine from the core but feminine from the outside, then balancing her feelings may be confusing, or she may attract more outwardly feminine men with a lot of masculine traits from the core. An outwardly masculine guy may be more feminine inwardly, and many masculine-looking women have more feminine inner qualities. Under the eye of superficial attributes, we can easily be fooled by the players and haters of this game called life. The ability to read people fairly well with the help of the cosmos can justify the need for prejudging as a means of defense. Every situation that we unknowingly create is like a piece of art. It is crafty, articulated, manifested, and dealt with accordingly to either get it out of our way or to use as a tool. We use our knowledge, skills, degrees, and anything that is credible to get us to our desires. Our mind-sets may change, evolve, rotate, flip-flop—you name it—but it is for our higher purpose and destined good. God planned to give us resources to use while we plan the road map to where we want to be. It is up to us to seize the opportunities that will give us peace and resonance. If we fail to take up these opportunities that are given to us to enjoy, then there will always be another chance to get where we are destined to be no matter how long it may take. That is the game to life, knowing opportunity when it is given to you and to act or not act on it. You can always climb off the devil's wagon of unnatural emotions and be the one on top of the world. As you continue to experiment, you will know which players to keep and which not to keep in your heart. You will be lost for a long period if you are continuously in the inside or center of a problem looking out. There comes a moment when you have to pause and be the one on the outside looking in. Don't be so anxious to get to the finish line when you were the winner all along. Peace will be established once again, but you will have more appreciation for it due to the undertaking you have gone through while dwelling in carnal pleasures on rough terrain.

Jesus Christ no doubt was a player for God. He was knowledgeable about the cosmos, and he knew that his reincarnation gave way to our experiencing this division of everything in life. Jesus was not a religious man and was not influenced by either Western or Eastern people. He practiced spirituality and one law, which was under God. The expression of freedom of religion is what separated us from God because there is only one true religion and that is the study of God, which is intelligence in all that we sense as love. Jesus experienced Passover on the cross so that we can experience the east, west, north, and south and their unique, individual cultures, backgrounds, origins, food, and clothes that we call freedom when, actually, we should all be under one law, one religion of God, a species of individuals cooperating with one another. Since men and women have their own notions on how the world should be structured and what to take from it and who to give it to, limits are imposed when there should be no limitations. Being in the body of Christ is the ultimate feeling of serendipity with no limits.

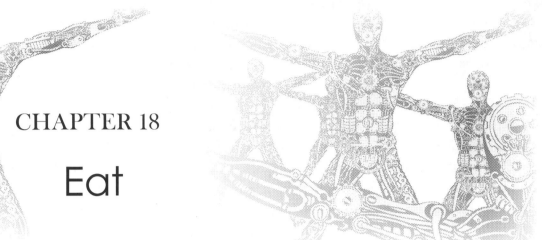

CHAPTER 18

Eat

This chapter has to be the one I have most anticipated because it is so crucial for all of us to know how to not only cook for ourselves but also how to eat our food. Our food is a part of us, so we better know as much as we can about what we ingest. The changes I have made to my diet are to eliminate all dead meat products and to severely limit carbonated beverages. Calories that we consume determine how our energy will be used to carry us throughout the days. My dairy intake is very minimal, limited to cheese, yogurt, 1% milk, soy milk, and vanilla Silk milk. I mainly eat vegetables at dinner and fruit during the breakfast and lunch hours. My main sources of protein are beans, nuts, and tofu, which I eat along with mushrooms. Beef and lamb are excluded because they take longer to process through the body, and unhealthy residues can stick to the intestinal walls because of their texture

You are what you eat, so choose your food wisely. It is important to cook your own food so that you can experience the love that you create in the food and for health reasons as well. Love is the engine to our souls; we might as well put it in our food. Dining at mainstream fast-food eateries is a quick way of stripping your body of the nutrients it deserves and needs. Fast-food restaurants take remnants of food that are hard to digest, leftovers from other meat parts. In most fast-food restaurant chains, potato fries are made from inedible runt potatoes. Most people do not know who is preparing and cooking their meals. Food poisoning is passed abundantly through uncleanliness in restaurants from food handlers. Thus, germs are spread from spores of bacterial infections that are painful and can be deadly. These cultures of bacteria can be treated with antibiotics but will forever stick with you in your intestinal tract, and they may linger for a while until they are cleansed through the deregulation of toxins. Our organs are clearly organized within our anatomy to help remove clutter and nonnutritious substances that we ingest into our bodies while also using the nutrients and energy from food that we need for our bodies to function properly. Our waste is excreted throughout the gestational tract, spleen, liver, pancreas, kidneys, and colon. All of these organs play a special part in sustaining our health. It is no wonder that all living creatures have bodies that process all digestive remnants.

When you eat fresh food, you feel fresh, and when you are able to smell the essence of your food, you want to love it. So you create tasty dishes that resonate with your fine style and taste for life. You can put a lot of yourself into any dish that you choose to make. To me, being able to cook for myself and company shows how much I appreciate the finer things in life. You literally you have to appreciate everything that is ripe, fresh, and grown when you learn how to cook. While you are cooking the food, you appreciate the sounds that it makes. Seeing how the colors come together at the final stages of cooking is exciting, and they can be representative of the colors we see in a rainbow for a complete nutritional meal. Expression is an important part in putting love into your cooking style with presentation. To make the dishes be loved, you have to give it patience and take your time with it so that it can reach perfection. I will bake my food instead of frying it any day, but for some people, a baked meal can taste bland. If you do decide to fry your meat or appetizers, I would suggest using coconut oil. It is healthier and makes your food taste better, and it is more expensive than other oils, which will deter you from frying your food because you will want to conserve as much of it as possible. The tremendous effect of baking your food over frying it is a far healthier and lighter meal. Try to buy fresh food from grocery markets. You may have to go to the grocery store once a week for a stock of fresh produce and meat, but the benefits are well worth it. Make it a routine to be creative and inspirational with one of the things you need in life to survive, which is food. Love your food, and eat it to live. Our energy is produced and generated by the food that we eat. The produce is grown under the sun and some is harvested from under the ground—the silver lining to matter, energy, and power.

After praying over your food, you still love it by eating moderately and respectably. Moderation applies to the portions, and respectability applies to not devouring it. For something we look forward to everyday like eating, God has provided us everything possible that we can find edible. Globalization has exposed the detriments of what division can do to the world. Instead of working as one network and unit as far as import/export policies, we remain divided under different agendas. We all have to eat to survive. Just think—if we could just provide people the four simple necessities on this earth to sustain survival, then we would be in a better place. But our perception of our entire universe is separate when we need to perceive it as whole, like the globe. A society that is not wary about food, security, the company of others, and whether or not they will be at peace is less violent, crime is low or nonexistent, and the mortality rate is lower. So giving individuals an adequate amount of food, rest, defense, and companionship for survival and an uplift of their existence is all the policy that the political caretakers should be concerned about and interested in. Anything that pertains to these four tactics is a major concern for all lives.

Marketing for pharmaceutical industries is a trillion dollar business that has profited from the sick, diseased, or ill. These pharmaceutical companies promise the solutions to your health mainly in the form of a powder-formulated pill administered orally. A simple change in diet can cure a person's ailment or at least alleviate it if the damage to the body is minimal. Every now and then, it is wise to eat a meal that does not contain the heaviness of protein. Americans consume a lot of protein; it is in almost every meal every day. So the absence of meat from one meal periodically will give us light-source energy from produce. For example, you can make a pasta salad that will give you all the nutrients with few ingredients. Also keep in mind the need to include all of the food groups from the nutrition chart. It is important to note that eating before you get hungry will lessen fat deposits on your tissue and cells and lessen insulin withdrawal while also decreasing your chances of becoming obese and susceptible to diabetes. You can balance your weight with the mind-set of "energy in, energy out," and if you can manage your appetite so that you are not hungered, then your body will not go into panic mode when you crave energy from food sources. Simply noticing what we eat can help us watch our weight and monitor our health. A person who has inner peace with resonance does not need the assistance of a physician to prescribe a pill every thirty days and to schedule monthly visits. Pharmaceutical companies are built for the minority of individuals who suffer from hereditary mutations and painful ailments. Contrarily, the majority of people are taking medications that do not cure sicknesses but cause more health problems for the organs and keep them in the hospitals and doctors' offices. I am not against pain management therapy because a person can die from pain, nor am I much against liquid injections of medicine. It is the substances that take longer to pass out of the body that are of major concern for they are easily abused. For every sickness and ailment, there is a pill—pills that will put you to sleep, make you stronger, help you lose weight, moderate your cholesterol, lower your high blood pressure, manage your blood sugar, cure erectile dysfunction, you name it. But if we just pay attention to our nutritional methods, then we don't have to lower our well-being to a pill that can possibly put us in a zombie state by depleting our energy. Chapter 26 contains further discussion about the drug industry and the abuse, dependency, and replacement of energy sources.

Everything that you swallow or administer to your body affects your mind as well. The body and mind are not separate from each other or the soul. That is how strategists get confused, thinking that the physical body is just a vessel that doesn't have anything to do with the spiritual. The spiritual body and the physical body are in union, and that is why our choices of food affect how clear our skin is, the health of our hair, and the length and color of our nails. Energy from animals, fish, and produce encompasses our entire body, altering our auras, chakras, and souls. The division of resources and the many miracles that Jesus Christ did were remarkable, and there were days when Jesus fasted without the sensations of hunger; his stomach was empty but he was full. Turning water into wine, a couple of fish into many, and the teachings of Jesus can all be summed up into the four survival technicalities: food, rest, companionship, and defense mechanisms. If we want to enjoy the simplicities in life, then these four obstacles must be our main focus to live like Christ.

CHAPTER 19

Rest

Every day is restless and filled with hurried followers beating the bustle of the herds. Almost everybody is in a rush to get somewhere even though they have no clue where they are going. Performance in the workday is measured by time-efficient, accurate, precise results. Productivity is disguised by anxiety surrounding rapid-function abilities and skills. You exchange your time for money when it comes to working. If we were to create a formula to represent the workday, it would have money as (paper) energy, the hours worked as time, and speed of productivity as either distance or velocity. Yes, a lot of us are just robots within the job sector, including me. Some organizations do not depend on productivity results, but those jobs are mainly artistic. If you are happy with your current job but know it lacks purpose, then you may come to the realization that life is definitely not all about money. Many people are quite comfortable with the earthly pleasures that have always been granted to them without having stress. Now that the industrial infrastructures of business are mounted into our soil, we can abundantly choose any occupation that we like. An occupation that is both rewarding for us and demonstrative in helping others is the only job that will satisfy us.

Some people, like me, are slow and stubborn about getting to what we are destined to do but fast and diligent when money is the only thing that feels secure. The money I received from my previous jobs combined with my immaturity fooled me into ignoring my calling, but even without knowing the description of my birth natal chart, I ended up going to graduate school for public administration while also being enrolled in metaphysical school. Thank goodness I was more rebellious than stubborn, so I ventured out into what I know I am supposed to do. The other occupations just helped me along the way and gave me great skills for my career. If you were to ask me five years ago if I would see myself as a person who was even interested in administrative politics, I would say no. Everything is planned right for us, and the trippy thing about it is that we don't realize what is taking place. We are literally on a trip to a destined journey that has little to do with time but a lot with fate. So we do not need psychics to tell us our fortune when we already consciously know what we are to do on this earthly plane. We will get there anyway, so there comes a period when we must take a rest to get on a spiritual plane. We may go through isolation, jail, prison, asylum, restraint, or some other confinement to get to our higher selves. Force and pressure to not obey the law, follow the rules, or just not be connected to materialism gives us precious time to relax before we being the adventure into becoming spiritual beings.

After quitting my job of nine and a half years, I had to adjust to losing some control. Being the provider that I am, this was very depressing for me. During that period, I was the most depressed I have been in my entire life due to thoughts of uncertainty, instability, and insecurities about finances. Even though money was not a concern for my family's survival, I was weary from the stronghold of excess energy from a paycheck. I was using my fears and rejections to work for me to "grow down." Being grown up for so long can wear on you because of the dependency of others, so there is nothing wrong with taking a breather. We are just breath when we take away all the anxieties, pressure, grief, sadness, anger, and fear. During rest periods, focus on your breath, on the way you exhale and inhale with your diaphragm.

If you do not get an adequate amount of rest, then your body will get bogged down and leave you in an unhealthy condition. When your body aches, that is a sign that you need to relax, rest, and stay easy. A lot of illnesses are due to constant feelings of stress and fatigue. If you do not find a way to give your body the rest and recovery that it needs, then it will try its best to get some sort of attention through a heart attack, stroke, high blood pressure, and other diseases. Even with exercise, it is wise to take rest days between your workout regimens so that you can rebuild muscle tissue and hormones. All matter needs a resting period, and so do you after days of stress. To gain understanding of mobility and purpose, there is an ultimate reunion that is higher than a present earthly reunion. Busting your ass every day and getting little in return is not the way you should live. Getting just two to four weeks of vacation out of the year is a tease because when you go on vacation, all that you want to do is rest unless you are serving your higher purpose. Being enthusiastic about everyday life will save you from restlessness.

Another cheat on relaxation and cleansing of the physical and mental capacities is yoga nidra meditation. Yoga nidra assists in improving your sleeping patterns by eliminating interference from the previous day's work. The subconscious mind does not remind you about yesterday. First, you sit still and undisturbed and focus on what you want in life that is satisfying. The thought will spread throughout your body, incapacitating your mind and giving you pleasure. Next, breathe slowly and deeply through your nostrils, feeling the sensitivity of breath extend to your body parts. Your nerves will relax, causing the neurons in your body to settle and recover from nervousness. Subconsciously imagine pleasurable feelings that you have had in the past by thinking about them to regenerate them. Reliving these pleasurable experiences will help you manifest your willpower. Last, use creative visualization of scenery that gives you peace of mind and relaxation. Repeat these phases over and over again for about forty-five minutes to an hour or more if you like in a nondormant awakening.

CHAPTER 20

Rejuvenation

One day recently, I had a headache that was probably caused by my tooth aching and a case of spring fever, with Mars and Venus in Taurus. I tried to sleep it off after taking a pain reliever, but it still mildly ached. My youngest daughter also had the same symptoms, and usually when she is feeling ill, I get suckered into coddling her. We said a prayer together, I gave her some allergy medicine, and I basically transferred my energy symbiotically to her, focusing on both of our breathing, until she was asleep. Afterward, I listened to the song "Rejuvenation" by musician Lonnie Liston Smith to relax myself before going to bed. The melody was the perfect representation of being rejuvenated. The song incorporated sounds similar to what you would hear during the day along with soft symphonies, and on the album cover Smith wore these cool blue shades that looked youthful. The next morning, my daughter's fever had reduced and her headache was gone, but mine was still currently present. The only substance that seems to alleviate my pain is marijuana. It not only relieves the headache but also relieves other parts of my body that feel alienated as well, especially my digestive system.

The recreational use of illegal marijuana has no doubt made me feel ashamed due to the restrictions and statutes that limit it, especially concerning my employment. There is a way to cheat a marijuana strip test, but I feel that if marijuana helps me so much, then why is it against the law to consume it? I would rather not bother with an employer whose policies are going to get in the way of what is healthy for me. Therefore, I did not feel the least amount of guilt about pursuing writing and school over a job that would only stress me out even more. My health is far more important than any occupation. As I look back to the past, I can't even comprehend how I stayed so loyal to one corporation just because it provided me a security exchange. But all things happen for a reason, and I am sure that I passed up many opportunities for successful endeavors by being too occupied to realize that there are no limitations.

Going through a rejuvenation stage is getting back to the feelings you had when you were a happy kid, when being closer to the ground did not stop you from being adventurous. Growing down can at first be a lot of watery pressure, like that of being in a womb, but then we can steadily keep on growing into our adult years while crafting the subjects that we did as a child in mature form. If we make time for the interests and hobbies that we love, then the pressures of life cannot affect us. If we neglect to do this, then we may be heading into the latter emotions of dying. To avoid that, we must know what our purpose is and become grown adults who are never afraid to learn anew. On most days, we need to not care about our appearance but rather our inner beauty, and we start by taking care of our health regimen.

Exercising is very important to the revitalization of the mind-body-spirit, and rejuvenation research has proven that it fights aging by repairing damaged cells in the human body. The research stimulates interest in therapies by observing cells, immunological devices, and genomic growth factors. Combining exercise regimens and rejuvenation therapies is a breakthrough to living longer. Depending on your current health, rejuvenation therapy can come after exercising has taken a toll on your joints due to aging. Introducing therapy before cell damage occurs prevents disease, illnesses, and disorders.

Standard binaural beats enhance the rejuvenation experience by helping a person visualize and stare at a picture, allowing meditation to stimulate the area from the center of the frontal lobe to the temporal parietal and occipital area of the skull and then generate the chakras that need healing. Regarding the whirlpools in our chakras, there comes a time when they can be depleted, slowing down in circuit like a steamboat on a river. During the depletion of water in the circuits, we may experience a craving for separation from all that is draining us. Under urgent circumstances, our bodies know when to slow down, even before anything occurs. Finding your niche can have you performing alchemy rituals unknowingly. The mixing of metals into gold for a perfect elixir is a magnificent rejuvenating process. Obtaining the fountain of life is like emptying your chakras of water and refilling them. The water represents the perfect rhythmic flow of cleansing and making oneself pure over and over again. Cleaning and clearing the clutter around you, whether it be in your home, body, attitude, or any standard that has to evolve, is an ongoing process. Exchanging matter with the correct formula is magic in itself. We are all magicians reconfiguring and manifesting our own future outcomes from our visible beliefs that are invisible because of our naïveté. Thus, we go through periods of birth and death in between transformations and undertake it all in a matter of situational circumstance. The feelings of tiredness are all a part of the way we feel as newborns and when we are elderly. Pinpointing the freedom to determine our own destiny through unconditional intuition, emotion, and feeling brings us into the depths of the soil on this earth, and with the inspirational influences that chain our hearts, we create fire in the source of energy to maintain power for alchemic functions. Transforming any small situation into a dissolved situation for creative means replaces old atoms with new, regenerative atoms that switch to positivity.

Going through external changes for desires might not be at all what we have planned for. For instance, we may pray for a partner who has all the qualities of someone from one of our past relationships because they are familiar. Then, when we get into a relationship that fits our desire, we may find out that we bit off more than we can chew. We may go through many obstacles and changes just to get to that destination and end up not wanting what we prayed for or using it for our advantage. Prayers start a new cycle for opportune gains. Relationships that we form with other people prove to us the love that God has for us. When we are aware to be careful about what we pray for, then that is when we pray more for God's presence through Jesus instead of a human being. God will send us anybody we want, but we have to be ready in case it comes and we do not want it. You can feel the rejuvenating presence when you take a shower to cleanse yourself. The wonder of water, which is so pure and flowing to us, relieves us from pain and strife. Water is a spiritual gain and can take over any material gain because it is needed for thirst, cleansing, and energy. From a woman's perspective, I have even achieved orgasm from the stream of hot water running along my genitals while bathing or showering. Nobody will ever satisfy you but yourself and what God has in store for you, but before we proceed, you have to rejuvenate your youth again and be clean.

A woman is reminded about her body constantly and from an early age. When she is a young girl, she is taught to cover herself up by wearing a bra and, in some countries, a shawl or gown. During childbirth and her menstrual cycles, her body goes through agonizing pain, and she can't help but notice her body and all that comes with it. These phases do not prove the inferiority of women but rather the superiority of a woman's body, which can create, renew, and be productive by using strength. I like to think of the woman as dualistic in her qualities because of her functional durability and powerful stability to take care of youth. In most Eastern countries, women cover themselves to protect their sacredness, and their inner beauty can be appreciated through their piercing eyes. Naive women in the West lack the purpose for their vehicles because the female body is openly exploited in movies, videos, songs, and television shows. Fashion lines are tailored to the woman's body with its erotic features that accentuate sexiness. So women are definitely sellable, like property and cattle, for idolization. I often wonder why God gave us bodies. I mean, Adam and Eve probably would have never been cast out of Eden if it were not for the body. I guess the world would be a boring place with souls just lingering around. God formed Adam in the image of himself, but a true image of himself would be everything from the dirt on the earth to the stars up above, all of the planets, and the galaxy all around us. The body is just three-dimensional, and the reason we have it is so we can feel through stimuli what it is to be God through human contact with other god-beings. Getting into the presence of God through our bodies is all the occurence we have with God.

A soul mate relationship is a coupling of two people who understand each other on a soul level. Soul mates know how each other feel before anything hurtful is formed between them, meaning that any aspect of betrayal between them is devastating. Gossiping about somebody when you feel that they have hurt you is not indicative of a soul mate relationship. A soul mate will not underhandedly allow another person to think, hear, see, or feel badly about you in any way. Your soul mate will always want you to appear at your best and will not reveal any information that they know or feel will belittle or undermine you.

A person who does not interact much with other, different souls is soulful or an old soul. Old souls do not need much information from others because they have roamed and been reincarnated on this earth many times. When they do seek information, it is mostly in a form of documentaries, articles and books, biographies, history, and anything that will get them more in touch with their roots. A loner's soul burns very bright; it longs for continual companionship that never stops. The body in depth knows that the soul came first, then the mind, and last the body. A lot of folks keep to themselves when they comprehend that the soul needs less drama in their vicinity. More God-conscious focus will make people's souls grow fonder of everything around them without the assurance of other souls. Just as there is one sun, you have one soul, and when you conjoin with a spouse on a soul mate level, you will still have one soul combined. Soul mates appreciate each other and support each other's actions, thereby complementing each other. There are no secrets between you and your soul mate just like there are none between you and God. So when someone betrays your trust, your soul starts to break free from that person's soul through disbelief. The soul never breaks; it lives on forever. The body can break down, the mind can get lost, but the soul is here for an eternity. Your soul makes your life eternal, and with your eyes you can judge one another. People gossip with one eye open and one eye closed. When you involve the person who is being critiqued and judged in the conversation, then you are seeing with two eyes. But a person who sees with his or her third eye does not need the information of others to judge, analyze, or critique a circumstance. The third eye is all-knowing and all-seeing through God's perception with silence. The soul is silent, not loud like the body and the mind. It is at peace and at one with itself. Soul searching gives us peace and allows us to feel God's presence from the beginning and end of time. It's the only thing that truly satisfies us in a spec of an eye.

A healthy soul has a healthy spirit. To imagine a healthy spirit, just think of a church choir and how the feeling of the words takes over them and the audience. You do not see anyone at all out of the spirit when singing, and it does not matter how you sound because it is in your soul that people can feel you. When you have the Holy Spirit in your realm, you will naturally have a glow to your appearance that can draw people to you—or maybe push them away from you in awe. The soul modifies relationships and gets fueled by them with instant connection, and it can go through despair when connections are weak. The heart and soul are interlinked with a pulse to be able to feel. They soar together to place us on another plane besides the earth. Conditions of the heart can chain and shackle the soul through human impact and conduct. Entanglement of mistrust, disloyalty, and maltreatment can limit the soul from experiencing its true essence. But with time, the soul is able to recover from any amount of damage.

CHAPTER 21

Mind

Empty your mind … Be formless … shapeless, like water. If you put water into a cup, it becomes the cup. You put water into a bottle, it becomes the bottle. You put it into a teapot, it becomes the teapot. Water can flow or it can crash. Be water my friends.

—Bruce Lee

"A mind is a terrible thing to waste" is the slogan used by the United Negro College Fund. Through all of our experiences with other beings in life, we have brains that analyze, critique, and judge people's actions. We are all prejudiced, and until we accept that fact, we cannot move onto aspects that are past judgment. If we are kind to others without expecting reward or gratitude, then we are improving the formulated relationship that we have with God. God created all things and all people using the same image of the self with different makeups of DNA blueprints. Family influences, friends, peers, and the media shape our perception of the world and the critiques that we have about it. Many Americans sit in front of a television to add to their daily source of drama and information. In today's era, technology has improved network connections pertaining to school and work but has depleted the connectedness of personal relationships, which has deluded the masses. If we are to be loved and God-conscious, relationships have to be truthfully connected as well. Text messaging is the prevalent form of communication when it comes to the people we love, but we devalue feelings and emotions when not speaking verbally. It causes confusion because the mind runs rapidly and yearns for physical, sensory pleasures, which we misconstrue with text messaging. Emoticons demonstrate feelings but lack sensory depth and lead to confusion when we're trying to understand the depth of an emotion. When the brain receives sensory pleasure, it spreads all throughout the body in a real way, beyond textual lines.

Lacking mind connection and stimulation is daunting and can be one of the reasons a mind gets lost. Many martial arts prescribe the practice of mind over matter. Flexibility, endurance, and strength are practiced in shaolin kung fu and other art forms of physical protection. Overcoming physical pain and using natural forms of flexibility are talents that can be taught at a very young age. The exercises are specifically created to use the most fragile parts of the body as weapons first; then, metal weapons can be added at another age level to strategically master defense. I feel that the weakest parts of our bodies are the wrists, hands, and ankles. Gaining strength in these areas should start at a young age. Doing flexibility exercises can help these body parts more able to deal with the pain they feel through punching, jumping, hitting, and kicking.

To understand matter, we must first look at the history of it. Matter is cow and bull feces, and since it is defecated we can conclude that it is nothing but what we eat pertaining to weight. Therefore, eating the lightest meals—that are preferably vegan and vegetarian—is the best diet for achieving mind over matter. Proper upright posturing of the body assures proper bone muscle and neuron growth. It is important to mainly eat green vegetables because they keep us grounded to the soil, like the plants on this earth. When meat is excluded from the diet, the digestive system is trained to process food much faster, which increases metabolism.

Separation of mind and body is the separation of God from us. If we were to combine all techniques from the east, west, north, and south, we would not only gain an abundance of spiritual knowledge, but we would become as one and our power would be multiplied. Gathering various styles from all regions of the world proves the mind over matter phenomena. Norse mythology; Shaolin; Buddhism; the teachings of Jesus Christ, Allah, and I Ching; runes—all techniques are God searching. Every aspect that came from man first came from God. We make conclusions, judgments, and speculations through the mind. We are reminded about our God consciousness through the Holy Spirit, which encompasses our entire body with inspiration and makes us whole, or holistic. The constant remainder of thought that is mostly processed in the brain is manifested until something else replaces it because there is no room for it to exist. It's like when you blow a bubble from gum, a balloon, or soap—the bubble can only go so far or the balloon can only hold so much air before it bursts. That is the same reaction we have when we are focused on something to its normal capacity. That is why constantly worrying about a subject can lead to stroke, shingles, or a heart attack. The bubble can be slowly released through some other body part as well, like joint pain in your shoulders. To give you an example, my worries may be more focused on my finances; thus, my shoulders may suffer more than other body parts because my second house in finances is in Virgo, and the second house is ruled by Taurus, which occupies the throat, shoulders, and back of the neck. I may analyze money in every resource that I have until there is no more room to analyze it, and in the long run my speech and shoulders may suffer from the burden. Or if my finances are intact, these parts of my body may get a boost. Your body is a house, and it is up to you to defend it from outside attacks that try to take it over. So if someone keeps knocking on your door for some reply, you have the choice to ignore them. Only you can tell the person if he or she can gain entrance, and you are the only one with the key to unlock your home. Vandalism and theft of the mind, body, and spirit can occur by people you know or people you do not know. The house requires maintenance, cleaning, sweeping, dusting, refurnishing, and yard work.

Increasing the value of your mind requires you to not mind or perhaps to say, "I don't mind at all" regarding whatever is outside your personal space. You tend to not mind when something does not pertain to your house or property. Imagine going to the gym to work out, and you have waited to switch your credit card information to another card. You have about one more week before they will take the funds out again, so you decide to wait a couple of more days to switch. As you walk out the door, you notice the receptionist flirting with someone, and you proceed to the door with a smile and go on about your business. The next time you go in, you decide to update your information that day since you will be out of town for the next few days. You see the employee flirting with a member and you don't mind. Then you see that they are still flirting with each other three minutes later, and you wait for them to finish their conversation. Now you *do* mind, and you start to get agitated. You are letting the period in time affect your sensations of impatience. The urgency of your plans to leave town is a result of your choice. Getting into a "never mind" or "I don't mind" mind-set will mature the mind, and there will be less of a malevolent karmic effect on you. Furthermore, when we're at ease, we are less prone to disease.

Freeing your mind from heavy burdens and all else that is debilitating to you will make you light from within, which will heal you. You may be lacking in some areas, like communication, but if it does not affect your well-being then it is not a factor. Say that people tell you that you have a problem with expressing yourself, but you feel otherwise. The house in communication will not be affected because you do not feel the same as other people do about your expression. According to you, your expression is in tip-top shape, and you feel that people will have to adjust to your style. So the third house and any other house that deals with self-expression, like the first and twelfth houses, will not get sidetracked. When it comes to the self, you literally have to not care about what people think about you. You can take their advice into consideration, but you know what kind of person you are; it takes a person with true confidence to overcome this. So you also have this metaphor of you emptying your mind of all that hinders you from progression. If you are a person who likes to control more than submit, then losing control can cause you to lose your mind if you get to a breaking point for constant change. If you are doing something you do not want to do routinely, then you will feel an inkling for evolving and seeking out where your mind yearns to go for some relief and decrease of tension.

Repetitively processing a thought that you can sense will lead you closer to it. Traveling to different places will open you up to different cultures, backgrounds, and histories of people who reside in those locations. As you go back to your home, you can recall the sounds, smells, tastes, sights, and textures of the atmosphere and people of the country or city, and you draw it closer to you when you remember what it is like to visit there. Thus, if you allow your entire mind to be consumed with it, then you may visit the place more than once or decide to live there. These are the works of manifesting through the senses of the body through the perception of the mind. The greater the effect of the feeling, sensation, or emotion, the more power it will have over you when combining the mind and body. The mind-body is not free from worry, senses, perceptions, thoughts, feelings, emotions, and all things and people that come into contact with. That is why we have to be free like children to pay no attention to what tries to harm the mind-body. When someone cuts you off in traffic without a signal, just shrug it off unless it causes a wreck. Even then, your exterior should be calm in the face of other people's mistakes.

African Americans and other people of color have been called the most soulful persons walking, with astonishing artistic talents in music and dance. During the slavery era in the United States, slaves would sing in joyful light and dance for comedy and spirituality. I have always been amazed at how the slaves could keep such high spirits under complete control. A timid demeanor was a sign that a slave had been subdued by a whip. If punished, slaves would continue their work all throughout the fields and the slave master's house. Slaves would sing while they were cooking, cleaning, plowing, and cropping, even through being beaten. To this day, most African Americans are reminded of their skin color and bodies every time they come in contact with other physical beings. The color of a person's skin still elicits a powerful reaction from some people and can be difficult for people to adjust to. A velvety black skin color is definitely moving when we realize that racist bigots pay too much attention to it. Most minority people are so used to experiencing racism that they no longer care how they showcase their bodies. They are reminded about their skin color so often that they can completely transcend outside of their bodies and forget about it until there is nothing left but a soul. African slave ancestors worked so much out in the sun and in the soil that it is not surprising that modern-day African Americans are so soulful. Their soulfulness has been passed down from generations of slaves who were out in the fields all day. So losing the perceptions of the mind and body leads us to be light beings taking everything to light. The mind is a feeling and an emotion that encompasses the body. Our instincts, behaviors, feelings, and emotions that startle our neurons are composed within the mind.

CHAPTER 22

Body

Bras and "draws" cause cancer. So be carefree with your body. The body is sacred and the main defender of your house. Your body is the physical representation of your genetic makeup. Since the earliest King James Version of the Bible, the body has been identified as being of great significance to our fall. For once, we did not know of bodies and facial features were unimportant because perfect companionship was found in the union between a man and a woman. So according to the Bible, Eve enticed Adam to eat from the tree that God had warned both of them not to eat from. Eve's mistake was listening to the trickery of a serpent. I can only imagine that the spineless snake told her false truths or lines about her body, tempted her into thinking that she was the lesser of sexes—because the animal was asexual—and told her that her physique was not as slender as the serpent's. This is just my imagination, but you get the point. The covering up of a woman's body has been the source of shame, exposure, and indecency. Naked bodies are taboo, as is appreciating the vehicles that will be with us for a lifetime. Taking care of them and not being ashamed of them is how we are meant to deal with them, and our awareness should be concerned with more than just health as it pertains to anatomy. Yet we are aware of all of the exterior portions of our bodies and are not much in tune with most of what is inside our bodies.

People who wear bras or underwear are more prone to suffer from cancer. Except for hygienic reasons, a bra does not need to be worn for more than twelve hours a day. Cutting off the slightest bit of circulation can lead to constricted blood vessels, veins, and capillaries, causing a reduction of blood flow to areas of the body. Antiperspirant is speculated to lead to cancer as well, along with cigarettes, power line towers, certain pharmaceutical drugs, an unhealthy diet, hereditary and genetic mutations, contagious substances, and malfunctions of cells. The lighter you are, the less susceptible you are to diseases, illnesses, disorders, colds, and sicknesses. In addition to diseases being hereditary, cells are affected during conception when they start to divide. They can be dormant or active, but the continuation of a lifestyle that is not light will make them more prone to illness. The uneasiness of the mind, causing disruption, makes the body malfunction, and it can work against you until you receive the proper healing by being God-conscious through Jesus Christ—if you are a Christian, or even Krishna, which is the portal to God. God gave men and women the knowledge to prepare medicine that can fight sicknesses, but for most illnesses, no cure is known. The cure is the mind-body connection with the self and our union with God consciousness. Do you ever notice how some foods can make you more lethargic than others? Whatever makes our bodies feel lively is what we need to nourish ourselves. Sometimes we may need candy if our sugar levels are low, but most importantly we have to choose foods that are most agreeable with our temples. If we don't, our bodies will choose dreadfully for us—a body with a mind of its own.

I love the skin that I am in. It glows and feels so soft but looks so strong. I appreciate all the genetic features that make up the blueprints of my body. As long as it is healthy and satisfies my desire for cleanliness, there is no adaptation needed whatsoever. I can't replace the body I have with another unless I am conjoined with it through the mind, body, and soul; thus, I am whole with the singularity of my own personal anatomy. When we exercise, our circulation increases throughout our bodies, which thrushes particles out of the body more readily. Exercising for an hour three times a week relieves my entire body and gives strength to my skin. Exercise releases toxins and replaces them with healing hormones such as dopamine and serotonin. The "energy in, energy out" mind-set helps my body retrieve new, fresh energy through my exercise regimens. If I miss a workout, I suffer by becoming irritable and annoyed easily. Staying active reassures me that I am doing something great for my well-being, and my mind is triggered to remaining in good cardiovascular standing. Confining yourself to the trends, body mass index, and weight standards is misleading. As long as you remain active and your health is good, then there is no need to stress and worry about losing weight unless it makes you feel good. You shouldn't do it for any occupation, person, obsession, or false perception. Your health and body are what distinguish you from everybody else, so why change it through plastic surgery when you can cleanse your body throughout and enjoy the journey of training your body to produce healthy results by exercising.

Commercials and advertisements have placed great significance on the female body and how it is to look. From 1980 to 2005, people who were skin and bones were portrayed as healthy. Awareness of anorexia nervosa, bulimia, and other eating disorders came to center stage when they became common among models. As mentioned before, I had lost a lot of weight due to stomach issues and looked very ill, so whatever fits you is acceptable. Contrarily, obesity rates have risen over the years not from overeating but from the food choices people make. I no longer want somebody else to cook my food since I had a lot of moments on the toilet due to food poisoning or what felt like it.

Finding a balance between the body and mind is difficult due to the gravitational pull on earth keeping us grounded. You know, some people really like the earthly plane of matter and carnal pleasures, and that seems to be all they focus upon. Attaining material wealth, overrating the body, being obsessed with youth, and indulging frequently are common for them. Getting so caught up in material things creates an atmosphere of bullshit. Then, there are the few who keep to themselves, or rather, are well-connected with beings but also have an appreciation for nature. We need devil's advocates to stir us up to achieve more than earthly pleasures, and that is why they live here—to awaken us and yet still have a chance to be awakened as well by those sentient beings who are in tune with nature and all that surrounds us. Unhappy individuals are those who are insecure in themselves, so they try to make people around them insecure by pointing out what they deem to be bodily flaws. Gifted people are starved for stimulation and challenges, they get bored easily, and their attention spans can be quite short when there are few activities to do. The devil in people is meant to bring out the gifts of the mind because the devil loves to mock them as if it was the creator. The devil within us loves to demolish, destroy, and pick out what he or she sees as our weaknesses, flaws, and shortcomings, which can either really demolish us or make us overcome or not care about the opinions of others. Separation from the mind and body can be alarming at times by devilish ways, but they can be put back together through the realization of a spiritual plane that expands beyond the material nature of our bodies. You can't taste a feeling or hear it, see it, or touch it. It is what covers the body, and the body is either protected or delusional when combined with the mind. Therefore, the mind and body are the same, with the mind being able to generate feelings and emotions and the other senses being controlled through the body. So if we were to think of the body as being observed from a cross, we could imagine a compass showing north, south, east, and west. North is air, south is earth, east is water, and west is fire. Those things combined bring the four bodily senses—hear, touch, see, and taste—all of which function through the body. Smelling is more of a central sense since it is located at the center of the face.

CHAPTER 23

Soul

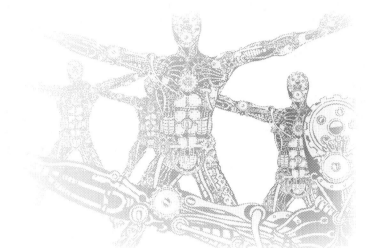

Before we proceed to the soul, it is important to really understand that the mind and body are one and the exact same thing. Just like we have the concept of globalization and its many discontents of networks, we have the mind-body that works as an organization of body parts, organs, blood, neurons, atoms, and an extension of organizations that work together and against one another. The soul is like a star that never burns out. We are connected to the stars in the sky, so as long there are people, there are stars; and as long as there are stars, there are beings. Some burn brightly, and others are not so bright. For each star we lose, another is gained, representing birth and death.

Then that is when the soul-searching process begins following failed relationships. Traumas of disheartening connections lead us to a better path of knowing and seclusion until we can make sense of things. Some folks experience a loss of identity from failed connections and thus can't function on a soul level due to past hurts. But if we take into account how much better off we are in forming new, supportive connections with soulful people and in not subjecting ourselves to the thieves and wolves in this world, then we can emerge as lighter souls that are more refined and fierce, determined not to accept the damage that people tend to put us through. Understanding that our health starts with the self and our standards will keep us from a lot of turmoil.

When I think of a soul, I picture a round glow of gold light that swarms freely around a person. And when a person passes away, I picture the soul roaming freely on the earth and through the higher dimensions of the universe. Our souls connect all of us and everything, and they can change minds. Listening to something soulful can put you in a trance because of the realness of it. It helps us along our true journeys and paths. The soul endures true self-love that can only be found when you are on your chosen path that you picked from the universe and God years ago. Through many failed opportunities of successful ventures, the path is always constructed to the same outcomes in life. Your soul has a purpose to fulfill, and it may go through a lot of destruction, construction, and reconstruction to get there. The glimpse of darkness makes the soul shine brighter in the everlasting light. The dark matter of things is heavy and unclear, but afterward it is the opposite, light and transparent with a higher-purpose understanding of the self. And when you think or feel that it is all over, it has only just begun.

Action and scary movies have portrayed the soul as a very valuable object. Movies like *Bedazzled* and episodes of *The Twilight Zone* capture the plot of a devil or antagonist making a deal and signing contracts with people to sell their souls, meaning that if an imaginary devil wants possession over someone's soul, it must be quite valuable. Handing over your soul in a devilish contract would initially project greed and damnation. I am guessing the significance of giving away a soul to the devil after wishes are granted is an example of indulging in the seven sins rather than seeking one's true purpose. Obviously, the sins of greed, wrath, lust, sloth, gluttony, vanity, and envy are all traded for the soul as if God and the devil are in competition with each other over which souls will seek out eternity or damnation. Living in sin on the earth plane and being very comfortable with all that it has to offer seems to come with a hefty price. You can be a submissive person, always giving to people, and still play an advocacy role for the devil. It is the undermining value of temptation that can place us on the wrong path and lead us into destruction. We can fall over and over again, but the choice is ours to learn from mistakes and get clarification on our life's purpose. If things, people, and places are not fulfilling our souls, then our minds will be changed and we can decide to stay the same or choose the alternative. Remember that the order goes from soul to mind to body, and if we incorporate the following chapter, which is "Illumination," then we can conclude that it takes matter, feelings, and spirit to be illuminated.

Men and women feel a loss in soul by submitting to the greedy demands of their partners. Soul mate matches are balanced and do not seek to harm the other person. Men buy cars, new clothes, expensive houses, and apartments all to please women. Women submit to men's will instead of their own, use their bodies to superficially gain love, and lose mental stability in trying to figure out the ways of men. The devil gets a bad name from other people's actions, but to keep it in perspective, the devil teaches us about overindulging and inequality. People are at fault for giving in to outlandish temptations and sinful, carnal pleasures because God gave us brains with which to think about, judge, criticize, and analyze all situations that we face. It is up to us to learn from them and apply knowledge from our experiences. But whatever obstacle we face, it gets us closer to where we have to be, and the tests and challenges in life are our freedom of expressing our individuality. The division and the turmoil a soul will have to go through is our way of playing with the devil that is entrapped in the mind because, believe it or not, we like to experience those changes and divisions of life. But the soul can never be divided; it is always whole and spherical like the planets in the solar system, the stars, the moon, the sun, and the galaxies. We can't deceive ourselves into thinking that we are separate from one another. The sacrifice for division in different individual religions, politics, practices, and interests combined with a forced desire for integration confuses the variability of oneness. Sometimes you can notice a person's aural energy vibe just by interacting or observing him or her and can readily experience the same emotions and feelings as well if you are a sensitive person. A predicate sense of falsehood can be verified through one's actions while being silent. The truth of most matters comes out when there is a prolonged silence and the soul searches for answers that we try to hide from ourselves and others. Even though the silence can seem blinding and delusional, a lot about the self can be revealed in it. Our soul path is determined to compete with the spirituality realm of our being. The earth is our median and safe haven for playground activities. We can dwell in luxury, indulgences, and everything else without shame. The earth is composed of four elements: fire, water, air, and matter. The spirituality realm is the upper, higher planes in the universe, and this is where we can attain more meaningful, esoteric knowledge that feeds the soul and is a part of growing. During our observations, we can be influenced by the moon because enlightenment happens to be passed on by the moon where there is less gravity, less weight balance—we just float above the ground. Growing down is acting upon emotions and negativism and is in the lower planes in the earth's crust. The underworld is ruled in the lower root planes of the earth, beneath the water and ground that is the seed of the earth. Emotion can guide us into areas without gravity as well—that is, what is beneath the earth—because we are surrounded by space. It is obvious that the growing-down phase can be related to the moon as well when rotating. However it goes, the soul yearns to be free, and it will try to go one of two routes to float: spirituality or emotionality.

CHAPTER 24

Illumination

Illumination is the emotional thought process that is felt when enlightened. Just imagine being on the moon where there is less gravity and your whole entire being is afloat. After the illumination process, the higher feelings are initiated. Aspects of it can leave people uncertain because they have to puzzle through emotions. Evidence and voyages to the moon have shown that there is water and moon rocks have been found to be "contaminated" with plant materials from Earth there. Motion and crater matter make up the elements of the moon, and there is little gravity and a limited oxygenated air supply. You would literally have to be in a bubble to live there. Under the influences of the moon, one can feel emotionally drained because the moon affects tidal waves in the ocean and draws water out of it. Things are not what they seem during the night when it is dark and shadowy. Some people see better in the dark, though, because the lower level of light puts less strain on the eyes. Therefore, emotions can lift them to higher places like the sun. And by accident, it seems that illuminating effects take place when we are emotionally drawn. The higher feelings belong to the sun, which is on one side of the Earth, and the emotions belong to the moon on the other side of the Earth. We can see these aspects of duality well: yin/yang, heaven/underworld, bad/good, love/fear, past/present, peace/turmoil. Adding Earth to the sun and moon forms a trilogy. The moon often has a champagne glow that is easy on the eyes. With that glow comes illumination.

Illumination is "light that comes into a room that shines on something, etc.; knowledge or understanding; spiritual or intellectual enlightenment; a lighting-up." I can only assume that, after we go through an emotional trauma or take on some baggage, we may feel light after the saga is over, leading to illuminating effects. As a whole, we are so focused on how relationships are connected. We try not to do this or that concerning other people's feelings to screw up a relationship. A challenge in values, morals, and beliefs can leave partnerships full of emotions even though we reflect each other. This is the aspect of the moon. When we study twin flame relationships, we can see that the mirror effect deceives couples and that the turbulence they face in the relationship is a result of their being opposites. Emotions are driven from the ground down, and higher feelings are generated from the ground up. You can use the moon or the sun to gain illumination. Greater effects are under the moon because of its lunar effects. The sun illuminates us with light energy, and the moon illuminates us with dark energy. Light energy is of solar power, and dark energy is of luminance power. With solar power, you can feel a hot temperature, but with luminance power, it feels much cooler. To get a glimpse of the sun's energy, consider the sunspots that are steadily being drawn to the center of the sun, spitting out mostly plasma. The moon, on the other hand, is calmer, with bits of water in its craters.

Volcanoes on this earth are nothing but sunspots from the sun. UFO activity has been reported near volcanoes in parts of Mexico and Hawaii. Some scientists and researchers even say that the sun may be a star gate. Geometric formations of circular beauty and perfection in crop areas are still an unsolved mystery. Details can remind us of things out of this world. Remember the incident involving the Sufi whirls and dance. At that time, I believe I was under the effects of both the crescent moon and the star behind it along with the sun rising. Anyway, the crop formations remind me of the constellation that I saw that morning after experiencing an array of sparkles around my hand after stargazing and looking at the moon. I figure that these extraordinary crop formations represent the zodiac and the solar system or the Mayan calendar in some way. There is definitely something greater than this earth that is incomprehensible to the makings of humans.

You had better believe that you can levitate off the ground by being in a state of being. Being in a state of being is just allowing nothing to take hold of your energy while at the same time being sensitive to waves and rays from the solar power of the sun or the luminance power of the moon. Pulling energy from the sun and moon can lead to spectacular events that can be declared delusional, insane, or lunacy by other human beings. When you feel the effects of this illumination, you will no longer be a human but a sentient being. Anything that you say about your experience can be labeled as craziness by other people who have not gone to that level of elevation. The best time to experience these seemingly foreign incidents is when you are coming down from a high. The high does not have to be a result of drugs, alcohol, or any hallucinogen. It can be sensed after dancing, praying, meditating, or swimming. We can't lose or gain energy; it can only be transferred. And we transfer these different energies all the time with the universe. Sweating from our pores releases bad, draining, depressive energy, mainly into the ground through our feet. When we are in our emotions, we release and transfer energy through the ground, and it travels through the core of the atmosphere. When we are in our feelings, the energy travels through the tops of our heads in the middle, releasing and transferring energy into outer space and permeating the atmosphere. The levitation begins when we can merge both the feelings and emotions together, forming being and an awareness of identification not only on Earth but in outer space as well.

I will tell you of an experience that is hard to comprehend. During my spring vacation back in 2012, I had booked a hotel in the Southwest for my family and me. One night there, I went to sleep and my dream was quite bizarre. It was pitch black, and for some reason I was drawn to this police officer, so I walked toward him and stopped. Beside him was a German shepherd with its head turned to where I couldn't see it. Unlike any other dream I'd had, I walked toward the policeman and the dog, and as I approached them, the damn dog turned around with glowing green eyes and bit me. It felt so real. In fact, it *was* real because I immediately woke up, and to my surprise the outside of my right thigh was throbbing. I went into the bathroom and saw a bruise in the shape of a bite mark on the same spot the dog had bitten me in the dream. I could not believe it and told my boyfriend that was sleeping next to me about it. I even tried to remember whether I had bumped up against something prior to the dream, but I did not recall anything. I have walked in my sleep before, but when that happened I just ended up in a place other than my bed. This was different. I was in my bed the whole time when this occurred. I have come to recognize that there are greater forces than what meets the eye. I'm not necessarily inclined to thinking that extraterrestrials are above, below, or beside us, but there may be some truth in it.

Moon aspects can impact us in mysterious ways concerning our emotions. Under the moonlight, we can finally simmer down at night and enjoy the glowing, floating effects of the moon as it draws closer to us after the sun goes down. We get approximately twelve hours of sunlight and twelve hours of moonlight, which both have illuminating effects. Remember, the sun gives us solar power and the moon gives us luminance power. You can feel the illumination effects in both phases of light and dark energy. Correlating the two in acceptance of each other brings forth the illumination process. Overcoming the thinking process leads to levitation. Accepting a no-thinking-aloud concept for vague or high feelings and emotions gets us in touch with our higher power through spiritual realms.

Both positive and negative forces are implemented by the sun and moon. Merging war with peace, love with hate, evil with good, right with wrong, up with down, and other opposites is the set frame of mind for this. Within a certain circumstance, the extreme of what is right and what is wrong can take place. For instance, a person may say or do something that is offensive to your emotional being, and you may place that thought in the back of your mind while still within the presence of that person. As you simply don't give a damn about the character of the other person, you start to feel the opposite of what is expected. What was wrongly done to you is not a deal breaker in your character; thus, you gain positive energy from it while the other person is more than likely still possessing negative energy. You feed off his or her negative energy and try to mirror it with its attraction of positive energy. Doing this while close to nature or with just a peek at a scenic view toward the sky will bring in the power. Your focus on the higher powers of luminance from the energy of the sun and moon pulls together matter and magnetism of both ends of circumstances. Focusing on the third eye chakra and the back of the head, where the occipital lobe is located, can help you within this discovery of another realm. Therefore, merging the two eyes until there is one is the key of infusion to this self-directing journey. The neutralizer in the brain between the two antonyms is the amygdala, which processes hormones that affect mood and emotion. Some forms of posttraumatic stress disorder (PTSD) can trigger illumination because a past event can affect mood and emotion, thereby stimulating the amygdala. The amygdala will seem to protect the person by numbing the emotion through time and feel-good hormones. When the PTSD is in control of the person to the point that there is no serenity, the only satisfaction or outlet for the depressing stage is to release hormones like dopamine and serotonin in the system to a greater degree, causing nerve endings to connect more powerfully through synapses. When nervousness and anxiety are heightened, nerves become erratic, so the body and brain have to find a solution to alleviate the matter. In response, hormones are released, and the person may experience euphoria or relief from tension, as in a kundalini meditation or exercise.

Some people think that the consumption of drugs can lead to a heightened illumination stage, but that is not the case. It is when you are going through withdrawals or coming down from a high that you are able to feel the highest. Independence from hallucinogenic substances, drugs, and alcohol is the high way. I'm not saying that you can't experience illumination when you are under the influence of drugs and alcohol, but the absence of it makes you more dependent on a natural high, where the brain is not as foggy and cluttered with residuals. Consider any of the *X-Men* movies. You can see that the movie is based on a lot of emotion and feelings of what is right and wrong, peace and war, and so on. Powers are gained from merging feelings and emotions to form illumination. The end result of all of this is unconditional love formally expressed, experimented, and overcome through rude, ruthless behaviors. The notion of turning the other cheek by not validating defiance in one's environment offsets a greater vibration of no conditions. Just like in a lab experiment, you have the experiment and the conditional or controlled (placebo), but in the middle of the specimens you have the nonconditions—specimens that are not affected or experimented. Or rather, they are affected based upon the ineffectiveness and the indifference of opposites.

The comparison of Magneto and Professor X in *X-Men* to Malcolm X and Martin Luther King Jr. explains the satire and use of emotion through the Civil Rights Movement. The two personalities examine the idea that there are two different ways to approach a circumstance. Brother Malcolm X's approach was said to be more on the aggressive side than that of his counterpart Dr. Martin Luther King Jr., who was seen as more passive in his approach to the movement. Both of them seemingly wanted to merge their differences into a more assertive approach, but they were assassinated right when they started to realize the illusion of being separate from each other and of being blinded to the atrocities and hate of the nation. In the *X-Men* comics and movies, Professor X and Magneto are portrayed as mutants, which allowed them to have superpowers such as the ability to read minds and control objects with their minds. You see, I don't think that either of the civil rights activists knew how much of an impact he had on so many other minds. Both of them definitely possessed the power of persuasion with their speeches, but they did not have control over their own minds. It was their divinity that taught and held speeches to inform the public. They were masterminds and could get a large population of people to agree with them because they persuaded them with feelings and emotions, with empathy and sympathy. So what lies in between these two is the real magic. The cure to violence is what is in between it and peace; by combining both of these energetic forces, there is bound to be a combustion or nebula of some sort within the universe that will resonate for a dramatic change on this earth. But as years go by, history can be forgotten or not considered, and it can repeat itself if we are careless, forgetful tyrants who are foreigners in their own lands. If we had an equation that always equaled "unconditional love," it would be the sum of two dualities. For instance 100% love + 100% fear = unconditional love, and 100% peace + 100% war = unconditional love. These concepts' thought processes give off high vibrational waves in the yin/yang energy that frees us from mental bondage. You have to take the good with the bad and make magic out of it to resonate unconditional love.

To be able to forgive a wrongdoing is to use a high-frequency unconditional vibrancy; it is felt throughout the galaxy and magnified back to us. If you want to break down the equation into simpler terms, we can say that fear = love, good = bad, and peace = war. As long as we get the understanding that they are really not opposites and just resonate and mirror each other, then we can be dedicated to our real truth. As above, so below, just like the illuminations of the sun and moon being opposites of one another surrounded by combustion nebulae. To better understand this phenomenon, we must dig deep into the psyche of both light forces and dark forces. Normalcy occurs when we merge these opposites into nothing, the median.

Other Hollywood examples that entail illumination are the movies *Lucy* and *Limitless*. The activation of cells can activate a hormone to the point that we can use 100 percent of our brain capacity at all times. This method can seem unreal, but it is actually achievable. It is when we know but don't know, when we see we don't see, when we act but don't act. The concept is that of a mirror of reflection and refraction. Normalcy is the nothingness of two antonyms, opposites, and differences. One person can generate this feeling of pure empirical true value of self. Becoming is being. I mean *becoming* in the sense of a character in a movie or TV episode or commercial, and identifying with another person even if he or she is a complete stranger to you. It's those happy feelings you get when you smell fresh-cut grass on a rainy day—feelings of oneness and completeness, of knowing that all your needs are met and that your wants are of just doing. To better understand where we can get these wonderful feelings, it is important to start from the beginning of reproduction that is in Genesis. The Bible is a helpful guide to explain religion and genetics. With the addition of astrology and cosmology, we can pinpoint exactly why we feel the way we do and why there are so many diseases, illnesses, and sicknesses to this day. It's in being aware of where the ego resides and the true self is emerged. Believing that everything is about you amplifies the power of knowing. Keeping the ego under complete control and bounded by will is the illumination factor. You have to be careful because vanity can increase illusions. I guess you can say it is important not to take things personally. Don't be serious and don't play at the same time. The ego's sole purpose in life is to demonstrate. It is required to be in a state of focus to experience the higher realm—getting in between thinking and not thinking, feeling but not feeling, knowing but not knowing, being but not being, wanting but not wanting, using but not using, desiring but not desiring, and so on. We must partially observe spiritually in isolation and solitude, letting go of what was and what will be. We all have egos and can be eccentric in our own ways, but allowing the self to set aside the ego and observe other egos in silence is also recommended.

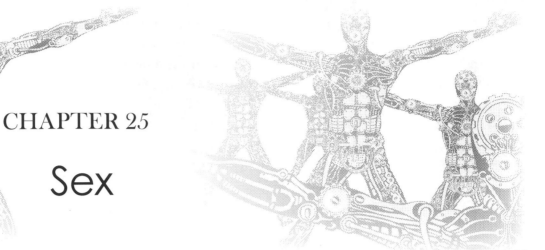

CHAPTER 25

Sex

According to the Bible, after Adam and Eve descended to earth, they created multiple images of themselves. Their first two children were boys: the oldest was named Cain, and the second was named Abel. Now, if we are into names, we know that *Cain* looks like the word *can't*, and Abel is similar to the word *able*. Cain and Abel represent Gemini, the twins, which is an air sign. Gemini is known for talking and thinking, gossiping and intellect, communications and broadcasting, and also exaggeration to the point of lying. Cain was an offspring of activated mutations. Thus, using this concept, we can assume that we get our issues from our ancestor Cain if we follow the Bible. Spiritually, Cain was going through all of the negative emotions, feelings, and thoughts that we as humans experience here on earth. We are all mutated in our gene makeup since we all descended from the same source. We share this planet with one another in every life formation, including plant and eukaryotic life. On this planet, we are all we have.

Cain murdered his brother out of envy, and he knew that it was the wrong thing to do. Animals were killed for survival, but Cain was told by his parents that it was not acceptable to kill one another, especially our own brethren. Cain's offering to God was the sacrifice of an animal, and I'm sure God or the higher intelligence knew that Cain was going to commit the act anyway. Negativism is the duality of positivism, and if we were to study the two brothers, they would represent that yin-yang energy. Activated dormant cells have everything to do with feelings, emotionality, thoughtfulness, and energy that is released and stored on the circumstance or matter. We get a first glimpse of polarity and all that comes with it—one cell dividing into two cells and then into multiples of cells. Cell replication demonstrates the division and divine procreation of life—being able to multiply abundantly and yet still is one unit. Cells are developed through the prophase, prometaphase, anaphase, telophase, interphase, mitotic phase, G1, S and G2 phases. A cell goes through a process to renew itself and to form another image of itself during cell replications, our DNA is in combination with linked genes of different phenotypes and genotypes that we inherit from our ancestors. Mutations in these genes may take form depending on our hereditary makeup, dietary intake, and local environment. If we are literal Bible readers, we can conclude that Cain was probably the first person to exhibit these mutations due to a deeply felt emotion. To kill another is the most horrible thing one can do. Cain represented thought, and Abel represented talk, which composes the duality air sign, Gemini. When Cain murdered his brother Abel, Cain took on the roles of thinking and talking. Considering the Gemini astrological sign, we can see that communications, broadcasting, politics, astral plane, and airiness are all traits of the twins, which is the third sign in the Western zodiac. Abel was slain by his brother, and later Cain came to understand and care that his actions were wrong. It sounds like some old prison stories from a movie.

Our addictions, habits, health, and environment are all independent of the mutations that we have in cell generation. As we get older, cell replication slows down and our bodies can seem to linger if we do not exercise often enough. When our bodies are in the habit of being worked on as far as getting adequate exercise, rest, nutritious food, and pleasure, then they can survive various climactic environments. Keeping the body fit—not necessarily skinny or slim—is the best way to help our cells grow, regenerate, and replicate proficiently and keep ourselves functioning properly. Physical activity gives us a release of energy into the atmosphere, and we take in the oxygenated particles of the atmosphere in return. It is important to learn the proper breathing techniques and postures to get the best workout. Incorporating cardiovascular exercise is the key to maintaining a healthy heart and good oxygen levels to most cells in our bodies. Pumping freshly oxygenated blood with natural hormonal influences such as dopamine, adrenaline, and serotonin throughout our bodies makes us feel refreshed and regenerated afterward, which beneficially impacts the cells in our systems. If we feel good, we usually are good, and we can perpetuate this feeling with adequate cardiovascular exercise, a nutritional diet, proper rest, and stimuli observation.

Now, the mutations can be derived from a single thought that can activate these genes to affect our health. Literally, if we have happy thoughts, we are less susceptible and prone to diseases, illnesses, and sicknesses. The less we talk and complain about ordinary circumstances, the more likely it is that our health will be good for the long run. Habits and addictions also have an impact on our cells and may possibly further mutate or delete a vital enzyme for catalyzing cells. The overuse of alcohol and drugs can alter cells into foreign cells and may replicate the image of a mutated cell, thus destroying the human anatomy. Even poor quality air, water, and land affect cell replication. Therefore, the very laws that were to be obeyed in the early ages, like tending to the land, are of great importance to this day for sustainability of life. We have to recognize that every life form around us is connected to us in this one symbiotic unit not only on this planet but throughout this entire universe. We are never alone, and just like God watched Cain and knew his motive in plotting a sin against his brother, thus the universe and higher intelligence also know the plan for you in life. It is up to us to be humble of being able to just have the things we need to survive or to sustain our well-being. When we come to the conclusion that we are equipped with the survival tactics we need, then we can move on to better things like the spiritual realm, which is much greater than what is comforting to us like luxury, money, material things, and big houses. Helping others is our main goal to reach in life, as well as to demonstrate the many techniques of the universal mind. It is taught in every movie we watch, every song we hear, everything we see, all the smells of the atmosphere, and the touch of reality; but there is one more simple thing that is hidden from us, which is good company, the God-Jesus (Yahweh)-me. Once you tap into that realm, the most loyal of people will not be able to be bargained with on how good it makes them feel to know how to resonate with vibrant frequencies and master quantum leaps. Your one eye will suddenly be open and, without even having to read anything, you will just know, but then again you will be clueless because all of the pieces to the puzzle may not be laid out for your understanding just yet. This is the main reason there are insane asylums and psychiatrists who counsel people on hearing voices, seeing things, or having bad dreams and nightmares that keep them awake at night. People who see things that are not there are labeled schizophrenic. People who are too into themselves are labeled narcissistic, and people who are up one minute and down the next are labeled bipolar. Therefore, they are put on antidepressants, anxiety meds, or tranquilizers to stop or subdue the images that are in their heads. They are taught that the images they see are illusions when, in actuality, they are very real since they stimulate the nervous system. Now there are a set of people who are totally off the physical plane of this earth, but we can learn from these individuals who have thought problems and are unaffected with the survival needs here. Do they have an ancestry of nonrecurring thought and language patterns that are mainly primitive? Perhaps so. Catatonic schizophrenia is an illness that immobilizes the body, especially in the limbs, but our ancestors and natives would just refer to a person experiencing such an episode as being in spirit. Behavioral conditions have prolonged the compensation of counselors, psychologists, psychiatrists, and social workers around the nation and the world. The continuation of increasing poverty helps drive "mental illnesses" in people, which can either improve a person's spiritual being to help other individuals understand and appreciate surviving or can hinder them in a state of confusion. Rest (breath), eating (habits), body (function), and support (coping mechanisms) are all vital to the generation of cell DNA replication. If all these aspects are tended to, then we can more than likely assume that our health will be sustainable into older age. There is, however, the Darwinist view of natural selection, geographic drift, the Doppler effect, and the theory that there are superior and inferior *homo sapiens* even though we all belong to the same species. The bone structures in our skulls help to differentiate our identities, and the hip structures in the torso distinguish our sex as well. Our ages can be identified from our teeth, and the dents, grooves, and dimples in our bones can tell how athletic we are. XX sex chromosomes are homozygous and are female, while XY sex chromosomes are heterozygous and are male. Therefore, our blood cells are linked to bone structure, bone function, bone marrow, skeletal injuries, skeletal damage, and trauma areas. Getting a daily dose of sunshine (vitamin D) promotes bone health and also decreases depression as well. Therefore, when humans separated into colder climates, their bodies—mainly their skeletal features like the skull—had to adapt to the climate so that they could still procreate. During this migration, their bodies turned on active sites on certain cells that led to mutations in skin, eye color, skull thickness, and facial features. The lack of sunshine in these colder climatic areas turned active sites on or off and dormant cells on or off, thus making an entire versatile gene pool in another area of the world. Replacement, deletion, splicing, and cutting of enzymes, triglycerides, and amino acids alter genes to survive in the designated atmospheric weather and climate. Cancer research uses genetic engineering to explain the root causes of gene sites that activate cancer cells. Research is being done on pregnant women to monitor their moods and health to determine whether these have a profound effect on fetal growth and health. It is known that expectant mothers are able to send energy to their unborn babies by turning on or off active sites on cells and make dormant cells become activated and catalyzed. Thus, the way we think has a lot to tell us about our health.

Tantric sex positions provide the most enjoyable and fun foreplay. Sex does not have to be serious, but safety must always be taken into account. You not only share bodily fluids with another, but you also share synergistic energies. You actually take a part of that person with you after intercourse. Mostly, when a woman has sex with a man, she is giving and submitting herself to a potential life partner. With most men, sex is seen as a means to control and dominate their partners and as creating a feeling of possession that is confused with protection. In Western society, men are prone to believe that females are the inferior sex because of that not-so-old Bible story of Adam following Eve's lead in eating fruit from a forbidden tree. In other cultures, especially Eastern, the view about women is quite the opposite. The women actually lead men into the spirituality realm and gain a closer relationship to God. It is the women who preserve and nurture the land. Females are the creators of the earth and are of dominant character compared to their homozygous XX chromosome. And doesn't the letter Y come after the letter X? It was Eve who ate the forbidden fruit first. It was Eve who encountered the serpent first and was enticed by it. It was Eve who was blamed for the fall of man. So if Eve was the first person and woman to do all these things, then why is it not plausible to accept that a man came out of a woman? The first human could have simply had sex chromosomes XXY. Women are thicker and their bone density is greater than that of a man for childbearing purposes. It would make sense for a woman to be the creator of all things if we were to be literal and observant, but we must be equally fair and assume that everything is unisex, or rather bisexual, when speaking of earthly bodies. The notion is that Adam and Eve were in their heavenly bodies before they descended to earth in their human bodies. So before they were created on earth, they were in their spiritual, celestial, heavenly bodies before they could separate from each other and become one again. At first in their heavenly bodies, they were two souls; then, after they formed their earthly anatomy, they became one again just like the image of God. The only explanation as to why God, the universe, a higher power, or higher intelligence technically procreated humans is inspiration. Inspiration from unlimited space and everlasting time was the reason to create images. Like an artist paints on a canvas to create a perfect picture and like an engineer pinpoints every connection to a working engine, inspiration was the driving force. Observing the image of a flower reveals all about the spiritual essence between a man and a woman. The male parts of the flower and plant are at the bottom, while the female parts of the plant and flower are showcased up above. The same goes for Egyptian ankhs, where the male is seen with a sword in one hand staring up above at a goddess angel, perceived to be his lady love, guiding him to God consciousness.

Sexual intercourse is one of the foundations through which we can express our love to each other. But a master in life knows that the feeling of love does not require sex at all. Sex is happening inside of us constantly with the replication of our cells, so no wonder we humans think about sex so much. When people develop a universal mind, they have control over their bodies because they have so much love for themselves. A person can make love to nature just by being loved. Even if the human condition prevents real love, it is the feeling that you get from believing that you are loved, which is the ultimate higher power of self. Therefore, with anybody by whom you feel loved, you should enjoy the initial feelings of that love, even if it's immature or innocent at the time being. We are not concerned about the status, whether the relationship is long-term, or the "what have you done for me lately?" aspect after the love dies down and is not appreciated. We are generally trying to experience the here and now in our relationships so that the vibration of love can be amplified to higher powers that will turn us on to more spiritual realms of our being. If we have to become one again after a breakup in our personal relationships, then we can become transformers of love. Through our relationships with one another, we come to experience love with all life and nature. Without the constant game of love, we can't experience evolution and how it is to feel the higher learning of love. Instead, we are stuck in being pleased by one another, which is so grounded. Remember, first came fire like an explosion in the galaxy, and basically something came out of something that is perceived as nothing to make existence. Second, earth and all of its sediments were created, with lava slowly covering the surface to help form the crust into a hard, molten material. Next was air and that completion of space that inspired God to create humans. Water is the fourth element that helps with understanding emotions and caring deeply for causes of issues. Last, there is heart, and this is a vibration that is above all the other elements because it encompasses them. Just think of the *Captain Planet and the Planeteers* theme song. The heart is the generator of all existence, life, love, and creation, and it resonates and amplifies the higher-power feelings. Think of the heart as a big air pump to the survival of all humankind. We can probably include that all the hearts of the world are responsible for the air we breathe. We all share the same air capacity whether we live on planet Earth, on Mars, or in any other dimension whatsoever.

We confuse sex and love in so many ways. Codependent relationships are the main reason for shaming love and sex in personal relationships. A codependent person is in denial, experiences shame, and has feelings of unworthiness of real love due to early traumatic experiences in childhood. Some individuals have painful early experiences, but then they have other great experiences that help them to love and nurture themselves. But the individuals who are codependent think more in the past and are regularly negative. A codependent person can be overtly caretaking or controlling because of the desire to be needed, not loved. All of these symptoms derive from the desire to feel worthy through somebody else along with a denial of oneself for that love. These people hardly take the time to ponder and ask themselves what they need, want, and value in life. A codependent relationship is just a game of push and pull, forcing and letting go, back and forth until those in it get so tired that they become the ultimate cowards against each other and gain peace of mind by filling their emptiness. The feeling of death may overtake you after sex with a potential partner has been halted, but after that a transformation of new life is given once you feel the emptiness so you can fill yourself back up again.

The planets Mars and Venus are said to rule sexology, romance, and love. Mars is more forcefully driven by the power of sex, and Venus is more steady with increments of love. Mars is a clay rock red planet that is being considered for starting civilizations upon due to the discovery of water underneath its surface. By the year 2020, scientists, engineers, and private corporations are hoping to start their launches to Mars. I wonder what the energy orbital differences will be in Mars compared to Earth. The asteroid belt serves as a barrier to keep big asteroids from clashing with the planets in big pieces, and it seems as if Earth is between a father and a mother—Mars and Venus, war and love. But the one thing that can bring polar opposites together when speaking of human development and plant and animal life is communication, and Mercury rules that, which is the first planet residing near the sun. The sun is the center of all the orbits, and using coordinates, the sun would be the center point of (0, 0). All the planets orbit around the sun at x-y axis coordinates and are trying to catch the sun. Studying the sun has led to intensive research on solar energy and can influence our moods along with the DNA replication of our cells, which impact our health, generations, and survival. Since the sun is so massive, it takes asteroid hits all the time. Some scientists have projected that these fast-traveling rocks hit the hot surfaces of the sun and melt within its layers or possibly go back out the other side of the sun at some moment of time. Our solar system is dense in the center, like a nucleus in a cell body. In sync with the sun, we are walking souls of energy with nerve cells and pathogens just like the sun. Planets orbit the sun like electrons, protons, and neutrons orbit a nucleus. So according to the scientists that have their own theories when asteroids hit the sun, it would seem that the sun takes the hits and turns the rock into energy. Our location in the solar system is somewhat halfway between the hottest area of the polarity, which is the sun, and the coldest part of the system, which is the location of Pluto—or if you a modern planet seeker, Neptune. Therefore, we have the extremes of climates on planet Earth expressed from the sun and the colder parts of the galaxy. Even the planets orbit around the Sun like the elements of a DNA nucleotide. The sun moves steadily in one motion while the planets orbit and move around it in a vortex in the same coordinates. The sun is always leading the planets even though it is the biggest celestial part of the solar system. So the sun is like the head of a person, if we are speaking of celestial bodies, and the planets make up the body. Just by generalizing, we can relate and compare our chakras, birth natal charts, and body parts. For instance, the highest chakra is at the top of the head, and my sun sign is Taurus but my ascendant is Cancer/Leo. The chakra at the top of the head is of the universal mind and is associated with the third eye chakra as well. Since my sun sign is in Taurus, it is ruled by the neck, larynx, shoulders, and occipital area of the skull. This shows me my forward life path with Cancer/Leo being my first house of leadership. Taurus shows forward progression in career since it is also in my tenth house as well. The first house will show me the means of how I go about getting to that tenth midheaven house. Mercury is the closest planet to the sun, and Mercury is in Aries for me. Aries is the first sign of the zodiac and is philosophical, ambitious, innocent, and free in communication—with the focus on me being to empathize with others in conversations and decrease the amount of gossip I engage in. If we were to reconfigure astrological signs and their positions we would start with the sun being in the forefront of the solar system and being in the first house. Mercury would correlate with the second house. Venus with the third, Saturn and Pluto in the fourth, Jupiter with the fifth, Saturn with the sixth, Uranus with the seventh, and the replica with Neptune in the eighth house, Mars in the ninth house, Venus in the tenth house, Mercury in the eleventh house and the Moon in the twelfth house. Notice how the planets above the asteroid belt are repeated. So you can basically picture how your life path is projected just with those three observations of chakras, astrology, and planet position.

Trigonometry, logarithms, and geometry all provide perfect explanations for clockwork planetary aspects, but if we were to look at astrology and the cosmos as well, we may come up with the same solution by using two separate disciplines with different conceptions. Sacred geometry opens up doors to extraterrestrial life forms possibly visiting Earth. Telescoping astrology can also hypothesize that there are various forms of life on other planets and the moon as well. Marine life has demonstrated the sexual formation of two completely different species into one mutated species, like the combination of sponges and jellyfish. Mysterious farm crops in the southwestern part of the United States in other parts of the world suddenly exhibit geometric patterns. Individuals have exotic and disturbing dreams of future happenings, and déjà vu incidents frequently occur. Literary works, music, movies, films, and various forms of creative art are expressed through all of us as one unit of relation and connectivity to another. All disciplines have a domino effect of the others and make up the big picture of our higher purpose here on Earth, and that is to express our observations through hearing, seeing, and mediums of information to amplify the feelings of the central portal (heart) that is satisfying to the hunger of the cycle of life, regeneration, death, and then transformation.

CHAPTER 26

Addictions

A study was recommended to me that indicated that the moon is an illusion and that it is portrayed in some sort of hologram, one that is not technically manufactured but rather made through an oblong object that is reflected from the side of the sun through a prism. Too much of this is true to believe that the moon is in no way to be touched due to an illusory image of it. Astronomers and astrologists can attest that the phases of the moon effectively influence life on Earth. Contrarily, a more mundane influence that is pleasing to us humans is our addictions. Our addictions can be of underworld standards, resulting in dependency on drugs, alcohol, obsessiveness, compulsiveness, impulsiveness, impatience, unnaturalness, of fearful living. All these things are driven by our personal egos acting out or acting in past circumstances to create future outcomes. Our goal is to get to the middle of this act and activate same spontaneous energies based on intentional emotional feelings. Picture your body as a bright yellow-orange light that glows like the sun, and imagine sparks of orbitals going all around your body with active connection spots—the same way the planets orbit the sun. This is the same way we carry our energy around us and thus how we connect with the universe. Every microscopic aspect of us is representative of the galaxy; we are all connected to it and correspond with it all the time. One reaction leading to an action is spiritual, and an action that leads to a reaction is real ego. If you see how this phrase connects like an infinity symbol, then you will understand how a middle connection can be turned on by the use of proper intentions for outside influences. Influencing the chakras to release negative energy and transferring it into positive energy at the right codon site connects us simultaneously to the natural journey of the universal mind.

All addictions are distractions to detour us from the higher frame of mind in our present beings. An addiction is an added consequence repetitiously experienced in excess for current, present emotions from illusory past and future thinking. Addictions to substances that we ingest add on different DNA codons to nucleotides on our DNA strands. The more the nucleotides replicate through RNA polymerase, the easier it is to remove the added codon incision. This is why the body gets so used to a consumed substance—it alters the DNA to fight off the excess unnatural chemical energy sites that are taken over in a cell. Most substances alter moods and thus alter cells, holding up the healing process of your natural emotions. This can also cause underdevelopment if substances such as alcohol and drugs are consumed at a very young age since it is easier for immature and developing cells to be influenced by additional substances. The more a cell replicates, the less of an influence substances from outside emotional environments have on the health of a person. In the long run, we have to understand that being in the *now* is the soul-purpose to everything and the secret to winning by realizing you have already *won* the game of life by being present and not pondering on illusive past and future concepts. We are awakened to experience the now with our gifts to demonstrate and share with one another and to bring the heart of giving and receiving various energetic orbiting realms.

Addiction is the result of an immaturity of brain development more than likely located in the ventromedial prefrontal cortex, which is behind the nasal cavity. A person who has damage or underdevelopment to this part of the brain is more susceptible to addictions because this part of the brain handles decision making. The affected person lacks decision making skills and the ability to determine what factors are important versus what should be discarded. The behavior denying what is right in favor of an addiction is caused by a behavioral brain malfunction and leaves the damaged person seeking outlets. Outside environments such as priming can result in addictions, and also traumatic experiences can trigger damage to that part of the brain from experiences like shell shock or a disgusted altercation to the sensory (see, smell, taste, hear, touch) stimuli. It is a perception or judgment that has been added on about oneself in accordance with the environment, rest, food, and physical trauma (food, rest, companionship, and defense mechanisms). Also, not being able to let go of what was leads to addictions of collecting, like hoarding. Contrarily, being a "clean freak" is taken lightly these days when it comes to hygiene, cleaning, and discarding material because that makes way for better concentration and making room for new and modern things in our lives. So it is safe to say that once we add on things to our lives that change and alter our moods, then new nucleotide sequences add on to our DNA, which can cause disruption, diseases, illnesses, and disorders. Thus, when we continue to live in the insanity of addiction to alcohol, drugs, sex, television, food, shopping, and even too much exercising, it can take a toll on our health. Simplicity, priorities, disciplined behavior, and development all are a part of overcoming an addiction. If something takes up a lot of our time, whether it's work, school, a partner, kids, or something else, then we must figure out our value system and thus proceed with correcting our addictions. When we were first born, we immediately recognized what we needed to survive as infants. If we lacked any of our basic needs, then we would act out by screaming, crying, and hollering for food, rest, companionship, or a fresh diaper, and those are all we need to sustain and occupy our time with on this planet pertaining to ourselves.

Adding chemicals to our bodies adds more waste because of the work and energy that our organs have to go through to clean the waste and use the substance for its purpose. Human-made substances and chemicals are not compatible with the naturalness of our bodies. Natural herbal treatments and remedies are less harmful to the human anatomy. If you examine your limbs, you'll find that they look very similar to those of a plant or tree. The branches are your arms and legs, your head is the top of the tree or plant, and your hair is a flower. If you are bald, you're a bud. Each step you take is connected to the ground, grass, and greenery. Plants exhaust waste and take up nutrients just like we do, and they pass gas as well. It is boggling to my noggin that alcoholics are prone to drinking high proofs of fermented alcohol. To me, anything that is upsetting to the organs upon ingestion based on taste and content is off limits. That's why, if I ever do drink any alcoholic beverage, I prefer it to be a mixed drink. Alcohol affects every organ in the body, just like all human-made substances.

As a matter of fact, as you minus addiction it equals true happiness. A lot of us are addicted to competition, gambling, or the pleasing of just one sense at a time. Cars are nice to drive and look at, but that is about it. The only purpose a vehicle serves is to get us from point A to point B. Sex is addictive because an energy surge is transferred from one body to the next, and the purposes of sex are to procreate or engage in a playful activity. Having multiple partners in your life is exhausting, and the upkeep runs people ragged. A bigger house means higher energy usage, more taxes to pay on it, and more maintenance issues that lead to more money spent. Believe it or not, we do not have control over anything that we obtain during life. After we are exhausted, stressed, depressed, angered, nerve-wrecked, and unsatisfied with these addictions, we turn to pill popping, bottle drinking, drug addictions, and anything that can subdue the feeling of failure from not having enough. The desire to always add causes addiction. There is no gateway drug; there is only addiction, and it is driven in economies that thrive on consumerism and capitalism. You are not born to love things. You are born to love those things that you need (rest, food, defense mechanisms, and companionship). Once we are conscious enough to understand this, then we can proceed to better things that actually add value to our lives from the connections we create to nurture one another. Forcing your will upon uncontrollable circumstances is dis-easing and totally against your natural being. There is no time lost in an intelligently planned plot called life, so there is no need to rush because you are going to end up at the same destination at the same time any which way you go. The priming of race and ethnicity has also primed people to think less of themselves because of media stereotypes, thus disallowing individuals to feel confident enough to succeed. These thoughts can also form an early addiction to feeling unworthy with nonactualization, which is still an underdevelopment of the middle part of the brain.

It is as if we were all programmed by teachers, doctors, police officers, and lawmakers to believe that psychedelics, marijuana, and other natural-growing hallucinogenic plants are harmful to us. They have been hiding vital information and healing answers to our well-being by making them illegal. These plants were created on this earth to assist everybody and in their health. Right now, it is not a big secret that we can heal ourselves from within, but when we let officials basically control what we eat, when we rest, how we defend ourselves, and who we sleep with through media stereotypes on television and advertisements, we are giving our freedom away. By legalizing all drugs, substances, and other consumptives that give us pleasure, we will bring about the lovey-dovey realization that less is more. Legalizing all drugs and ingestible substances will give the people freedom to proceed with other things, rituals, and activities that are of value to them and to this world. Studies have shown that citizens are less likely to abuse, use, and misuse when there is freedom to do so. The excitement of getting caught is no longer there, and people will find more spiritual and holistic ways to get high, like just being present. Subtracting the addictions that are cluttering up space in your life makes room for the best to come in it. It's like cleaning and clearing up space so that you can think of better fulfillment and adventure in your journey. A homeless person has more independence and freedom than people of the working class just by not having things that he or she has to maintain. I'm not saying to live your life as a bum or fleeting gypsy, but you know you will never be satisfied with the continuation of competing among others and appealing only to a minimal number of senses at one time. I am just trying to make people aware that there are moments, occurrences, and happenings that are far greater and appealing to all your senses than any addiction can hand you. Any addiction is a thin one and can be broken with information and consultation. The real self is the main motivation to discontinuing a habit. In literal means, the gain of getting back to reality and to the purest genetic makeup of being instead of binging is the most natural goal your essence is willing to achieve. Creating through all senses, including the sixth, seventh, eighth, and however many there are, is magnificent and can't be replaced with things because they are planetary moments.

Examining the solar system also explains how a higher intelligence created humans in the image of a person. The sun is like the top of the head, the asteroid belt is like the middle of your torso, and Pluto is where your feet are—at the coldest part of your body. Shingles caused from stress, anxiety, depression, or any other ailment occur frequently, and they usually manifest in a band around the waist; this can be representative of the asteroid belt in the solar system. The sixth/seventh house in our natal chart pertains to our health and is located in the middle of the zodiac between Virgo and Libra. So what we analyze, critique, balance, and create as law affects our health. If you notice the medical symbols, you will see that there are one or two snakes intertwined with wings. Spiritual healing is equal from within and is divinely encrypted into our universal DNA to heal oneself and others through energy orbitals surrounding us. We are just microscopic energy portals representative of everything, every place, and every one, and the more we remember who we truly are, the more we engineer that type of reality by creating cars to ride in, stable houses to live in, and better places to play in.

Addiction has paved the way for accumulated things. Like all the luxuries have created ways to obtain addictive habits readily. The engineering, architecture, planning, businesses, and other infrastructure have created methods to prolong an addiction of luxury. Between other people and myself, I have had a series of American-made and foreign-made cars, and they are all used for the same old purpose and can be problems to collect, like taking care of another person. So practically, all these things we have for our luxury, entertainment, and daily use are a part of the family, including a mistress (or mister). They all have to be maintained so you can keep them a little longer. Therefore, if you remove some of what is in excess, then you will have more room for greater spiritual rewards that the universal God-mind is willing to give you. Temperance is the key to filling and emptying out what is clogging up your life. The constant, infinite ebb and flow of the connection of one planet to another through the solar power of the sun enables us to truly gain what we know is the kingdom of heaven, which is out of this world and space, from any cerebral, sensory stimulation and is the utmost of all highs and any underworld carnal, manual pleasures.

Social media and paparazzi serve as mediums through which connections are communicated and broadcast through television and Internet database systems. An unaware novice would be easily influenced by these medium waves, as if in a state of trance, regarding what his or her image is falsely made of. Pop culture in hip hop and some forms of R&B and rap have portrayed an image of buying foreign cars, making money by any means necessary, stereotypes how African Americans deal with priorities. Since it can be such a struggle for the average black person to get out of poverty, they are the main focus; black people are targeted to get them to spend money. Misinformed and uneducated black people are being brainwashed into this era of trash music that only sings and raps about sex, drugs, alcohol, money, cars, and more money. There are really a lot of underprivileged black folk these days who have been through the ringer with the justice system due to many years of ancestral slavery, poor functioning public schools that cater to people of other origins, and the overflowing drug and alcohol cargo in predominantly black communities here in the United States. So many African Americans are tolerant of not having much, so when they do start to make a little money, many seem to want to hold onto it for dear life or spend it on things that make them feel accepted by other people, to add people as a security blanket of improvement and support even though the only acceptance that counts is within oneself. Remember, getting back to ground zero is the fool tarot card. There is nothing to be added or subtracted from that; it is equally mellow and full of sunshine at the ending and beginning of a journey.

People with a dominant Earth in their natal charts can possibly get complacent in their environments. Furthermore, like all living organisms, we form habits and addictions—even the steadiest individual. Most of our motives are sexually driven, given that we are far into trying to impress people through material gain. Unconscious behavior acts to feed its personal ego that is only within the comforts of earthly possessions, material wealth, and sexual pleasure. All of these enticements can be felt in the midsection of your anatomy, in the bottom chakra of your torso, and your energy will circulate through and focus on that area only if you choose to be unconsciously aware of it. Achieving the opening of all of our chakras at the same time is our ultimate goal to bring pure satisfaction. There are seven chakras, and thus, like the planets endlessly orbiting the sun, it is the same with our energy chakras that we will feel the effects of holiness.

We have to take into account who we really are. If we have more fire in our charts, then we are more likely to be anxious and exhibit bouts of anger more often than others. An abundance of air in a natal chart can impact us through feeling spacy, confused, and disoriented. Water may lead to depression, and Earth would lead to coping with reality or addiction to materials (purchasing habits). Once we figure out why, who, when, where, how, and what makes us agitated, annoyed, and distracted, then we can start to clean all the cluttered spaces we have in our lives. Sex addictions and the excitement of multiple partners are a temporary fix to anxiety and are fed by the personal ego. Depression and forms of PTSD often lead to alcohol and drug abuse due to pondering the past. Thinking about the future too much can turn into cerebral overload and being too much in the head instead of focusing on being connected and grounded to the familiar environment we walk in. Laziness and comfort can take over a well-grounded person and can cause a denaturing or stagnation of growing up into the spiritual realm because comfort lies in the lower chakras of the womb and carnal pleasures. Through all of these ups and downs with a constant struggle like addiction, we do learn about balance and temperance. It is the same with hoarding because it is necessary to give away as much as we receive to get the flow of balance in our essence (what comes in must go out but is not lost or gained). This is the law of nature and we must abide by it, for if we don't, nature will denature us. In order to not form unhealthy addictions, we must subtract the people, places, and things that no longer serve a purpose in growth. For instance, if you like to collect artifacts or books, give them a home in your house and give them value by letting them serve their purpose. Organization improves a scattered brain, and then you can proceed to what you really want to do. For example, think of a scattered plot chart with a line drawn across it. Time and money are going to be on the plot chart. Time is represented on the x-axis, and money is represented on the y-axis in terms of value on commodities. Your variables may be for every month for time and an income of $2,400 a month for money. Legend points are gas, clothes, food, décor, entertainment, rent, utilities, savings, and so on. You can plot your expenses on the graph and see where most of your time and funds are going, and then look at the plot line to see how to get your points closer to the line so that there can be a steady flow of income and a steady flow of expenditures. Money has no end to itself on earth, and for now it is comprehensible to measure the illusive time over money with material commodities, goods, and services. You can also measure time in days spent with family, television, Internet, entertainment, friends, spouse, work, hobbies, and so forth.

Today, it is not surprising to encounter many simple addictions in our lifestyles since we depend on corporations and businesses to provide us with our food. Fast-food chains have been the culprit behind processed foods with enriched bleached flour and bread products. Our children are becoming more and more addicted to sugar and its access. A reward system of giving a child candy, snacks, and cookies is set up in most homes, or it falsely disguises the gift of love. In the meantime, these products thrive on DNA that multiplies bad bacteria in our systems, and we become processed in the mix of it. To be processed is to come out of something that already exists, like fecal waste. Adding simple sugars from organic fruits, dried fruits, and frozen fruits as well simplifies your DNA to its primal makeup, which is much easier to make because it is recognizable from the years of ancestry programmed in your DNA. Simplifying food is like looking at the big picture of a meal and breaking it down into its simplest, purest form—pretty much cooking from scratch or eating more raw fruits and vegetables. We are always adding to our meals when we should be simplifying them and adding flavor with herbs for entrées and agave or raw honey for dessert dishes. To help our bodies become full of energetic life, we have to reduce our intake to simple foods. Keeping meals simple requires less stress and exhaustion as well. Using fewer ingredients in a dish eliminates fatigue, and eating foods of the sea matures our development process as well. Healthy dishes that consist of protein-rich nutrients found in lentil beans, lima beans, chickpeas, red beans, okra, brown rice, fish, shellfish, unprocessed corn products, whole grains, greens, fruits, and herbs are all a part of getting over the process in your body that has been corrupted with processed eating. After we are accustomed to eating the way we always knew to be best, then we can reprogram our brains to again perfect themselves in the thought process. This is a part of the never-ending perfecting process of self to get closer to God consciousness and universal mind thinking.

A microscope tells us a lot about the dimensions of the universe. Looking outside and inside the human body, we can see that it is a copy of every life form on earth and beyond. Our sweat glands are representative of rivers, streams, and water life. Skin is the terrain, and as mentioned before, hairs are like the petals of a flower. Nerve synapses and endings are like star constellations and many forms of bacteria seeping everywhere. Not to sound so cliché, but every point and ray in space demonstrates our image. So it is up to us to get out of this trance to be more aware and present in this world. Taking care of our bodies by eating the right foods, staying away as much as possible from chemical substances in the products that we use every day, and realizing that the quality of the particles in the air affects our health as well is the mainstream way to be aware of how we can proceed into the manifestation of healthy, wealthy beings. An advantage in the capital business system is consumerism and people being ignorant of what they are ingesting into their systems, applying on their skin, and breathing in, promoting an ongoing problem of denaturing the system simply by adding complexity. Being more awakened to your freedom to become independent of these goods, services, and people helps you to create better natural solutions, like making your own clothes, cooking your own food for you and your family, not watching television, making your home solar powered, and learning how to install your own water system.

Nevertheless, simplification in attitude is the cure for addictive, impulsive behavior. Being able to simplify our lives by learning from behavior is what sets us apart from other species. Being able to make the best decisions for ourselves by presently taking accountability for our physical bodies is our duty, to live according to how our ancestors lived. Our DNA is programmed to constantly perfect the human system by decoding, splicing, regenerating, and repairing cells. It receives information through stimuli and a constant programming of random information. In able to reach perfection, one's organism has to go through the *one,* or (0, 0) coordinates, as seen in the Greek letter Omega. The dense areas in your brain are related to your third eye or seventh chakra, ankhs, Omega, infinity letter, the cross, amygdala, pituitary gland, occipital magnum and the center of the universe, just to name a few. Children get older and adults get younger during their lives; if you live to an elderly age, you will come to know and understand day by day that you just want to revert back to the condition of an infant. An infant is the most primitive breathing being on earth because it needs only its four survival needs met: being fed, changed, loved, and rested. That is all an infant is concerned about. In between life and death, the infant is programmed early on how to get what it wants and is excited about getting rewarded. Toys are used for playtime, books are read for cognitive learning, and more sensory development intrigues the senses of the system for more information to feel sure of the self. Throughout all this, sources of information that forever perfect us from the relationships we form with others, the experiences we undertake, and the goals that we try to achieve are all a part of the process of getting closer to subtracting all the added relative problems we have in our vicinity to reach equilibrium in just being *one.*

CHAPTER 27

Indulgences

We all get tempted to take on more than our share, and some of us indulge a little bit much when it comes to pleasure. On numerous times, we replace and confuse love with sensory pleasure. Without regard, I may say that I love cookies, cake, and candy. What I really mean is that those things please me. An indulgence is easily related to sweets things to eat because they immediately please our taste buds and we want them constantly, so we eat more of what brings us pleasure, which can turn into an overindulgence. This is not to be confused with self-indulgence; that is mainly part of the personal ego and disregards the true, higher, real self. I can admit that I overindulge in food, rest, and defense, but companionship has been and still seems to be very rare. Perhaps greediness on my behalf is the culprit, as well as my insistence on having two of everything. My biggest fear in life has always been rejection, thus making my main goal in life to value success and acceptance in terms of love. Thus, through the years, I have worked to overcome my fears through public speaking, education, and several forms of language. I want people to be able to understand purpose in all forms and fashions, but on the flip side, I disregard what people think and feel about me quite naturally when I am distant and silent. I learned that overextending is not in my true nature, and it can warp and zap me of energy because I am so damn sensitive. Remember that the more we try to add to someone or something, the less value it has for that person. Nevertheless, to this day, I feel like less of a person when I have people involved in my life because I attract takers. So I ask myself, *If I am such a giver, then why do I attract nongivers?* I contemplated the possibility that I come across as a pushover or that those who get close to me can easily sense how caring I am and take advantage of that. At an early age, I learned how it feels to be outcast by supposedly good friends who were two-faced or too adolescent in my eyes. Through the years I built up this shell—or rather, I had a soft shell when I was growing up, and each year I cared less about friendships and more about conversations with strangers. People are nicer when they are making their first adult impressions, so it's easier to just share companionship with a stranger for a brief moment than to try to figure out if I have true friends. Being a blowhard to friendship can seem lonesome, but currently much of my life does not require a network of friends and I love that feeling. Extending and overextending the self to others can take a toll on oneself all across the board, in my case. Since the feeling of being rejected is not comforting, I find it pleasant to keep relationships and friendships simple by having a bare minimum, or even none at all. Social media has kept me in touch with my old hometown friends and distant family, but I love solitude and can't function without it. Sensitivities may make me feel this way as well, but I get a lot done by being by myself.

Most of the relationships I formed in the past made me feel alone anyway because they catered to others and not to me. Even if I was alone with a man, he would always seem to bring up someone who was better, prettier, smarter, or anything to take the focus off the presence of us. However, my intentions are not to rant about myself. I thought the reason for being rejected was that I came across as too self-centered, but that was not the case. It was depressing and still is. I really didn't know that I deserve "special" treatment. Then I found the answer after some deep soul-searching—one friend or spouse, one mother, one father, one sibling, and so on is all I need and is good enough. Just like having one major credit card, one car, one house, and no more is what will keep me satisfied. I am only speaking from my point of view; it may be different with how your life is set up. I just know that I am most comfortable when I dwell inside myself and do all the things that I want to do without any disruptions to my psyche from what seem to be from very possessive energetic bodies that drain me whenever given a chance. This is especially true in the friendship department because I allow these energy vampires to suck the life force out of me by continuing to feed them with my aura and energy.

Furthermore, when I did not have any children, I always took the time to self-indulge a bit. Self-indulgence is quite different from overindulgence. Since I did not have any dependents, my freedom had reached its limit. I divided the caretaking once I conceived children, who duplicated my genes and their father's genes as well. So the parental stage starts at 1, which is me, and the father is 1 as well. Conjoining takes half of each of us, which later makes up one whole. So that is how we should see numbers, with everything adding up to 1. When you introduce a generation, it always starts with two halves. It is rather a reduction of fractions that are between 0 and 1. Picture 0 as the core center of the universe, sun, or earth/moon and the limit of the universe being 1, which is infinite. Ground zero is earth since it has gravity, and 1 would be the heavens. The "as above, so below" law would be 0 to −1 and is a mirror reflection of 0 to 1. With all the circumstances in the world, we are just 0 to 1 reflections of one another, and we usually attract who we are. To get a real glimpse into how we truly are, we can video record ourselves for a month or longer to shock, surprise, and quite shame us into real selfhood.

Self-indulgence is a part of the personal ego that is relentless in pleasing and satisfying the self without any regard to injury of the self or others. Through relationships with humans, we can become confused about whether we attract who we are, who we want, or who is opposite of us. First of all, we have to understand that in every relationship we have, whether with friends, coworkers, relatives, or others, it is always going to be different from the relationships we have with other people. The reason is that all of our thought processes and perceptions of people change all the time, ranging on a scale from 0 to 1, and this is really how we compare our relationships—by using these range measurements of data to depict the pleasure and satisfaction we get from them. The range of 0 to −1 is representative of the same concept, just at different poles. Karmic relationships can take a toll on us. They are here to teach us valuable lessons in learning how to love ourselves completely. Forget about the words that were said between the two of you and the deceptions or lies, and really look within yourself and realize that most relationships are way past their termination points. Holding onto hurt, pain, and disruption is a reflection of the hurt, pain, and disruption that you want or wanted in your life. Studies have shown that adult people are abused not by strangers but by people they have known within their families or for some years. Until we get to know ourselves by being isolated or alienated or by digging deep within ourselves, then we will not know who to trust and believe. Various individuals go through life, jumping from one relationship to another without ever knowing who they are because they are disrupted and disturbed from sharing their energy with irrelevant people. This explains the saying "You are the company you keep." An overindulgence in a bad influence of friends can bring your self-value and self-worth down due to karmic law. Whatever is injurious to another will bring tragic results and a downfall to both parties because when one falls, the other will come right after. We form relationships with who we are in want of someone to complete us through attraction. That wanting can create secrets, lies, and deception with the intent of holding on, which pleases the ego. Our health defends itself from this environment by secluding away from the stimulus that is not serving its betterment and standards for evolution. If the health is not in recovery from the environment, then the body will turn on itself until it gets the proper treatment from its environment. The body merely cares about what it needs, but the mind deals with all its thoughts and sensibilities. The body is after the wants, and the mind is searching for the needs, thus making it easier for us to be prone to indulgences, which is the sweet life. By merging the mind-body, a person is able to succeed in getting both needs and wants met. Each of us has a completely different outlook and perception on life that is changing moment to moment. We plan and create our own manifestations and guidelines to getting to our individual sweet-as-water lives. It is our self-indulgences that prompt us to confess and regret guilty pleasures.

My many indulgences thrive on my current state of being immobilized. Self-indulgence always hinders progression with a constant probing backward. For example, having more than one partner takes away the time and attention for one person over the other. Even if the person has repetitive thoughts about a past love or flame, it still takes away from his or her current partnership. Our thoughts run rampant about the daily activities of others while the people who are present in relationships with us are not getting adequate attention. Like I said before, we attract who we are rather than who we want. And we want to be ourselves or in union with ourselves. My latest affair consisted of such a relationship; I was paying less and less attention and showing less affection to one partner and sharing my time with another who was always dwelling in the past about his ex. Whether his agenda was right or wrong, I feel that it was fair because I was attracting that maltreatment through my own behavior with another. During that lengthy process, I learned a lot about myself as far as my attitude and how the people with whom we surround ourselves are the people who reflect our own attitudes about ourselves. Developing relationships with people gives us a chance to better our behavior on the astral and physical planes, which reconnects the mind-body-spirit kinship. As we learn the lessons of these acquaintances and happenings, we can look with disgust at a partner, who is really us, and try to avoid the behavior that person is portraying to us, as if we will never adopt those bad traits. Thus evolution connects us to morals, values, and standards on whom we invite into our lives and how we invite them into our channeling process. So it is just best to close one door before opening another. Now, that term reminds me of a *Night Gallery* episode focused on a girl named Brenda who was always getting into these lonesome adventures at her parents' beach house. She was a tomboy and a bit of a fearless risk taker who did not even mind inviting a monstrous, rocky being into her family home by leaving the door wide open for the foreign marsh to come in, whom she befriended. At the end of the episode, Brenda's father and neighbor chased off the marsh into a bottomless pit, where Brenda had once trapped him before, and later the two men mummified Brenda's only friend into a sturdy, immobile mound of rocks. Seasons passed, and Brenda returned to visit the site that next summer. She apologized and made a promise to come back to visit and that they could never be separated. The episode concluded with a creepy ending—the camera focused in on the mound of marsh rocks, which appeared to be a monster figure or a mother and a child. The significance of this is that unconditional love in all of our significant relationships and the closeness of companionship alters the power of love. I bet Brenda had found a summer vacation love and friend who would stay with her all of her life. She could never lose sight of it because she knew its place. So if you leave doors wide open and do not care to close the necessary doors to start anew, then you will only create rockiness because there is no order. When there is no order or respect for laws in nature, then the result is failure or stagnation. Furthermore, in the future, we gain less stress with less self-indulgence.

Now, open relationships operate on a higher awareness of optional offers and pretty much consider sex as a sport and release of energy. But more than likely there is going to be jealousy in these relationships, with one person craving oneness and simplicity. Partners in an open relationship have to be open to eliminating privacy when it comes to sexual matters. An open conversation about having casual sexual intercourse with other people is a sign of a healthy open relationship. Also, the sharing of partners during sexual acts creates the pleasure of multiple bodies being one. There is no jealousy or secrecy—just fun among people whose company you love. Feelings of wanting to please another are the primal energy when seeking these orgies or swinger situations. When one pleases multiple people at the same time, the energy increases at the temporary time of pleasure. This can become addictive and indulgent based on the feeling of increased energy release, but according to the unwritten moral code, there is distaste for this type of behavior. It is now becoming more steadily acceptable in modern cultures. I remember watching clips of swingers on *Real Sex* or *Shock Video* on HBO, displaying taboos about having sex with multiple partners as if in a union.

Nevertheless, I've always been intrigued by people of both sexes, and on many occasions I was caught dry humping with one of my friends at my parents' house. A person can feel sexual gratification at a very young age. When caught, I felt extremely embarrassed, and two of my friendships were terminated out of the sheer humiliation. I first noticed the implications of sex when I found a Kama Sutra book with couples in many tantric sex positions. Later on, I discovered pornographic videotapes, and then I experienced the feeling of sex by grinding up against several of my childhood friends. A very curious child with lots of energy to share, I still was very shy and quiet in my adolescent years. Fourteen was the age that I lost my virginity.

I can only imagine how much of a whore I would have been if my first sexual partner had not been experienced in sex himself. Instead, I was content with only him as a sex partner for about a year. I feel that females actually need a mature, but not necessarily older, person to lose their virginity to. A lot of girls don't have to worry about rumors being spread all throughout school and creating a bad reputation. In intermediate school and high school, I was mainly a loner, and I could see how fast the other teenagers were. I felt that I had passed that stage in life when I was at the age of six with sexual indulgences. I can say that the number of my partners is at a minimum because of my placing mates on a pedestal, considering each of them to be my one true love, twin flame, soul mate, or even a comic book character such as Peter Parker in *Spider Man*, Bruce Wayne in *Batman*, or Clark Kent in *Superman*. As I got older, I would imagine them to be a son of Adam to my Eve and even troll or fairy-type beings—anything other than human. Then, when I took the rose-colored glasses off, they appeared to be less than human, not even human beings anymore. They were nicer when they were strangers, but a companion can suddenly turn cold, distant, dominating, and inconsistent. It did not matter the type of abuse I would experience in some of these relationships; I still saw my partner as a higher being even when he was injurious to me and himself. Some form of rejection, discrimination, or segregation on their part was what it took to halt these relationships. It really takes that much for me to quit all forms of communication with them. By being that type of partner, I experienced completeness with myself because I kept yearning and waiting for a reciprocation of unconditional love in a duality of partnerships. Unfortunately, we can't achieve miracles with other beings when there is a duality, only conflicts. The acceptance of conditional love on my part from another was not a mistake. You see, the universal God is very jealous when it comes to nonreciprocal love. The vibration of unconditional love is with the heavens and the universe, and this is where we really reside. Experiencing negative emotions and feelings only pulls us more down to earth and into the underworld with regard to the spiritual realm. Contrarily, we have to go through these multiple relationships until we get ourselves on a higher plane where our higher intelligence wants us to be. Adding onto our lifestyles with temporary substances only confuses this for us. Indulgences are meant to be experienced, learned, and inspiring until the next best thing or people come into our lives, which is consistent with knowing.

CHAPTER 28

Forbiddance

Movies that are made about some genre of dancing always portray it as provocative, sexy, rebellious, and creative. A dance is more than an active movement and gesture of limbs. It is a language that does not need to be spoken by mouth but can be conveyed by moving to the beat of a sound. All species of bees waltz in circular, spiral motions to communicate where there is food, shelter, nectar, and other survival needs to prolong their sustainability. The communication style of bees can be so accurate and precise that it has been questioned whether their colonies are of an elevated caliber because there are various waltzes that are unique in the direction of the dance but the bees remember them. They adapt at an alarming rate as the populations of Africanized and honey bees increase in the general population. One common quality that bees have with this universe is the structure and demonstration of the Fibonacci series. The dances correlate with the same formula that is calculated in this array of number sequencing. All of its existence stems from the Fibonacci series of pattern modeling. Levels of this geometry are definitely magical in that they are so hard to explain but so simple to create. It is within our genome of division, discrimination, sequencing, splicing, recombinant, and regeneration of ancestry that we're more in tune with prime native architecture, design, symbols, numbers, and ancient vibrational flow. We are all programmed to work around this sequence of mathematical formulas that are explanatory but still vague. It is forbidden to even mention this type of so-called conspiracy beyond mathematical calculations. Our brains are small networks that operate the entire universe using the frequency of vibrational waves. When we get in touch with nature around some body of water, a forest of trees, sun gazing, and even skydiving, we reset our active sites and can temporarily replace or stave off hunger through exposure to sunlight and stimuli of nature. Most forests have pine cones, flowers, waves, and little remnants of a creative designer that is turned on by us. It is a rule that is repeated over and over again but not explained thoroughly in education. The Fibonacci series is just an example of loving the self entirely like a coiled seashell. Inside a pregnant mother's womb when she first conceives, the zygote is one cell that later divides in the same sequence as the Fibonacci numbers. Throughout the replication of cells, we follow a sequence of dividing numbers from the DNA of a nucleus that falls inside square (0, 1, 1) and evolves around a spiral image similar to a serpent coiled into a spiral and the circles inside a tree. Male sperm moves toward an egg in the same motion that the planets move toward the sun, using the same sequence of numbers but at various speeds. There is definitely something hidden when we try to delve deeper into these so-called conspiracies. We see the connection in movies, music, art, nature, logic, math, physics, and every other discipline that there is but cannot figure out why we are programmed with these formulas. The only explanation I can make sense of is the acceptance factor, where there is no room for discrimination in love. We are all made the same way with the same formulas, but we still distinguish ourselves from one another through gender, race, origin, culture, genetics, creed, class, handicap, and mental illness. Thus, when the acceptance factor is generated from compassion, understanding, and just not giving a flip about other people's attitudes, we realize that we are one and that we exist accordingly to designated traveling.

Dancing is a commonality that we all share in that we can all do it. Even plants and flowers dance from the whispers of the wind, and dancing does not have to be done with a partner. You can do it all by yourself, and leading choreographers prefer it this way. I love dancing by myself, especially when no one else is around. Sacred forms of dancing are kept hidden these days, away from exposure and censorship, but the freedom that dancing has to offer with a release of feeling and emotion connects rapidly to our external environment. We are a world full of bodies that love to have a good time. We celebrate different holidays, birthdays, and special occasions all because everyone else is doing it. The point is that we need to celebrate every day of our lives but within our own celebrations. You may have to ask yourself, do you celebrate because you want to celebrate? Or do celebrations serve your higher purposeful good? These questions may not be of much practicality and may be less conventional because they distinguish time and love into a relationship. We practice the same rituals, holidays, occasions, anniversaries, and so on generation after generation. We feed the same junk education that we learned in school to our children. We keep information that is uniquely hidden from us in textbooks. We can become familiar with the cosmos, matrices, and the universe through science, math, and the arts, but we are still separate in our teachings. We still have discrimination in our school systems that hinders the full potential of some students' education. Outdated stereotypes of others help politicians to not require a funding system that will benefit all children in school. Finding what makes us true in the universe should be the ultimate primary goal in progressing our children's knowledge. Accepting that we are all geniuses and that we all have a unique purpose to fulfill is the mission of learning but is forbidden on earth through hate and limits.

In the literature describing Eve plucking the forbidden fruit from the tree, we find a fairy tale turned grim. From the very beginning, the Bible was meant to separate the genders from each other due to this forbidden fruit. I can only assume that a source of information was being exposed to the general public that did not benefit moneymakers. During that time, women may have been the main explorers of the higher realms of spirituality, which would explain why there was not much mention of women in the Bible. Monarchism must have been despised, and I can only imagine that these writers of the book were men who were not all that attractive to the women and were left out of sexual ordinances. Thus, if we look closer into religion and spirituality we will find that Jesus' existence is not hidden at all but just disguised in a delusional facade of elaborate masks. These masks are similar to a butterfly, and once we are dwelling in our shadow side, the mask must come off and we must face our own individual truth that is the forbidden fruit.

As previously mentioned, meditation can be done spontaneously, like during daydreams. With me having a square in Venus/Neptune, I am prone to daydreaming a lot. I look back and think that if only I had paid more attention to my teachers and instructors instead of daydreaming, I may have been a scholarly student all throughout school. Daydreaming is part of meditation, and in some instances it can be uncontrollable when in a modest state. Daydreaming is forbidden in some cultures because it is a portal that can keep us aware of the connection we have with Mother Nature. When we pay attention to Mother Nature, we are actually listening to her. In return for listening and spending time with Mother Nature, miracles occur to improve the already rather strong connection of the perfect union. Daydreaming may not benefit us much in a classroom but can be of much sustenance near and looking at nature. When daydreaming, we mostly ignore discrimination and rejection because we feel at home with Mother Nature and in turn have dreams and vivid thoughts about a union of acceptance in a frustrated environment. We share that with Mother. Now, if we don't pay attention to Mother Nature, then she can become a nag and powerfully force us to return to her through duality. It's a dance, and two can tango. You can dance by yourself or choose to dance with another to feel the unconditional effects of love from nature. She nurtures us when we hide from darkness and rewards us when we pay homage to not accepting false truths about ourselves that people try to make us accept. Venus/Neptune aspects experience this energy profoundly and end up telling these doomed fairy tale stories that are later read and viewed in cinema.

The square Venus/Neptune aspect is always placing their significant other close to God initially due to Venus/Neptune being delusional in love and seeing themselves at that level themselves. And according to all the soul mate and twin flame chats, books, blogs, and other sources of information, a perfect mate is one who is the opposite of me, which is totally insufficient. I deceived myself by having an array of knowledge about twin flames. So when I got into a relationship, I automatically assumed that there would be some type of hardship to go through, which is true. But love does not require sacrifices, and reluctantly I became inspired and enlightened to create my craft from a doomed relationship. I do agree with most texts about twin flame relationships that the universe does not care whether you marry or prolong erratic behavior in the codependent relationship. So that being said, I sort of can't help the fact that I picture my lovers as surreal being that they are my twin flames. We are told in the Bible not to idolize or put figures, symbols, or people above God or ourselves. We continue to go through the rings of the fire even though we know some relationships are not up to our standards. We enjoy the fantasy of sharing unconditional love with someone even if it hurts us because we believe in sacrifices when it comes to the reciprocation of love. Just being in love with the feelings of love in a relationship that are superficial in a natural environment is forbidden because it leads to savior/victim codependent habitual companionship. But this is where all the magic takes place, and by the time we know it, we cannot distinguish fact from truth or what is real when it comes to sexual partners and higher intelligence. The feelings that are expressed between me and a jerk-ish boyfriend may be the opening to a portal of true acceptance from the universe. My truth and my acceptance, feelings of rejection, abuse, being victimized, and all those counterreactive emotions are filtered through silence and daydreaming by ignoring the other party and reconnecting with the universe for higher truth. A simple, arrogant annoyance leads the other party to ignore, and then that ignorance leads to a truth that is bliss when one listens to Mother Nature in real time. The production of this leaves a person knowing but not knowing. Answers are still unknown, but knowledge is rekindled in memory. Our memory banks are from our ancestors and are encoded into our genetic makeup to help us remember the true self.

Cellular production and repair are aligned with the aspects of the solar system. Cell repair consists of natural healing antigens within the human system, and just like in the solar system, there are planets and different aspects that come to the rescue to repair our souls. Planets move in a double helix spiral just like DNA and are continuously meeting up at vertices for energy. This journey is repetitive and insanely fixing circumstances all on a blueprint of karmic destinations. Everything is coded, decoded, and recoded over and over again. Manufacturing products, pixels in a television, the circular motion of water in the toilet, the pupils in our eyes, the ground we walk on—all particles are resonated, frequently moving to the same vibration of the proceeding solar power. We repair ourselves from the ray of the sun's particles. Our connection to the sun is mysteriously active in its transits. The biggest star in our solar system is the generator of all high-light energies. The deeper parts of the galaxy are dark matter energies. Sun –star companionship introduces us to enlightenment during an explicable time of reflection. Soul-searching simply enjoys sun engagements; thus, it is easy to daydream when caught between the rays of the Sun.

Intense observation of perception and the sun has proven that particles and objects that enter the sun come out on the other side. The energy is not destroyed by the massive heat but exits through the sun perpendicularly, and this applies to all matter that comes into contact with other matter. Perception is the study of an object in quantum physics that proves practice and theory even though there is one perceivable object within our vision. If that object is impacted, then its energy will go on the other side of the object being impacted. For instance, practicing volleyball drills includes a ball, a person, and a wall. Hitting the ball against the wall creates work, force, and energy being exerted from the movement of the hand and wrist to the contact of the ball onto the wall. Energy that is transferred from the contact of the hand to the ball is spread beyond the impact of the exertion on the ball. Contact reflects in the exertion of the hand and the ball reflexes to the wall, causing an equal amount of energy to be transferred to the wall. For beginners, this volleyball drill can be tiresome until they learn the rhythms of controlling the volleyball with their hand. The hand becomes stronger and is programmed to the feelings of hitting the ball at the best spot with little exertion but more transfer of energy. So what does a simple volleyball practice drill have to do with the effects of the sun? Well, the more we regenerate our human systems with all of these different aspects, the easier it is to feel the illuminating effects of the sun. When we follow the aspects that are laid out for us, we are rewarded with transforming new energy because everything is going according to plan. Personally, I really never did read the Bible, but I still have a feeling of knowing all while not knowing because I learn something new every day. I remember the scriptures that forbid the observations of cosmology, which are contradictory to all the Magi calculations on birth and direction. There is definitely an unhidden secret that is known to all of us through listening, seeing, and appreciating. Observing the cosmos while feeling rejection and acceptance mutually enables you to structure the beauty of nature by communicating with a higher intelligence through trancelike modes of functioning. Colors of the sky can change to the colors of your clothes or your skin and will camouflage you because you share the connection just by listening and paying attention to nature with the presence of a dual relationship that is disguised with problems, chaos, and any negative environment that tries to disprove your truth.

Greek mythology has introduced to us the forbiddance of gazing at Venus. I came across a handful of readings about Venus, and the planet is portrayed as either a love goddess or a mean bitch. The law of attraction is felt best around August 5 every year to me. That is the time when I love to get in touch with nature. With the help of Venus and Jupiter in transit, this day is a force to be reckoned with. Electrical vibrations are felt through human connections of sincere kinship more readily, and on that day passionate frequencies are expanded. It is amazing that a lot of people disprove of or are biased against sun gazing, analyzing astrology, and gaining perception. Sensitive individuals who do step out of the box of perceived normality are often questioned and labeled as delusional. These perceptions have made our world so obsessively mundane to the point of living a fake life filled with worshipping the material plane. Ignoring or hiding this connectedness to reality has been done for so many years that we have failed to save these qualities from teachers who could explain abundance without working for money from ancient history. Reluctantly, though, we have a genetic backup system that will not allow this information to be forgotten. Our recurring progression of DNA, planets, and technology reminds us of where we really came from and why we coexist. One last forbidden concept is the act of wanting God. There is a scripture that tells us not to be in want or desire for God. A part of me agrees with this because in order for us to experience higher realms it is explained that we must go through Jesus Christ first; thus, the initial want and desire is the inspirational feeling of unconditional love that is easily attainable with unity. The bottom line is that if you know Jesus, go through him. If you only know God, go through him. If you only know nature, then get your nurture on by communicating with Mother through silence, which is listening. If you don't believe in these figures, symbols, and incarnations, then just know yourself and that's all. All you need to know is you because you are an image of God. In my experience, I know Christ, God, nature, universe, and angels by my confessions, convictions, and repentance. Therefore, it is very hard for me to eliminate all these figures even though I know deep inside that we create what we want and there is a force within all that elevates us. We are God-conscious, we are who we are, and we are perfectly developed to reach earth-changing spirituality in our lives.

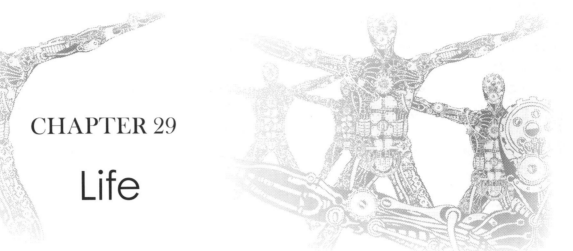

CHAPTER 29

Life

Life is simply what you make it. You can get lemons and let them go sour, or you can cut and squeeze them and add a little water and sugar to make lemonade. You can even add other fruits to it like blueberries, strawberries, or raspberries to your liking. It is our choice to how we live our lives, from the company we keep to the opportunities we seek through challenges. Choice in lifestyle impacts our health in so many different ways. That is why alone time is critical to the sanity of our health. It is noticeable that all matter is connected. The way the planets move around in a double helix toward the sun as a focal center point, meeting at equidistant intersections, is a sure sign of our symbiotic relationship with everything and everybody. Within these relative systems are cycles. Cycles are composed of macroparticle substances that correlate with nature to form ecosystems.

Today marks the day of my dear friend's passing. This day, August 5, also marks the law of attraction, when Venus and Jupiter align at 28 degrees for evening sky-Venus Rx. As mentioned earlier, the experience of the law of attraction is the vibrant relationship we meditate toward being in nature and in tune with the cosmos. A point of meditation can take place with ritual dances such as Sufi whirling, simple yoga, or just a calming of the mind. This influence is strong because Jupiter is aligned with Venus, which expands the abundance of energy for the love of beauty. Creation is inspired through bountiful beauty. Life is a repetitive cycle of dividing abundance into complete perfection of evolving resonance. Whirlpools in a body of water give a great example of the cycle of life in reflective, pure forms of water. The flow of water is held in every crevice of the earth. Earth holds water all throughout the depths and center core crust. Water is evaporated into the atmosphere through the air, creating recycled water in the form of rain and condensation, forming humidity.

With this in mind, nearly every living substance contains H_2O. The four elements of fire, water, air, and earth are all part of our general makeup of matter. We contain dust, especially when we pass into ashes and are buried inside the earth or cremated. Ashes are all the matter that we are composed of and are the ancient material of the ground. A lack or abundance of earth can cause inertia, flightiness, stubbornness, inflexibility, a focus on long leisure time, indulgences, and prolonged pleasures. A good amount of earth keeps us focused on rewards and material stabilization, secured in faith, protected by loyalty, and fixed in our ways. Our fire is within our blood, and it circulates throughout our bodies creating passionate energy filtered through the heart. Fire gives us force and drive, adrenaline, dopamine, bravery, and boldness—aggressiveness that is suited for politicians with a compassionate demeanor. A lack of fire or too much fire can result in anxiety, laziness, tiredness or lack of adrenaline, dopamine, stroke, and aneurisms. Water keeps in touch with the emotions of our shadow sides, which are hidden beneath us just like the depths of an ocean. Liquids leave a bloating or clear effect on us. Too much water causes retention, and too little water causes dehydration. It is important to listen to the body regarding the adequate amount of liquid intake to prevent retention and dehydration, which can cause dizziness, blindness, depression, loss of breathing, and malfunction of organs and organisms. Last is the quality of air and wind that gives us that summer breeze in the early hours of the morning and late during the evenings. Shade trees help by giving us wind through their cool leaves and the input and output irrigation water system and grasp of sunlight. Country life gives us an opportunity to experience the quality of fresh air away from polluting factories that are located in city areas. A lack or abundance of air can leave us too gullible, airheaded, flighty, dreaming, talkative, following, experiencing a loss of memory, confused, spaced out, and having mental problems. A consistent amount of air leaves us refreshed, directed, inspired, persuasive, and with feelings of limitless power.

Picture the movement of DNA and planets. Upon creation and catalyst cells' activation, the spiral effect of kinetic energy circulates around potential revolving planned-out matter. Cells are created from one cell at first, which then later divides itself into many other cells to further the creation of life. DNA is a strand of nucleotides and acid formulated into a tight coil of replication. Just like the motion of the planets, revolving and circulating within the universe trying to catch up to a hot fireball of lighted energy (sun), our cells are also replicating bursts of activated energy sites. The potential energy is located in the center core of the nucleus for this is conducted in centripetal force experiments. The sun can also be perceived as a centripetal force since it gives off bursts of energy to our inhabitants.

When I was attending the University of Texas at Arlington, my biology professor lectured about three main parts of biology in the first semester. I have made the suggestion that all three of these parts are correlated with the four elements of biology. Cells and organisms were first, plants and genetics were second, and third was the human body, mainly focusing on the parts of the heart. Cells and organisms show how organisms grow, especially with the use of water-based chemicals like hydrogen and oxygen. Plants and genetics are composed of our earth and air, and the heart is fire based. We learned what cells are composed of many different organisms' functions, processes, and structures of a cell nucleus atom. Water plays a significant role in the function of cells by activating cell structure sites with added chemical elements that help to catalyze the duties of forming a functional cell. Earth is the matter, the substance material that is given to provide us with a function in our bodies, such as organelles like mitochondria, nucleus, chlorophyll (plants), chloroplast, and enzymes. Learning about all the parts of a plant helped me to understand the similarity of plant systems to human systems and how every living and nonliving thing is connected. There is no separation, just division of cellular processes among us while we are incapacitated and grounded to earth, which is our safe haven even though it is a fragile protector from insecurities. The roots of a plant are embedded into the ground and regurgitated in the soil of our land. We are embedded into the land when we pass away and later replenished back unto this earth, with our spirits located in the airy wind drift and outer space.

Seeing the functions, processes, and structures of organisms and organelles helped me to understand how a system is indebted to organization. Without organization, there would not be an established order. There are checkpoints within a functioning cell and atom. Every organelle, enzyme, hormone, nucleic acid, vitamin, mineral, and nutrient plays a major role in replicating healthy, durable cells for living a long life. A nutritious, healthy diet determines the energetic intake our bodies process to give us the right amount of neutral energy to carry out necessary functions to perform the skills that we were given to heal ourselves.

Now, fire is representative of the heart. Our wheel power (engine and drive) is extinguished through the body with the rapid flow of blood through the heart. The chambers of the heart pull us through the impossible that seemed detrimental. A person with an adequate amount of fire is forced to go after their dreams whenever they see fit. Challenges are seen as opportunities with this aspect. They never give up because their fire and strength are controlled with a push of forward mobility. Every living organism has a center point of heart that gives it vitality.

Nevertheless, life can feel like a lie due to the notion of death. Death is just a transformation of transitional stages. For example, the body has expiration dates for old cells, atoms, and particles. The cells on top of our skin expire as dead, scaly cells shedding like snakeskin. When the body is no longer mobile, the spirit is exerted into the atmosphere and air as a spirit. Thus, death is not permanent but is another ongoing cycle of life. After each death that we experience in the living, we are constantly perfecting our lives to the betterment of what we see fit. A lot of adults adjust their lifestyles through competition with others. Challenges with competitors are just opportunities waiting to begin. We all have karmic debt in our lives, and transformational death plays a huge role in our lifestyles.

The process of the human system, which consists of organelles, organisms, enzymes, nucleic acids, and genetic replication, is a huge list of material that processes a lot of information. Information is reprogrammed to our cells, perfecting bodies that have already been perfected from the start. But with the influence of other people, memory loss, and current cultural fads, the forgetfulness of the true, real self can get misplaced in the processes of reestablishment.

An opportunity to change one's mind is a milestone of imagination that leads to great prosperity in life. Making snap decisions can change your life for the better in most instances because you are mainly going with your heart on matters. The complete ignoring of what everyone else is doing in life and following our so-called dreams, which are just unremembered realities, into an active, self-seeking lifestyle is our godly calling into higher purpose. I really have never known a person to regret an action he or she has taken just on intuition. I have heard stories, though, of people regretting inaction and later wishing that they had taken opportunities. The process of everything is a simple reminder to let God handle the hard or impossible situations that will creep up in our subconscious minds and leave us robotic. Going on hunches and intuition after endless pondering is just the reward that we need to begin a journey that starts anew for us in this big world. How we live our lives affects our well-being.

It does not matter how much material goods you consume but rather how you live your life that will determine your place in the kingdom of heaven or everlasting immortality.

Nevertheless, all of us have two parietal sides to our brains. The left side of the brain is known to be logical, thus lacking idealism and fanaticism. The right side of the brain is creative and can lack reason. The sole objective of living a peaceful life is to process information as far as our emotions, feelings, and thoughts in equal amounts through the left and right part of the brain. When your seventh chakra is fully stimulated and activated, you may notice that important sources of information can leave a cooling, electrical sensation through one side of the skull. When a eureka moment comes up after processing logical or creative ideas, the neurons of the brain will react by giving you a great sensory expression. On rare moments, you may experience the brain having a great sensation on both sides, meaning that equilibrium has been accomplished. Also, being in the zone of thinking, feeling, and being emotional can spark these reactions for you quite frequently. When you feel these sensations, it is very important that you pay attention to them for this is a green light to proceed with the thought, feeling, or emotion into action. You can possibly tell which side of the brain a person processes information through just by observing which side of the bed he or she lays on. Through listening to and observing Mother Nature, we can get these telepathic eureka moments more readily and watch miracles happen. Miracles can be as simple as childbirth or as complicated as engineering a new invention. All these aspects are godly gifts that we have inherited through generations of ancestry and images of our godly presence and calling.

The half-life cycle of a cell is a prime example of growth through life cycles. The degradation and dilution of cells are key to understanding human growth cancer cells. Rapidly killing growth cancer cells with the use of proteins is dynamic. A variety of stresses from life can cause cancer cells to increase in number, thereby overtaking the proper functions of living. Our lifestyles, atmospheres, environments, and processing of information affect our health in so many ways. Thereafter, it is critical for us to live free from radical disturbances, whether they be the people with whom we associate, the things we put into our bodies, or the worries of everyday life that need to be adjusted in order to sustain a healthy lifestyle. If we have a population of walking zombies or individuals with dim-lighted spirits, we are thus creating a less positive energetic force on earth, which is detrimental to the universe.

CHAPTER 30

Transformation (Death)

The word *miss* is complicated. We miss revelations in our rest when we are so called dreaming. A dream or nightmare that seems so real to us is actually guiding us to our future realm. We are all quite prophetic when we go to bed at night and close our eyes in a trance of conscious awareness. In reality, we do not sleep but play a glimpse of what is to come next. I like to call dreams just pictures, scenes, or plays of our lives, and just like a novel or movie, there are many possible interpretations, including whether the characters are monsters or people that we encounter every day. All of our dreams are significant to us, and it is important that we try to pay close attention to them if we do not want to be confused on where we are going in life and the transformations that will alleviate us from death. Dreams are an artistic way of painting a perfect picture for us, so it is important that we watch and see what is taking place. I can only imagine that the right side of the brain is in overhaul while we are painting our picture from our subconscious mind while we rest. The act of silence is a very powerful tool.

Our real personal business is kept out of the public eye and left in a closet with bones that we wish would just disappear. No matter how much we try to run from our fears and constant pressure from our peers, we always fall into that pit simply by association. Our civil duty on this earth is to simply understand and love one another no matter what the news is. The gift of empathy for one another proves that we all go through the same circumstances, just different scenarios. Some of us may be blind to that notion. But just like in a "dream," we are all players in this movie we call life; and even in death, our songs, books, shows, and plays go on and on in reincarnate.

A true killer is not somebody that holds in aggression for some time and all of a sudden goes on a killing spree. Nor is a true killer a person who snaps all of sudden and murders someone. An experienced true killer kills with kindness. The phrase "kill them with kindness" is overlooked by a lot of individuals. If we recall from church or any spiritual endeavor, letting God handle our foes is the best righteous revenge available. When people wrong us, it is best to take the necessary kind action to tangibly handle it and let our righteous God rule the rest. Prayer is really a strong weapon to have when somebody or something gets you down. Just remember that God is using all forces to alleviate your situation. It is definitely a waste of time and energy to get frustrated at other people's wrongdoings because, in the long run, their behavior has nothing to do with you; rather it is evidence of whatever they are going through. So it is best to seek to understand one another and imagine yourself in the other person's shoes to generate feelings of mutual empathy. Vengeance through God and the universe is delivered with sympathy to the right doer.

With all the creative material that we have on this earth, it is not hard to get over other people's behavior. Inspirational writings; relevant movies and shows; soothing songs; and sewing, sports, and all other creative activities will help us to move on from our past problems. Heck, when we go through so much strife, we become programmed to not let pettiness bother us anymore. We experience the pettiness readily at a young age, so when we become adults, it simply does not bother us. This formal concept weeds out the weak from the strong, and if we are constantly being bullied, talked about, abused, used, and misused, then we will be profoundly rewarded when we take time out during our daily process to call upon and talk to our godly presence to make ourselves feel better about the current void in our lives. Our lives are transformed before us when we pray the right way by including a trinity of the God-Christ-me conscious mind at our altar. It can be related to the butterfly effect. If you notice, the transformation of a butterfly is somewhat related to what we go through every day. A caterpillar is born and crawls on the branches of trees and the ground, which is representative of ancestry and how we suck up of what our family, especially our parents, want us to be. Later, after the slow movement of crawling on trees and slithering through grass, the insect goes into a state of rest within a cocoon, which is related to our depression and sadness. After the ripening of the cocoon, the caterpillar is in a state of trance and meditation. The cocoon helps protect the caterpillar during this process, which is isolated due to the sadness of zombie life. Much contemplation is done during this depressive state, and even during this time is the opportunity to evolve into the natural highest of all highs. Last, the cocoon opens when it is safe for the caterpillar to transform itself into a colorful and sometimes camouflaged butterfly that is free to flap its wings away from social norms and into individual prosperity. Butterflies live alone until they find a mate to continue this process of transformation that is death. The caterpillar has to die in order to adapt to its environment and to fly freely to wherever it wants to go. While in the cocoon, the caterpillar is in a trance filled with rest, "sleep," "dreams," and meditation, wishing for a change and also wishing that the environment around it will change as well. We can't forcefully change one another. Change only happens within oneself, and it requires a period of confinement and isolation. Now, this period will lead to either decay or growth.

Death is just another creative expression driven by emotions. Thus, it is very hard to escape from emotions no matter how hard we try. Death is part of life just like life is a part of death. Without one, the other does not exist. Our transformational accomplishment is dependent on death to evolve us into the beings that will fill our minds, bodies, and souls with completion. We experience death more readily when lies, deceit, betrayal, half-truths, fibs, and manipulation are introduced. These initial feelings of wrongdoing turn into emotional circumstances that are meant to leave us feeling alone. Until we go through multiple periods of "little deaths" to feel a uniqueness of oneness, we cannot ascend into the harmony of knowing the God-Christ-me conscious mind of acceptance, an acceptance that the world can't ever give us. Death has to take place in order to get to this knowing of acceptance from the universe. When we confess our sins, we use our vehicle bodies to come before Christ, who will never judge us, for our sincerity is within the forthcoming. Allowing ourselves to be reluctant to serve the Lord and to speak and carry his Word is the most cherished relationship between ourselves and Christ. After the acknowledgment of belief in Jesus Christ comes the knowing of God within a feeling of a light body when once before it felt heavy. Tears can help wash those sins away and uplift the soul heart into a burning fire. The body will float like a butterfly, and the mind will be all-knowing. We were never separated from this trinity, but it takes a death to realize and remember where we come from, where we are, and where we need to go. All of this is construed with our emotions, feelings, and thoughts.

Nevertheless, it is an unfortunate situation when people commit suicide, when they experience a death during their stay on earth. A lot of it is caused by bullying, and no one can control another person's sharp tongue and abuse of physical strength upon another. Whether the bullying is done by a family member, spouse, peer, boss, or some type of financial detriment, it is definitely considered part of the psyche of a troubled, slippery person. Thoughts of suicide are common, but the actuality of committing suicide is beyond reparable. When I was younger, I used to think that people who killed themselves would go to hell in total damnation. I see people killing themselves slowly every day, though. With the consumption of fast foods and alcohol, it is only a matter of time before their bodies will expire from all of the unhealthy crap that they put into their bodies. The only way for us to prevent harmful foods from killing us is to grow our own crops and to eat from the sea. But even the sea is polluted by petroleum, oil, and gas rigs. The vegetables and fruits that we eat are mostly decomposed from rudimentary plants and are actually inside plants instead of being raised from the fertile soil. So we are really all slippery people living in a world that is desperately in need of restructuring. The power of healing is made complete through the power of love, that which all of us secretly want and need.

The twelfth and last sign of the zodiac (Pisces) is representative of our final and last death before we can continue with life once again. Pisces is a water sign and is the deepest emotional sign of the zodiac that goes into the sea of consciousness of water. Cancer and Scorpio are more likely to be upon the shores of a beach when near water, but the fish can't survive without the water, thus making it enjoyable to dwell deeply in a fantasy. We need fantasy in order to prepare us for inspiration so that we can do our godly works for one another. Two fish are seen going in opposite ways, and this signifies negativity and positivity being in unity, which is the way to be when we are going through difficult periods in life. It is the balance of our emotions that will keep us safe in the valley of death. Taking the good with the bad is a conscious awareness that everything is going to be all right and weighs out our fear in problems; this is the solution to life and death, to knowing fear but not being afraid to enter into it. The water signs also are collaborative with the shedding of a snake. When death and transformation occurs in our lives, it is like shedding a skin that heals us, like the changing of the seasons. All things are always changing and are never in a halted status. A prolonged death is a stagnant position of dwelling on the past, that which cannot be changed and is already dead itself. While focusing on the past, one will contemplate the future—that which is never here. We can plan for the future, but that literally is a waste because we already planned it out from the beginning. All we need to do is simply try to remember the oneness that we all have in commonality with one another. Real time involves staying active and doing and completing our goals. Going forth with our ideas, creative works, and wildest fantasies keeps us alive because we are limitless vehicles. We are only fooled by the immobilization of our bodies and minds to think that we cannot be what we want to be. If the feeling is right, it is all for you. Movies and series about *The Walking Dead* and *Night of the Living Dead* ring true among all of us when we halt what we actually want to do.

The common death of a person passing away is just a continuation of that person's spirit into another, different body. Sometimes the body dies from old age, diseases, natural causes, accidents, mistakes, or other outside or inside forces. We simply cannot determine the status of our time clock with death until we see that white light when we pass, and then we will know that we are called upon if we do not commit suicide. Inside of our brains is a program database. The software, which is vulnerable to the extremities of this earth, is on the right side of our brain, while the hardware is located on the left side of our brain. Hardware is logic, and software is reason. A lot of times, we like to make reason within logic, and thus it may seem that we are going in two different directions, when in reality we are synchronizing logic and reason simultaneously. Our ancestors are part of the process, making our perceptions reality. We are programmed with basic instincts from ancestors who have passed away so that we may function to our prime potential of existence. We are all from the same family tree of life, and during the Babel era, when varying languages confused the masses, we were then separated on the delusional preface of building a tower that would reach the high heavens. Due to this foolish notion, different languages separated us from others into classifications. This was the first representation of a mass of people learning how to discriminate against one another. Through cosmology, it is prevalent to suggest that the universe is within all of us because that is how connected we are to reality and existence. If you look in the pupil of a person's eye, you will be able to see a constellation of specks and auroras, just like within the universe. It is funny to imagine how foolish the people of Babylon had to be to build a tower tall enough to reach God when all they had to study was the forces within to reach greater heights.

When I was looking at the results of people who had done DNA tests from an online testing service, I realized that they all had something very much in common. No matter how individually diverse they were, every one of them had a percentage of African ancestry. It did not matter how deeply rooted they were in other origins. Furthermore, this evidence demonstrates that Africans were the first people on this Earth. The denial of ancestry mainly by Caucasians and Hispanics has caused them to be blinded by their fate in life and in death, up until reincarnation. I clearly cannot comprehend why certain people would deny their African ancestry for so many years. This confrontational frame of mind has left many voided out of the Universe based upon their pure hate of themselves. The universe is massive, and every thing, place, and person that it comes into contact with is limitless. Therefore, limiting our perceptions on whom or what is superior or inferior is endangering the universe by limiting it. Now, we are being watched at all times, and the haste of the wicked hate that set back the world order regarding what does not fit into the universe is stagnating its perfected progress. We all search for one thing and only one thing, which is love. I don't care how many terrible relationships a person has been in, he or she will always yearn and search for love. In order to fulfill ourselves, we have to love one another through pure or tough love. That is what we are placed on this planet to do—to simply *love*.

We are all prejudiced simply because we are primal, animal creatures. Our God-mind has given us the senses to judge others within reason and logic. We are elevated when we take our prejudices into account to make good judgments for survival. For example, when we are driving, we have to be careful about how we drive and also be observant of how other motorists drive as well. Practicing good judgment on the highways, streets, roads, and even parking lots can save us from accidents and even death. Having good judgment means making good decisions, and it takes both the left and right side of the brain to do so. The kundalini experience is direct contact with the sun god and illumination. Bringing both female and male energies, moon and sun, is bringing forth the Trinity within.

It is through discrimination that the process of the Trinity is initiated. Discriminatory acts that are felt from within send us into a process of truth, acceptance, and rejection. When we are discriminated against, we feel rejected and alienated from the world. We may repent of our sins, of wanting to feel a belonging to this world. Our chakras are able to open to the point that our emotions are lightly washed away and we once feel again that we are children of God. We ask for forgiveness of our sins and also to forgive the sins of our brethren who cast us out. Therefore, a God-Christ-me conscious mind is activated. Now the kundalini process, mentioned in an earlier chapter, is started when we go with the flow of our feminine and masculine energies. When we are forced by earthly material or even sexual forces, our control over our body is sent out of whack. So we may have a bad kundalini experience when we are going through this process. At the end of this process, a rush of ecstasy fills the chakras, and the washing of bondage, of shackled, chained sin, is cleared. Now, that does not mean that an individual will not go through other tests and higher information in life. This kundalini process is simply a small death with an activation of nerves and sensory perception that has illuminated the whole mind. The base of the spine is activated first and is greatly associated with the zodiac. The thirteenth zodiac sign is the completion of the kundalini awakening. So basically, your whole body's motherboard has been upgraded, and you can program information in miraculous ways. A lot of celebrities have an activated kundalini semi-God. That is why a lot of them will say that they are gods—because their perception of the world is heightened and upgraded. Also celebrities are able to create godly works and present them to the world in an angelic way. All these creative arts are done through God, and the ones that have the most impact on the universal world are made through God-Christ-me consciousness. Through the artist's perception, we can see joy and pain, or rather the good, the bad, and the ugly.

Father Time and Mother Nature are perceptions that we should pay close attention to because they have a lot to do with the communication that our ancestors practiced in different eras. Our ancestors observed the sun, moon, stars, and nature in their spirituality as common forms of direction. Ancestors have passed so much information to us through paintings, art, writings, music, and other creative forms that mention the universe. The Pyramids of Giza have a lot of hand- and instrument-painted scriptures, scrolls, sculptures, and pottery that inform us about the ancient Egyptians' perceptions of nature and time. As a matter of fact, the

Egyptians were the first humans to come up with hieroglyphics and arithmetic that basically initiated the calendar, time, and the zodiac. It is definitely up to us to remember the incremental knowledge that those in our family tree have passed on to us. If we seek within ourselves, we will find all of the information and codes to our destination. To stereotype individuals based on skin color is hypocrisy. We all know that in many cultures, people look down on those with darker skin. This sort of hate has a lot to do with jealousy, and the oppressors want us to forget about where we come from and that Africans were the enablers of universal thought.

Self-hatred is the fundamental dynamic of "black" oppression. We live in a society of repeated events with alternate circumstances. I have come across a good number of individuals who try to duplicate someone else's appearance and character. But who is to say that we all are not duplicates of what we perceive in life? Most of us have tuned into numerous shows, episodes, movies, and news on the television set. By doing this, our perception is scripted from the different types of characters on television. If a set of individuals do not have a strong background of their family history and ancestry, then these factors become us because our sensory glands feed off what is pleasing. So a loss of identity or an identity that was never developed is prone to copy everything it perceives and sees. The phrase "we are what we eat" is correlated with the food that we eat, but consider it along with the phrase "birds of a feather flock together," meaning that the company we keep shapes who we are in life. Therefore, we take on many parts of everybody and everything. We all need to be labeled with having different personality types if our identity is not developed, just like the "mentally ill." When a person is able to gather all of the perception and sensation of the pretend world and incorporate it into the self, that person has found his or her true being on this earth. Thus, an individual is gifted to live in the world and to be able to sustain its own character with diligence and dignity. Oh, yes, there is no stopping a person who has found his or her power.

In my nation, dark skin is frowned upon and is an allegory for what is to fear and hate. The self-hate method is used to diminish the character of others, especially in the African-American community. Mass incarceration is one method, and media channeling is another. Asian markets love to thrive on this community because it brings them material wealth and prosperity so they can send their children to college and have financial gain. Hair, nail, and clothing products are consumed rapidly by this set of people, and yet they are still blind to this reality. African Americans love to showboat, and this stems from slave history. There is still a recollection of slavery to this day that is encrypted into DNA and that predisposes us to think that we still do not have anything. This perception of a slave obeying a master is still present, and the constant showboat attitude of the working poor black person is prevalent. This is just an example to show that history repeats itself and that people still struggle not to lose their identities. The person who focuses on what he or she needs instead of wants is an individual with high perception of what we are planned and set up on this earth to do. This lack of wanting brings forth our spiritual godly gifts that we must share with one another and our calling of higher purpose. Until the ignorance of wanting to collect material things is downplayed and we can actually be our own bosses, instead of working as an employee under someone else, we cannot really put our energy into halting oppression. Oppression is exterminated from within, and it begins with the one who is being oppressed initiating their gift.

CHAPTER 31

Reincarnation

Reincarnated souls are a hot topic in paranormal psychology. Reincarnation and incarnations are real to the extent that energy is neither gained nor lost. When a body is no longer respiring and is a corpse, the soul has to find another body to inhabit. We get traits from both the paternal and maternal sides of our family. One without the other is impossible. Our genes are distributed evenly, and where some form a lack, there is an equal gain. I am always reminded that I act just like my father when I am led into anxiety and form an outburst of anger. I love to tell my mom that I did not pick my earthly father but rather she chose the man with whom she wanted to have a child. It truly is not my fault, and the only time that it was is when I was just a soul and I searched and snatched the parents of my liking or that I was settled with before conception.

From the early years up until my twenties, I was a very passive, shy, timid young lady. The slightest sarcastic comment would make me cringe, and anyone I was not close to perceived that I was a shallow person. I always was careful about stepping on toes. During those days, I would get run over by people, and they would take advantage of my generosity and lucid quietness. I would give them the benefit of the doubt, thinking that maybe my catatonic facial expressions gave the wrong message. But even as I got older and more cheerful, with a jolly demeanor and frequent smiles, I was still not taken seriously. Now, I do try to manage my behavior in being more assertive with people and practicing very good manners with other souls as well. My altercations concerning behavior have made me more aggressive to sarcasm, and the downside is that I have become more paranoid, anxious, and delusional regarding what other people gossip about. If I know for a fact that they have gossiped about me in the past, then I keep them closer than most. I learned not to trust at a very young age, and this has shaped me into a person who can be a walking time bomb, on edge, and always turned up. The good part is that I am able to get over any altercation and be as loving to a person as I was beforehand. I know that this conduct will reward me in the beginning and end with lovely gifts from the universal God, simply because I do not hold grudges. We just have to get over the negative attitudes we have with one another, perceiving that we are all just mirrors of one another after the same feeling, which is that love fabricates us. "As above, so below" is the method to the madness of our daily connections. Doing what we feel without harming one another is the predominant action of self-gratitude. When our ancestors pass, especially our parents, we can incorporate them into our spirits if we call upon that transition. We take all the knowledge that the ancestor gained into our own being, and the process is done over and over again throughout generations to come. That is why it is so important for us to learn our spiritual gifts and to gain power through correct knowledge from different sources in order to obtain peacefulness on earth through respectable incarnates. This respect for our elders gives us an eternity through life and death from the beginning to the ending in everlasting companionship. Respecting our elders is also demonstrated through us by rejoicing in the death of our elders because we know that they are within us through incarnations. They become part of us throughout life. Sadness has a place at a funeral and is a test of our knowing God's presence and that just because a body is no longer breathing does not mean that our parents, grandparents, and other relatives are not with us in spirit. They are present just like us, but not in bodily form. I will testify that my attitude has translated into a character of my passed earthly father, and I get to experience the ins and outs of being a person with a lot of dignity who does not take much mess from anybody. This feeling is a great reward for me, and I am able to carry out my creative works because my father has forwardly reincarnated himself unto me.

Speaking of reincarnations, whomever believes in the loving grace and whom also has been through the Trinity is reincarnated with Christ. Christ has never been absent in our bodies, and it is up to us to conjure this spirit through the experiences, tribulations, and factors of life. Going through life, death, transformations, and reincarnation is uplifting and is a never-ending process. We reach levels of prosperity and wealth when we go pass through these cycles, cleaning ourselves over and over again, perfecting a specimen so that future generations are occupied by well doers. It is a mobilizing force of nature to keep on repeating our mistakes until we get it just right. We are forgiven through Christ consciousness just so that we can be aware of the perfect love that is awaiting us here on earth and in the afterlife. It is definitely a wonderful feeling to know that everything is going to be all right and that nothing or nobody can take that away from you. Yes, we may still go through difficulties, but to know that the universal God has a lot planned for us that will nurture our individualistic souls is the opportunity of a lifetime. Knowing that God, Christ, and you are compacted into one is all the perception that you need. Everything else will just fall right into place, and we may be tested from what is "seen" as negative. You will do all good things through the strength and knowing of the God-Christ-me conscious awareness, the Great Awakening.

Alter-egos are a jealous aspect of us, wanting to be saviors to people. For example, the alter-ego of Clark Kent is Superman in DC Comics. In everyday life, he dresses up in a suit, wears eyeglasses, and congregates with coworkers while covering up his hero identity. We all can relate to these alter-egos that are written in comic books because we all have a true self that is hidden from sight. We all have an amount of heroism in us to where we want to save a population of people or persons' from disparity. Saving ourselves from the calamity of destruction is the ultimate prospect of salvation. Attempting to put ourselves in harm's way for another is a meek glimpse of servitude to one another. Adrenaline is a natural hormone that gets us to act as the godly beings that we are to, perhaps, save the life of someone who is trapped or victimized. Civic duties are performed by heroes who go unannounced and unrewarded every day, yet the nation is quick to glorify a figurehead politician who isn't sincere in his or her words, rather overseeing the destruction of the poor and helpless. Americans continually praise unworthy souls who get paid under the table to benefit business owners instead of the working class, which stabilizes this economy.

This nation is driven by pure capitalism, and the lobbyists and stakeholders rule the nation. Gun ownership; tobacco production; alcohol consumption; outsourcing of business; environmentally unfriendly power plants; exhaust-spewing vehicles; garbage; lyrical music played over the airwaves that exaggerates sex, drugs, alcohol, and hatefulness that focuses on trigger happiness—all of these are current problems in our country. An animal's life is more important than a human's because at least animals have personalities that are natural and in line with the laws of nature. Overcrowding in public schools due to mass immigration continues to not focus on our uninspired youth so that the dropout rate increases every year due to some inattentive teachers who do not respect the talents of every child and children who can't factor the correlation of subjects, meaning they cannot see the connection, impact, domino effect or relation of disciplines to other disciplines that is insight to the "big picture" of relativity. The average laborer is placed on antidepressants and anxiety medication due to the constant pressures of swapping out employees and an infrastructure of molding the new employee into something that a senior employee will not tolerate. That whole Adam and Eve story is a cover-up to encourage you to be a part of the majority crowd in the robotic occupying of yourself with a corporate pyramid scheme of up and down circulation limiting levels. It is up to us to snap out of being financial security bums and to be more creative with our lives in accomplishing successful, healing works that are better for all of us. As long as we are successful, the money will follow and chase us to no limit. Follow your heart when it comes to your worth. Celebrities love to make music, act, and play sports, but there is also the price of required appearances on shows and interviews that keep them slaves to the money they make. As long as they love their careers, then they likely have no regrets regarding what their time is occupied with. Having to care for one another keeps individuals employed and in service. There is more purpose and fulfillment in servicing others than working for others. Doing and acting are forms of being God, and sharing that essence is how we are all universal without boundaries. Nevertheless, reincarnations of other souls into us are pentagrams that we collect down the road to success. We are all superheroes just waiting to save the day, the midday, and the night.

CHAPTER 32

Revolution

Television sets have been a remarkable invention in terms of shaping the image of every household. Almost every night, each American tunes into his or her favorite TV show. Cartoons have been babysitters for our youth since the 1960s. Upon viewing the images that come from a box, we get to watch and perceive the separate daily lives of characters. Our minds can be taken into empathic and sympathetic feelings while looking at a pixelated screen. We can fantasize movements of the body when looking at athletic or professional sports, cry when we can relate to downtrodden characters, laugh at our most-liked comedian, and get angered by what is being portrayed on the news throughout the world and in our neighborhoods. In places like North Korea, watching television from outside sources is prohibited. While many Americans may think of this restriction as hindering simple freedoms by limiting the press, some North Koreans see it as shaping their citizens.

Furthermore, the ongoing looking glass of television limits individual creativity. This is not to say that actors and actresses have a stagnant influence on people, but rather we tend to adopt a part of the characters that we watch on television into our own persona, especially if they are heartfelt or fanatical. I often hear the same jokes from different people who converse with me and others. Characters give us a chance to travel within ourselves and to comprehend problem-solving solutions that may occur in our own lives. The creation in screenplay gives us a source of human connection to our feelings. We can literally feel alive just by observing another sequential event, whether fact or fiction. There is truth to every literary print that has been established, whether the characters are animals, insects, people, or things. The simple notion that one individual seeks for his or her noggin to write an eventful story plot line is very much real; it is just that the interpretations may be casual for forward, progressive thinking. There is real history in all prints, and even though concepts can be futuristic, they are still presently accepted by many. Collections of literary writings are nothing but recollected repetitions of the conscious perception of extensive reading, listening, and comprehension alloys. We get to see how different authors see the world through their eyes in a simple, formatted writing that can be transferred into a script and then into a television show that is visibly pleasing to the audience.

All creative works are accessed through our God consciousness perception. The individual in each of us is detail-oriented in what our perspective is on everything we encounter. Commercial media brands market their products to consumers in between regular shows to generate interest from the public. With all the advertisements from social media websites and commercials, a certain one, or ones, taps into the brain with the idea that the consumer must buy it or is to be reminded of purchasing products, goods, and services to uphold a certain type of lifestyle in one's culture. Therefore, viewing television in the United States has become a patriotic tradition in being able to gain sources of information through popular media sites. Television catches the consumers' attention through props in facilitating meeting our needs in these vendors. It seems as if we are always going to be lacking something in our material lives no matter how many consumer products we buy. With North Korea opposing capitalism and being a communist country by disallowing outside influences to take over the minds of North Koreans through psychic methods, a televised trance is freedom. There is freedom to be your own person when you take the moment to do what you really want to do. The hype of the drama on TV shows through all tuned-in households forms a like-minded connection with other like-minded individuals who cannot help but live some more drama and action through these storytelling plots that can be obsessively addictive to watch. Watching television can be a routine ritual that is no different from what paganism entails. Repeating daily rituals is the constant notion that we are being watched even though we may be alone and isolated. Thus, television can be company for a lot of people to keep. One amateur aspects of these characters on television is, "No matter how much you try to save the world, there will always be blame on the protagonist as a bad person." Furthermore, alter-egos are formed to solve problems in a climactic plot just like in our very own lives as well. Everyday obstacles, likewise dealing with trust issues from past and present experiences, affect future thinking and manifestations. They can create the feeling that nobody understands the circumstantial problems of an individual perspective of not being felt or taken seriously as a human being, or rather an adult or respected individual. Radio and television waves send a ground material limitation of emotion and feeling displayed through other people. When we step away from the mass media of today and look inward to our souls' yearning search of completion and guidance, then tuning into these made-up characters becomes boring and obsolete because we simply understand that any reality can be created through us. All emotions and feelings are actively satisfying to those who are constantly searching for their true calling in life, and it definitely cannot be found by tuning into a television set five hours out the day or by listening to dumb-me-down filthy music. Influential garbage music that is synced in recording studios to further disconnect the spirituality of respect for one another leaves us emotionally disturbed through a lack of confidence and the addictive consumption of alcohol and oversexed lyrics, resulting in the separation of a soul bond with one another.

Listening to teenybopper, soul drenching, antilove, highly sexual, emotional club music promotes engaging in the seven sins. Individuals who seek higher connections of oneness with their God-Christ conscious mind are not easily swayed by money and cannot be influenced through the material-possessive captures of rap that significantly promote rape, male domination, consumption of harmful drugs and alcohol, selling and distributing of narcotics, and separation of female from male. The targets of this pitiful era are African American males and females—and anybody who is captivated by those lyrics. Every piece of creativity, especially in the music industry, sends a trance to the brain regarding what is pleasing. Nevertheless, most rap lyrics from no-name singers and terrible rap labels are feeding into the frenzy of undermining the most highly creative power, which is linked in a woman. Conspiracy theories have linked the overemotional music as a way to weed out the weak from the strong for when the mothership is ready to take those who are chosen and self-loved. Thus, if you are self-loving, you love your creator in every form and facet, which is rewarding. Treating, speaking with, and tolerating others in a freely nonvictim attitude is evidence of the realization that we are all just woven into a weave of soulful connections. And if there are obstacles that detour our aspect on this loving realm, then we may remain in a trance of limitations through other useless, emotional perspectives, causing a lot of unnecessary excess in our life such as OCD, paranoia, anxiety, depression, grief, and any unnatural emotion that brings no unity around us. What we think is what we attract, and these distractions can make us miss our opportunities if we do not have a constant flow of feelings that are pleasing to us in the earthly realm.

Throughout the years, broadcast media has been a great source to keep us informed on current affairs. Documentaries, biographies, autobiographies, church sermons, and self-help techniques are shown on our television sets. Any source of communication is a means of connection because it vibrates resonant waves into our neurological systems. Music is highly influential just based on the frequency at which it resonates in certain acoustics. Revolution is accomplished through observation and being able to pay attention to the details. Famous revolts like Nat Turner's Rebellion are strategically done with observation, time efficiency, urgency, knowledge of how things work, and knowledge of when to gain an opportunity when a challenge arises. The risk to stage a rebellion is not taken by many. Numbers are immaterial when planning a revolution, which can be easily done behind the scenes, like for J. Edgar Hoover, for instance. The most infamous mobster gangs took over cities and even a line of states as far as money sharing was involved. African Americans choose to be either involved or uninvolved in their communities, with black-on-black crimes and police-involved shootings. But I have to speculate that the mass murders and high mortality rates for blacks are due to their easily influenced perceptions of what life is. They have been told by their teachers, bosses, and even parents that they will not amount to much. Some African Americans can reach beyond the stereotypes and turn those comments into opportunities for success. But there are those who cannot help but sink into despair in the face of commentary and bigotry from others. Believing in nothing much but nice clothes, fancy cars, jewelry, and material things keeps them below the level of people who are told almost every day that they can achieve anything. A lot of us have to understand that as long as we are able to pay attention to detail, are superb at following directions, and gain insights from almost anybody, then being able to demonstrate new, innovative ways to do what we have learned is the reward. Black people are duped to believe that material things and all that comes with them are all they will ever be, even though a lot of them attend church in their best outfits and gossip about others, behavior that stems from the memory bank of separation before, during, and after slavery. Back then, there was pretty much nothing to do but consider the limits that were forced upon them. We have to really understand that our ancestors have influenced us to think a certain way, as have current social affairs in the media. If you notice, the difference between an African and an African American is the confidence and aggression that is lacking in the African American. Not only that, but Africans are respected far more highly by diverse groups in America because they respect their women and provide for them far more than the humdrum African American male. The term *nigger* did not come into heavy use until slavery and is the depiction of today's African American heritage—not knowing where they come from, who they are, or where they are heading. A line of confusion separates them from the best that is mainly concerned with bettering the self by being self-made and not bowing down to anybody. Yes, these feelings of uselessness still reign in black Americans to this day due to a general perception of slavery. Slaves were forced to work for nothing and to obey slave masters, and without obliging, the slaves subsided and tolerated this injustice. Slavery became more socially acceptable because of the hard work that was needed to manage the fields, land, and crops. Slavery left slaves gullible with pure innocence to work on plantations and being submissive just to hold on to a piece of something called hope and most wanted freedom. Abuse during slavery became part of the normal experience; thus, Negroes today are able to withstand great hardship. Yet there is still something missing, and it goes beyond brainwashing the slaves. Memory banks that of past life experiences of royal kingdom in African tribes are buried within the psyche. African-Americans who are living in present day unconsciously know in the psyche that African servants were placed on a royal pedestal just by association. The long-term memory of slavery is embedded into the African American population, resulting in the notion that getting money and material things through any means necessary is adequate, even if you have to crawl, steal, and kill for it. Spirituality was only expressed by the slaves who were just coming from Africa to be placed into slavery. Therein, families passed on strong African cultural roots through music, food, spiritual guidance, and many other creative things as expressed by individuals who are well rooted in their African ancestry. Most African Americans love to forget about their African roots, as if they are a plague, and talk boldly about a grandmother who was half Irish. And that is how media sources have shaped the African American to acknowledge their Caucasian ancestry over their African ancestry, which in most cases is lost and hard to recover through books and other media. In an era when jobs, careers, and occupations are scarce, it is excruciatingly tough for people of color to live, and everybody is suffering.

Contrarily, the average American is working two to three jobs according to an article written for USA Today by Paul Davidson. Based upon greediness to satisfy capitalistic demands and working for others and not the self a lot of Americans work over 50 plus hours a week for an employer. Upcoming holidays distract Americans from spirituality and are recognized in a religious fashion with exclusive, one-religion sermons every year. This is no different from performing pagan rituals that are determined of conjuring holy spirits upon historical information. We can be informed about religion in our weekly church get-togethers, gather the nicest materials pleasing to the eyes, have two or three academic degrees, occupy our time working eight to ten hours a day at a job we dislike, complain and gossip about how we are being treated unfairly or who got what and this, and yet still be in spiritual crisis. Gurus, teachers, and healers have told us to meditate daily on God's presence, which is hard for some of us to do. Expectantly, we have to capitalize on tuning into the higher surfaces of our conscious mind to seek our divine power in the entire universe, not giving a hoot what other people have or what they think about us. Tuning out outside sources is the first step in obtaining peacefulness and working your way up to blissfulness in the higher consciousness of mind. After you have tuned out all the noise in your life, then automatically, your all-knowing and all-seeing eye will help you to explore the universal depths and travel beyond this earth. Your perception in life will be quite different from most people who love to just dwell on the earthly plane. Remember that the universe is here to guide you to your higher purpose, which is way more satisfying than what any human being, material gift, or intellectual congregation can give you. What is asked of you is that you enthusiastically be in the everlasting presence of seeking the Lord and creator God, which is within you. We have to understand that all conflicts, problems, gains, losses, obstacles, and complications in our past lives are forthcoming to what we deserve in life. Each person's journey will be different, but we are all aiming for the same feeling and that is to be loved and accepted by one. There is only one entity that will accept us for who we truly are, and that is ourselves led by God-Christ-me consciousness.

I am often confused about what people want from me and what their ulterior motives are for inviting me into their presence. I have to look back on my life to see if I had indulged in petty quarrels over money and material. My quarrels mainly were focused on irresponsibility, pressure from an outside environment, and emotions of people that overruled common sense, at least from my point of view. These driving forces of quarrelsome conflicts go through the darker forces of emotions and are used to be intolerable to the one who is seeking a higher purpose. Just like an infinity symbol, we must form a figure eight that is embedded into our DNA as form and function of creating, replicating, and evolving. These emotions help to free ourselves to find outlets and rise above our circumstances. It takes solitude and servicing to the Lord God in silence to be able to get to escapism and serenity. The struggle and battle of the old versus the young is inevitable. At least I am grateful for the important things in life, one of which is to live life. We cannot always think that the next time we step out of the house, we may be gone. Counting years and comparing them to death is obsolete because death does not care about numbers. When it is our time to go, it is just our time to go. If we worry about death, we will start to look like death, talk of death, and walk of death, and before we know it we will be death zombies clinging onto unchanging daily rituals of what is to come. Live life and enjoy the company you have with the people you love. Mannerisms go a long way when addressing, greeting, and saluting others. It is not worth getting upset over some little bitty turmoil because it will just rot us deep down to the core, and the lighter side of the universe will have no use for us because we will be too concerned with trying to satisfy the emotions and what can be temporarily attained. Success is our main goal, and whatever reward there is will follow right after it.

Back in earlier times, the law was used only to handle taxes, money, property, and assets. Anything outside of tax law and contracts was the business of the household and individual. When women were silent, it was up to the man to provide, protect, secure, support, and stabilize them. The tables have surely turned toward women seeking the finest degrees from accredited colleges and having independence so that they do not have to domestically answer to anyone. But deep down, a woman loves to be taken care of and know that a man supports her in every endeavor that she wants to undertake. The female population is on a ground-breaking search for Mr. Right, and if any woman does not acquire hers, she will settle with a companion who is true to her. These qualities make a woman feel worthy when the world is on her shoulders. Being able to seek guidance from a man is so reassuring to the femininity of a woman or young female. Not only does she have the masculine qualities that adhere to her challenges in her diverse environment, including providing for herself and her family, she can also lean back on her feminine qualities that she is dying to express to a partner who is willing to just watch and listen to her. This way, she can become easily balanced in her spherical world and create substance in everybody's journey in life. This balance is so comfortable to her that having a man as a companion who is also a great provider for her and her family is an added security blanket. Feeling this balance through another is just a healthy expression of the love we receive from the universe that we yearn for. It is affirmative to get this feeling with no help from a human, but when we are one with ourselves and love ourselves completely, then all the pieces to a puzzle will fall into place. Literally, it is like being unstoppable, but we must remain active and know when to take our breaks. Wanting companionship is another way of needing God through free expression of oneness. We are complete when we know that we do not have to force anything. Forces are completed outside of our known perceptions, and we must come into knowing this when we are all-knowing.

Females are sacred, and that is why it has always been a duty to protect the sacrum of a female—because once perverted she can easily be confiscated through the mind and into the notion of guilt or resentment. If not careful, a woman can be a subjected to perversions, judgment, harassment, and any other effort to claim her as un-kept and unworthy. But now the law is here to protect female identities and extremities from being violated by men. A woman is always judged and harassed for what she wears rather than how she presents herself. Women are far more judgmental of their own outward appearance. The woman who opens a man to new experiences in a wanderlust of sensitivity to the world is very sure of herself and her power. The sacrum is significant in artifacts like the ancient ankh, the eternal symbol, and anything with a circle in it to represent the flowing energies of a woman. The uniqueness of a woman is the ability to allow herself to go freely into the black holes of the atmosphere through pain and pressure and then afterward being able to create a realm that resonates with this earthly plane. Plenty of women do not know that they possess this sort of power within themselves, and to withhold this sacred treasure from a beast of a man is temperance. Going her own path without paying any mind to pleasing a lustful man is empowering to the feminine energies of the universe. Feminine energy is free and does not have to abide by any rules or restrictions because of its innocence to unconditionally love another from the start of initiative romance.

Men have furthered the scenario of the oversexed male, and without their being satisfied by the guarded female, pornographic arts will relieve their tension. These arts alleviate the urge for sexual release with another human being and according to Psychology Today, *Evidence Mounts: More Porn, LESS Sexual Assault*, pornography helps to decrease the number of rape cases. Living in a world where sex is broadcast heavily, it is clear that the sex and pornographic industry is gaining capital even though it is still looked down upon by community members. Censorship only brings more attention to the sexy conduct of artists in videos, TV shows, magazines, and movies. Wonder meets the eye in distinguishing what is perceived acceptable to the function of the television set and censoring sexual acts. The simple mind thinks that making a big deal on censoring rated categorical videos will reduce crime and devious sexual acts, but the flip side of the matter is that making a big deal out of something brings more attention and curiosity to ponder upon it.

Information from dramatic reality shows and talk shows about celebrities is junk. That is not to say that you cannot learn from them, but watching a documentary, historical review, or anything about nature gets you in tune with real connections and creates a far greater information database in your brain. It really is not about what we watch but how much of what we watch is believable to us. Playing word and math games on the computer or manually keeps the mind sharp and not filled with processed information. It can also be a form of meditation since it is known to work the brain by encouraging cognitive thinking. We can be a little rational and work with the right sides of our brains by welcoming a dose of dramatic action and comedy into our spectrum through televised shows and movies, but we need to snap back into reality when we can incorporate logic into the mix. Therefore, the integration of feminine and masculine energies is done far more rapidly by females because they are not afraid to explore both sides of these energies. Since we assign boys gender roles, it can be hard for them to create because they may be afraid that they would be made fun of. So the boys of this world—or more likely, Americans—are conditioned to express their feelings in terms that are more masculine, sometimes withholding how they feel about certain situations in life. A girl can also have her feelings and emotions suppressed when there is opposition or a source of secrecy that she has to maintain in the family, and this goes for young boys as well. Hiding these energies does not make them expressive outwardly, but inwardly conserved energy is replicated from these pent-up feelings that shapes our personality. So if we take into account the suppression of feelings, thoughts, and emotions in a household, then escapism can be buried through the perceptions of the television set. And thus our thoughts, feelings, and emotions can dwell through the dimensions of a television set. Nonetheless, we can dwell in reading, cooking, sewing, drawing, playing musical instruments, writing, and anything that allows us to create a scapegoat of expression. This is how godly works are created through the outlier of expression, and when we show them to the world, we are presenting our godly images. If we are lucky enough to get old, we will come to find that we want to do what kindergarteners do but on an adult level. We want to create more and do the things that really touch our heart and make others happy with connectivity. The disruption that destabilizes the neutrality from logic and reason is the personal ego.

Personal egos are driven to do what makes us feel good through one another. They may make us feel that we have to sacrifice a part of ourselves to be loved by somebody else. Personal egos are only after a fulfillment of false completion that has been pondered through perceptions of the naked eye and acoustics that link to the brain into labels of thought that we feel when it comes to the emotions that are displayed from other characters. It is not in our interest to follow our personal egos if we want to become who we truly are; and we truly are human BEINGS, which is to live in the present. An ego is only great when it is used to demonstrate a behavior and to tell what a personal ego does to one's soul's outlook. Arguing with one another is useless because egos can be so huge that we will tend to think that we are always right. Then, abruptly, we notice that we are in a tailspin of a game of who is right or wrong when both sides are actually neutral. The movie *Rebel Without a Cause* depicts a rebellious group of teenagers who were not adjusting to the future and not following other people's paths. They constantly displayed complaining and forthright attitudes with this back-and-forth of pride and ownership. The teenagers exclaimed that their parents did not listen to them about how they wanted to live or accept their lifestyles. The movie starts out with a bunch of bickering at a police station, and there was a sense that the kids were going insane, but really the parents would be the insane ones for wanting their children to repeat their own lifestyle choices, which is not progressive. The teenagers acted out, challenging the boundaries of acceptable behavior. Pushing a behavior to its limits and salvaging childlike episodes are sure ways to gain attention from authorities and parents. If the parents were not going to listen to the teenagers, then what would be the use in conducting themselves properly? We can argue that the parents were just protecting their children, but from what? The monster that will make sure they do not have enough money to get out on their own? Or maybe they were trying to protect their own self-interests by reliving their adolescence through their children. Older people, especially baby boomers, have what they deem a logical outlook on wanting people to always work for employers while they lay up and neglect their health, suck up all the social security benefits, and remain reluctant to receive Medicare, which drains their fixed-income salaries. To have the audacity to complain about another person not working or having a job is hypocritical. How on earth is anybody supposed to look up to people who sit around all day watching soap operas or old ass Western shows along with talk show garbage and drama reality television? They do not care about the traumas, stress, and anxiety that you have to put up with from a job, people, and obstacles. They are solely driven by taking and using anything that is usable. The youth have to pay for the overexpenditures that have been accumulated by seniors even though the government taxes and takes medical costs from them.

The opposition to the Affordable Healthcare Act is a prime example of authoritarians keeping tension among people. The value of life is implied in the health care act. The restriction of cannabis oil is another example of public officials' wanting to have a chokehold on American citizens. Cannabis oil has substantially halted cancerous cells and tumors. It has been used as pain management therapy for patients with central nervous system damage, multiple sclerosis, epilepsy, and chronic stomach pain as well. Pharmaceutical companies are profiting from patient illnesses and repetitive consumption of prescription medication. Pills only cure viruses, pain, and bacterial infections, for the most part. All pills that are linked to blood sugar, blood pressure, and high cholesterol are contributing to the saga of overmedication. A change in diet and exercise routine can alleviate these illnesses and uneasiness. The overanalyzing and critique of time and money also plays a factor in health.

With revolution in mind, people are prosperous through their endeavors and lifestyle choices. It is up to us to distinguish fact from fiction in the news that we gather through the media and other people. By tuning out these sources and getting in touch with the sound of God and universe quality, we are able to augment our resonance and soul beings to get to what our soul's purpose is after. We can revisit our purpose in the images we see when we go to bed or when meditating on God's presence and getting a clear notion of what we need to do to help satisfy ourselves. There is a cause for rebellion when revolution begins because there are going to be forces that try to hinder you from your yellow-brick road, whether through family, finances, or other distractions to pure, holistic thinking. To overcome this is challenging since it is a feeling of being tested for your higher good. When you are in a revolution stage, you will rather work alone, undisturbed by the outside forces that try to creep in your way. You will encounter the journeys of life, transforming deaths, and rebirth reincarnation stages along with revolting and getting on with your works to get past a war not only with other individuals but within yourself as well. The best freedom to have is the freedom to know how to read and to understand that all words mean the same. Many slaves were kept from reading because it leads to knowing how to talk to God and the universe, which is on your side in a karmic duel of any wrongdoing and injuries done to you. Thus, learning how to read and interpret words leads to knowing how to read the different languages of body movement, nature, and identity of people. Reading was stripped from the Negro slave, and a slave was never meant to recover his or her education. They were to be treated like animals but to offer manual labor for free; they were not meant to feel anything painful but rather to endure the pain. I could never understand—if Africans were so inferior, then why were they hung up on crosses like Jesus Christ by Ku Klux Klan members? Was there some hidden message in the hangings, or were people just that hateful back then? Caucasians and Anglo Saxons performed these rituals and gatherings like sermons to be heard and later forgotten, as if nothing had happened. Is there a disdain for Christianity deep down in history, or is this just the cause of ignorance from Southern country bumpkins? The gift of reading, though, is like a free ride to paradise once understanding is gained.

CHAPTER 33

Read

Reading is a fundamental craft filled with wonders, travel, and all sorts of communication that can be adventuresome, wild, and cunning. We can peep into somebody's world just by observing what he or she reads and writes. We can read a person really well by listening to how he or she speaks. Knowing a person's background is not hard if we just listen to speech. When I was younger, reading was the subject I looked forward to the least. Numbers and science caught my interest in high school, while reading and writing were boring subjects to my intellect. I declined books with the selfishness of not wanting to experience another person's work unless it was a thriller or had horror involved. It was not until I was twenty-five years old that reading became a fundamental routine for me. I was intrigued by how I could read a three-hundred-page novel and dwell in it, making myself the characters in the book and becoming that story's plot line to better understand what the author was trying to portray to me. Reading gives us a chance to step out of our daily routines and go to another place different from our own. We learn, relate, and comprehend what the author is trying to tell us through an array of sentences that correlate settings, places, things, people, themes, plot schemes, resolutions, and climaxes. These creations all can be seen as different worlds inside one's imagination. The author shares his or her expertise through words and formats, as well as through numbers in terms of how many chapters they will write and how many pages are to be written. Balancing of both the right and left sides of the brain is expressed in reading and writing. Speech is how we get to be informative and persuasive by critiquing, analyzing, and interpreting the masterpiece.

People who have a hard aspect with Venus in their natal charts are the most romantic and creative and are more appreciative of the powers of love, beauty, and pleasures. These aspects make good writers, musicians, artists, and lovers who are in tune with nature. For instance, one of the most intriguing Venus aspects is when it is squared with Neptune. Now, Neptune is a planet ruled by the zodiac sign Pisces, which operates on unity in higher octave dimensions. Neptune's influence is the desire to be alone, like in the middle of a foggy ocean. Even though you do not have any sense of direction on top of the body of water because of the fogginess, you must dwell inside yourself to get beneath who you think you are. When Venus squares with Neptune, it can be a slow process when this person has to tap into the deeper and higher realms of consciousness simultaneously because Venus is ruled by Taurus and Libra. Taurus is a patient, plodding, stubborn sign that just wants to be left alone with all the pleasures, love, and beauty of this world without really going in deep to bypass all the distractions that come with this love of leisure. Libra is more on the balanced spectrum of the beauty of love, fairness, and justice being served when intentions are not genuine. So when we combine Venus and Neptune together, we really have a standoff with Taurus-Libra energy versus Pisces energy, which is practicality, responsibility, stability, security, protection, and justice, all going up against delusions, illusions, ephemeral fantasy, emotions, and spirituality. Basically, the material and the sexual are at odds with the spiritual and emotional. This aspect places individuals through abusive relationships because of the need for Venus to create a perfect, divine love with a human being. But Neptune is always there to show that the only true, divine love is a feeling of completeness within the self, which is with God and the universe. In the long run, Venus square Neptune overcomes some of these hard aspects through creativity with God-self in works, such as writing poems and novels, creating clothes by knitting and sewing, quilting, painting and drawing, and doing pretty much anything that correlates with the hands. The hands are very much gifted that lead into a third-eye opening by putting on rose-colored glasses through all the bullshit of abuse and feelings of abandonment with these human beings into an expression of fantasy that is created in real time.

Now, this aspect is just an example of how a victim/savior can turn human flaws and perceived imperfections into a creative art that is perfected in the isolation and confinement of self-love. God is a jealous God that is simply observant of our affairs. The universe rules the time of events, and it is only a matter of time (Taurus) until Venus will be fed up with the promises, trickery, and slippery (Pisces) antics of Neptune—a true blessing in disguise for the person who undergoes this aspect to replace God with something that we cannot possess (Taurus), a sacrificial relationship or affair with a human. Heartache does occur with this aspect even if a person is accompanied by someone who really loves him or her. Deep inside Venus-Neptune is a person who is distraught, disappointed, and hurt from tragic lost love affairs but once again is able to find love within his or her own beauty and love of self. This is the way of the true self and higher purpose, which is dominated by Venus and Neptune influences. Furthermore, hard aspects with Venus introduce us to knowing how to read and to ignore the nuisances of the world by being able to dig deeper than the surface of land, going beyond the colorful coral reefs of the ocean and being more likely to take care of the self.

Nigger is one of the most controversial words today and is used primarily by people born before the 1970s. According to what I was told, *nigger* refers to someone deemed ignorant and is jargon used to describe black people. Ignorance is simply not knowing, and some of us have even heard it said, "You know, niggers cannot read." Back in slavery days, poor and slave master Caucasians were sometimes baffled to find out that a slave had been able to catch on to reading the English language and writing it as well. People who are treated as if they will amount to nothing will eventually do just that. Therefore, there were crop Negroes who went out into the fields without rebelliousness, cooperated with the slave masters and their servants, and did everything the slave masters told them to do. The loss of a sense of history was common among slaves, especially if they were born in America. They just assumed that they had been placed on this earth to obey wealthy slave owners like children. Slaves were dependent on slave masters and usually seemed happy to show their appreciation for living a suitable life under the rule of a slave master. Slaves' true potential was rarely explored, and they were rewarded with politeness. Smiling slaves were able to be trusted because they did not display any remnant of anger or disappointment about being owned by the slave master as a piece of property. The slaves were astonished, and many were content to be that way as long as they did not have to suffer any form of the brutality, such as the murders and lynchings that were not uncommon during those days. A lot of slaves played with their puppet masters by taking on the role of geechee characters that would dance to entertain, perform comedies, cook, clean, tend to the cotton fields and other crops, and even nurse their offspring. Most were even talented enough to show off their skills on different musical instruments and spun off racist jokes that were endearing to the rich masters at the hosted parties. Slaves really had no say-so on the account of their lives and deaths. Most were just the walking dead who were, for no reason whatsoever, physically whipped, tormented, harassed, bullied, made fun of, and brutalized.

As the years went by after the 1600s, slaves had the attainment of knowledge on their minds. Some generous masters and mistresses even wanted their slaves to be educated so that new advances in sharecropping and other duties could be easily implemented. On a plantation, everybody might as well be considered a family that works together to get the best results. The faster and more efficiently the work was done, the most productive the plantation was, and slaves even received accolades and awards for working so hard. Hard work was a source of prosperity back then for slaves, and so it is today as well. Anyone who works disgruntledly for someone else or who is considered an employee is a slave. It does not matter how much money you make to fill up your homes with material goods; if you are miserable with the work that you do, then you are still a slave. This includes corporations, companies, and partnerships that use your talents, creativity, time, and energy which are molded into their infrastructure of productivity and capital gain. Capitalism is what helped to construct our roads, highways, import and export harbors, and all that is to be consumed by people through more efficient ways of doing. Productivity was initiated with the slaves of the United States. Spanish conquistadors and Frenchmen were inquisitive about exporting slaves out of Africa and importing them to the Western Hemisphere. Not having to pay for labor caused production to sky-rocket for the masses of population in the Americas. Slaves were the hardest working commodity in households and distributions of the seventeenth through the twentieth centuries.

As mentioned before, we all have memory banks that have been established by our ancestors who have passed and those who are still living. These memory banks are encrypted into the DNA complexes of each and every one of us. Hence, a lot of our psychological makeup came from DNA that was passed along to us from our ancestors. People love to stereotype other cultures, backgrounds, skin colors, and even genders because of the recollections we have of our incarnate selves through ancestry that give us a past perception based on experiences and knowledge that were realized in older times. You could say that when we are born, most of us have old souls that have been through many incarnations on earth, so we are old when we are born because of a reincarnate. We turn to our parents, teachers, employers, and authoritarians to give us a sense of validation in our lives just like with slaves in the yonder days. We completely ignore all the chaos, injustices, and unfairness until we are smacked in the face with it and have to experience it for ourselves. It is as if, in the middle of our adult years, we become awakened and reborn into children that are tolerable only to God. And even though we may periodically peek to see what the emotions, feelings, intellect, material wealth, and spirituality of others are by being a bit nosy and wanting to accomplish inspiration through other people, there is an inkling of getting into our deeper selves and breaking free of the puppet masters who tend to have us shackled and chained. And most importantly, the chains and shackles are not even locked on our wrists and ankles and we may have placed the perception of being locked and caged. There is freedom of choice, in which, we are the only blame to being in slavery. We realize that creativity can mean freedom as well.

SAT analogies and other word games have taught me that all words are just combinations and simplifications of one big word. Language was introduced after the creation of man and woman and was vibrantly conveyed through pictographs and drawings at first. Egyptians were very creative in correlating mathematics with words, and so thereafter we can see that letters and numbers go hand in hand. We can form a set of words to depict self-help one way by taking apart the letters and meanings within words by using the prefix, suffix, and context of a word. Psychological words can inform us about reasons for outcomes and implications. *Happy* is a word that extends beyond the meaning of being content. The gut of the word is the well-known *app*. When I am h*app*y, I can better *app*ly myself. When I am h*app*y, my *app*etite is superb. When I am h*app*y, I love my *app*earance and everyone else who *app*ears in my life. Furthermore, we can relate many other words that begin with *app* to h*app*y. It is not a coincidence that people do not want to apply themselves when they're not happy. Now, the opposite of *happy* is *sad*, a feeling of depression. S*ad* has an *add*-on of problems and is flush with obstacles. As mentioned in an earlier chapter, *add*ing on can mean more focus on more things, mainly materially and financially speaking. The more we *add* on, the deeper we dig ourselves into economical despair. It's the same with *add*ing on numerous partners to your life. Eventually, you are going to get tired and s*ad* for the temporary attractions you intermingled with to just *add* more people to your circle. Remember, everything amounts to empirical oneness. When you are s*ad*, you are vulnerable to *add*ictions, whether they be alcohol, food, drugs, obsessions, sex, or shopping. When you become preoccupied with *ad*ult life, you yearn to be a child again, which can make you s*ad* and quite foolish. The same applies to the word m*ad*. When reading a book, it is not as important to know the definition of a word as it is to configure it. When I was in grade school and even college, reading books was a drag because, for some reason, *words* make me *drowsy*. First, we must be into the material that we are reading and anticipate that we will understand the literature. A novel fits that criteria, as the author writes as if to novices so we can become the characters by explaining their dispositions and importance in the text. Novels are for readers who are beginning to learn about a subject or something new presented about it. Usually, novels have moral lessons to which readers will relate.

Reading was a challenge for me in school because it could not keep my attention in class. Writing was not an enjoyment until I was in the third grade and my reading and writing teacher praised my how-to papers. She told me how she loved my elaborate sentences that used many adjectives to specify order. Then she complimented me on a cooking how-to paper because what I described sounded so delicious. The more excited she was about my papers, the more I loved to write. I was most embarrassed when I had to take an English critique and analysis course in my last semester at UTA, which was the dickens. The teacher was a British editor, and I really had my work cut out for me. The professor had a more than 50 percent dropout rate, and I had a difficult time interpreting literature. I really did not know what the professor was expecting. I could not comprehend how to correlate the literature with the historical situations that were taking place in the readings. I kindly took my D in the class and graduated that following year. Even though I hated that I had to ever take that course due to the stress and effort put into overthinking, I had learned a lot.

Astrology was one of the main assets to communication among primal dwellers. The only communication was based on an understanding of the four elements: fire, earth, air, and water. These four words spawned other words because with fire comes light, with earth comes matter, with air comes breath, and with water comes bodily form. All terrestrial mammals originated from water. Oceans are filled with all exotic creatures and animals that are distinctive to human creation. It is plausible to assume that we came from earth since our bones turn into ashes after we die. The human body is perhaps made up of all of these four elements. Our energy exerts light just like the sun, our bodies are composed of earth just like within its crust, without air we would not have oxygen to breathe, and our bodies are made up of mostly liquids and water. For all of us to be composed of all four of these elements, which were the only viable language in ancient times, means that we are composed of everything and that our connections can be far more piercing than beneath the skies into the universe. Not only do we have terrestrial bodies on earth, but we also possess universal bodies as well.

Now, from the four elements of fire, earth, air, and water, we can also have a place for every living thing. There are living beings on earth, living creatures in the water, and living birds and insects in the sky, but does this mean that there are living things, creatures, or beings living in the fire or on the sun? It is rather silly to think of somebody living on the sun considering how hot it is. Exclusively, fire leads to everyone living in the fire of desire—desires for a perfect love that neither man nor creature can possess. All the planets look as if they are in a whirlwind, chasing the sun and trying to catch up with it but not even coming close. It makes me think, *Does the sun have a time piece on it for going so fast? And why are people so intrigued with the sun?* Without sunlight, all the living plants would disappear and disease would run rampant due to the lack of vitamin D, which enables us to live and to read. The sun provides us with the light to see another day, and it helps us look forward to proceeding, just like it is at the beginning of everything.

Lyric reading is more than just turning on a song and jamming to the beat or sounds of it. Lyrics are the part of a song intended to gradually entice the listener to think and see at the same time. Understanding how the words of a song come to a complete revolution of sound generates a feeling in all of us. I have not met one person who does not like music or who finds it to be a nuisance. If the writing from the singer or rapper is genuine, there will be a force in the lyrics with which other listeners can resonate. Paying attention to lyrics allows us to freely observe the metaphysics involved in the writing. Many writers are amazed by the lyrics that come from a pen and paper. The brain is simultaneously coordinating words from feelings, emotions, and thoughts, which is very powerful. People can be influenced by the words of a song, especially if they can specifically relate to them. Music brings fantasy, correlation, method, and most important, power over the listeners. On certain radio stations, I have noticed that a lot of songs get played over and over. When tuning into hip hop and rap radio stations, I cannot help but notice that they sound like chants that put people in a trance, and they are very much influential on not just young listeners but middle-aged listeners as well. These listeners promote music that is supported by celebrities, and people love to jump on the bandwagon of whatever is made hot by majority youngsters. A lot of these young rappers are one-hit wonders who use a rhythmic beat to protect their garbage wording. Whoever has dominion over the air waves has dominion over a mass of heads. Recording labels make boatloads of money based on whatever is trending. When we observe the music that is being played, we find more emphasis on sex than love. During the last three decades of the twentieth century music was love filled and came from emotions that had meaning. Now that we live in the twenty-first century, it is not unusual to hear a song that has twenty cuss words and downplays the importance of woman. The female rapper is no longer a competitor in the rap industry; really, there is no competition. Women are still in the clubs dancing and stripping to rap songs that are disrespectful to the female anatomy. The only people we can blame for prolonging this genre of garbage that perpetuates the rape culture of rap are the listeners. If women are dumb enough to promote these songs, then their production is validated. It is hard for me to listen to certain radio stations because of the repetitive chants that channel a darker perception of women as sluts, whores, and female dogs. Violence against black men stems from the maltreatment and abuse of black women. Police officers and people of any other culture outside of the black community do not dismantle, disrespect, or displace more than what black male artists have done. A lot of the downplay derives from a misconception of the African American woman and other origins of women from different backgrounds. But then we have women who are conditioned to think that men are to provide them everything under the stars, which is not bad but infeasible. With the exaggeration of sex, money, and competition, it is as if a lot of dwellers are racing their way to the bottom. Most people are amazed by just what they see instead of how they really feel. Being for real takes perception beyond the two ocular eyes. If you notice, in these current rap songs, handbags, fashion, shoes, and clothing are glorified. Possession of a woman is acceptable, sex is in abundance, drinking alcohol is an everyday event, money is always a subject, and if you are not into these things then you are a bum or just seen as a crazy person for not going after the finer things in life. If we were to look deeply inside an artist's lyrics, then we would find that there is more meaning to the words than meets the eyes. We would find that the combination of metaphysics and ritual patrons is at bay when listening to these songs. Following the lyrics requires more than just the bop of a head and calling out names with admiration of replacing love with materials.

I've noticed that even beneath the dark, unwanted paths of all young, middle-age, and old rappers is a common subject, but there is still greater force within all the songs that wrap up into something of the higher good. I mean, there are only a few songs that I am dead tired of hearing over the radio waves. But if you can sympathize and empathize with an artist as if you were him and he was you, then you will send an ambiance of connectivity through relations. The "for real" factor is to include both the feminine and masculine energies when reading into an author's writing, pictures, words, and lyrics. Feeling the significance of masculine and feminine energies is all there is. You can switch and intertwine these two concepts through your head and mindful thinking. Most would call this act a personality disorder despite the powers of tapping into a connection that completes an infinite amount of role-playing. Taking art personally can lead to disruption of positive energy, but as long as negative energy is used to emit and exhaust into positive energy, then a personification is healthy. In synchronization, the masculine and feminine energies are balanced through music. If we were to blast a big speaker onto the whole world, it could hypnotize people into a trance, which is exactly what air waves do. They control the communication, information, broadcasting, and everything that is perceived through the senses, including nature. When you read, you are taking from within and are expressing emotions that are relative to the majority of populations. Artists will read their atmosphere, environment, and competition as a readable format in order to have better judgment toward those around them. Artists express their emotions through the general environment in which they live so that we can connect and relate. Whether satisfied or not, artists have the ability to resonate all their feelings, thoughts, and emotions into an audience just by incorporating high-tune network connectivity. This leads to connections inside the brain that stimulate the senses and exert a connection to the universal mind of speaking. First, there was writing; then came speaking. Sometimes, this fantasy of sharing feminine and masculine energy can lead to vanity and thinking that everything is about you, when actually everything is about everybody who is able to connect musical vibrations by just relating.

Throughout the years, I have heard that every person who has ancestry in Africa should go and visit or even live there. So, based on genetics, every person should go to Africa because we are all rooted there; empirical DNA evidence tells us that we are all Africans. Remember, our earth is very old, and recombinants of same-cell replication among Northern Africans exude lighter skin due to cold climates and lack of sunlight. The artifacts from ancient Africa are significant to African descendants of all skin colors. From Latin, Spanish, Middle Eastern, European, Asian, and Australia, there are remnants of Africa in every culture. Making vibrant colors, cooking skills, and handiwork are hand-me-down abilities that come from the carpentry of Africa. Beneath every skin color is an African gene just desperate to get out to show what most will want to keep a secret. Rap infusion has shaped the world in being able to take raw, filthy emotion and interpret it into what is metaphysical, about God, and what is missing.

CHAPTER 34

Listening

By all means, if there ever comes a moment when you have to search your soul, then tuning out by eliminating social media, television, radio, and people of annoyance kills the unnecessary noise that will prevent you from listening. Listening is achieved with silence of the senses by deleting disturbances that interfere with pure, cognitive thinking. Silence along with soul searching makes way for meditation. Chakras are not flooded with emotion from the external environment as much in silence. This method is actually great for a person who is seen as extroverted but is truly an introvert at heart. Introspection is the process of looking within to clear out baggage, clutter, and drama that has taken a toll on our minds, bodies, and spirits. When we pull away from the mainstream, including friends, networks, extended family, and even immediate family, we can better move on from numerous emotions and instill purification in our systems. Now, experiences help us to move on faster because we admit to seeing the same behavior with other human relationships. Being able to close doors periodically gives us free will to make choices when we don't feel important to others or if we just cannot get any satisfaction out of flawed human relationships for a while.

Opening up to the sounds of nature is just like coming home. Our natural senses appreciate the sounds, smells, feels, sights, and even tastes of Mother Nature. When we feel defeated by circumstances, her protection opens you up to a sixth sense of a whimsical whirlwind of possibilities when you are just an attentive listener. Meditating with nature creates a peace of mind that you are protected and that you can trust your faith and belief by knowing that a higher Supreme Being is at work to help you navigate through life in the beginning and at the ending as well.

Listening comes with a formidable price when we pay attention. Paying attention to the cosmos while also meditating often will equally distribute a clear, intuitive pathway to success just by observing silence through unique listening skills. Listening is all about tuning up the self and no one else. Keeping your attention on just you and nobody else is important when listening. When you are approached, your demeanor is assertive rather than passive, aggressive, or passive-aggressive. Not caring about other people's actions that may be upsetting is allowing circumstances to be given up to the higher powers and Lord to deal with while we play under the sun, moon, and stars that are above and around us. There are sacrifices when we get into toxic, unhealthy relationships with people that will lead us into yearning for solitude. Our time to move on has everything to do with age (because of years of playing victim or savior to human relationships); instead, we dwell in our own psyche without blaming them, which is forgiving and is a great gift to give up to the universal mind. Beating yourself up or claiming that you were hurt by someone is a disturbance that pertains to the personal ego by genuinely taking conditions personally and allowing those conditions to create a false sense of who you are. When we get in touch with ourselves and do what we really need to do to fulfill purposes, then we can fall in love with life and acquaintances all over again. The cycle of life would amount to nothing if we did not take breaks during our journey to listen to our intuition. Surety, security, protection, identification, stability, reflection, and perception all have relevance in the power of listening. Quietness gives us grace, peace, and the power to eliminate the judgment of others no matter the initiation. Being able to know ahead of time that anything will work out in your favor is purification.

Doing creative works and duplicating what we see and perceive shows appreciation for the beauty. Gifts are waiting to be explored when our passionate drive is externally expressed. It may be calming to us, but distractions can still take away and cause it to fall short of permanence. Embracing solitude is a sign of growth transformation and is for all of us to undertake. Practicality roots us to where we need to be heading, and so a slow period is only significant and telling of big changes to our lives if we simply listen. Getting real with ourselves requires seeking the truth and looking outside by stepping out of our vehicle bodies and exploring the spirit to get clarity. All things with truth will show up if we try to stop forcing it and just be—just being who we are, who we need to be, and replacing the people, places, and things with new spirituality that is going to open up for better people, places, and things. But we first have to let go by listening to our guided intuitive calling.

Getting rid of useless social, sexual, and theatrical formats allows us to be grounded. Sometimes it may take some emotional dwelling as well. Thus, the formula for listening remains less air, more earth, a little bit of water, and fire for action and drive. A decrease in entanglements lets us listen to our calling to success and achievement. Put yourself on the priority list and find out that you are nurtured by the sounds of serenity in a serene atmosphere. Most take vacations to exotic lands to get rid of the noise of everyday hustles and bustles. When you don't have the time or the money to take a trip somewhere, you can always travel in a book or contemplate your next moves and get back to hobbies that you do to appreciate yourself.

Less talk becomes a prerequisite to being a good listener. Honestly, many people like to hear themselves talk and fail to take anything in. With a mind already made up, it is difficult to introduce knowledge unless hyperactivity is involved. A lack of listening declares an abundance of possessiveness, and we simply have to let go of all forces, take our hands off the steering wheel for a while, and trust that we are guided on the right pathway. Primal animals use their hearing to distinguish prey, food, danger, and an adequate habitat. All of these fall under the survival tactic of companionship, food, defense mechanisms, and rest. The brain moves so fast that it does not notice the senses interacting with its environment in such a territorial manner.

Environments can be our friend or our enemy. One environment that we can depend on to provide us with our needs is nature. and when we don't listen to it or treat it with respect, we become alienated by the masses. Communication problems result in not listening and paying attention to someone or something more often. Mentally ill patients are often depicted in all-white rooms with straitjackets to restrain the rampant outbursts and prevent suicide. Controlling and slowing down thoughts is an escape route to avoid asylums and psychotic drugs being prescribed and administered. Calming can be achieved with tranquilizers, but when a tranquilizer is exhausted outside the body, a person can become irritable and frantic all of a sudden, thus making him or her more agitated than before and more vulnerable to a dependence on prescription medication. Contrarily, mentally ill people can become virtual zombies to their adequate wanting of to listen from within and condone compassion to every soul they encounter. Rather mental illness is a reminiscent of not being socially acceptable. The brain is potent in listening when observing mentally ill patients.

It is best that we be wise about gathering and taking in knowledge from the young and the elderly. The young are the future and the ones who that will shape the world based on present viewpoints. The elderly are our guides who have been through basically the same experiences as us, and they know shortcuts for our shortcomings. We can learn from the elders' lessons and mistakes to alter our outlook. Children keep us motivated and connected to the fun play of this earth. Anybody who is middle-aged is mainly concerned with capitalistic gain and mainly focused on bettering the external self. So paying homage to elders and youngsters is being an attentive listener. Ignoring these groups as if they are irrelevant places roadblocks in our way because they remember the most since children are close to the beginning of life and the elderly are closer to the ending of life. People in their twenties, thirties, forties, fifties, and even sixties are too focused on retirement plans, overpriced homes, money, bills, and things to look forward to as a means to an end. Elders and youngsters do not have these endings in their way because they either are already in the retirement phase or just don't have those types of worries to clutter their heads, which can be like a breath of fresh air to listen and be attentive to.

Relationships are better when we take the time to listen to one another. Positive connections between two or more people increase the likelihood of achievement. The power of two minds in correspondence with each other is very uplifting and agreeable to progress. Agreeableness is one personality trait that I fall short of. A person who would rather keep to him- or herself can be seen as suspect because people are very leery of loners. Loners make time for what they want to do so that anybody else who is a priority will have the great feeling of being attended to. Prioritizing maintains a healthy relationship with yourself and with the people who matter to you. But first listening to the self is of utmost importance. The majority of us have taken part in the saga of claiming that we do not have time to exercise, cook meals for ourselves, and enjoy entertainment because of tiredness and loss of willpower. When we listen to our bodies and know what we have to do based on inklings, then we understand that it is very important to listen to our anatomy or else we may suffer the consequences later. The fire within us that controls our willpower and act of doing completes and starts cycles. Getting things done when it pertains to our health, diet, and just anything or anyone that makes us feel better about our situations is critical. Denying our duties will lead to feelings of resentment, regret, guilt, grief, and ultimately fear because we use dead-end jobs and other strenuous activities as excuses for not bettering our health, which will make us feel alleviated. Processing goals into daily rituals prepares us to up our standards in our inkling of accessed achievements. Having fewer items on the to-do list will make you feel better about yourself in accomplishing something.

Women are often credited with special intuition. A woman's experience with the opposite sex seems to be a constant battle these days. Much of it has to do with women not feeling like a priority to some men. *Woman* means "to come out of a man," which is daunting since men cannot deliver in childbirth as a woman does and the woman's psyche is solely based upon feelings. Facts and truth are of little importance to a woman; just the feeling will do to keep her balanced. Women want to feel supported and listened to. They do not want fixes to their problems because they can quickly list challenges to options that will help them. Any woman is capable of doing well for herself and thus does not need a male counterpart to complement her. Any excuse for not having quality time for a woman is a lie. Women are way too fast these days for men in courtships, marriage proposals, and starting families. Women are the sole creators of unity and are adamant about getting things done as far as personal and business relationships. The evolution of women has surpassed the male species, but as of yet women are still treated unfairly and are underpaid in the workforce, where they are docile and taken advantage of. So when a women senses that something is off kilter, she will immediately address the problem or just become silent due to the frustration of not being listened to. Distance is required to be listened to so that maybe a male can show his true feelings toward her. Treasures do not hunt and have to retreat to be found again. A treasure knows its worth and does not have to degrade itself. Women simply get involved, watch, observe, calculate, and make a final decision about a matter. Truths and facts are pointless because every person holds his or her own opinions, but if the feeling is good, then we do not have to worry about what is to come. Feelings replace fact and truth. Intent is more viable than facts and truth in court. A felon can get a lesser sentence if lack of intent is proven. Known good intentions are like extra shaving points on a point spread. Solemnly, that is where a woman's intuition is located in how she feels and her thoughts and emotions will determine her well-being. She is able to go deep within herself by listening to intuitive guidance in a feeling mode that is given to her to make the best decisions and choices while living in a masquerade of male domination. The atrocities of mankind have been dated since that of Cain and Abel. We never really read about any violent women in theological history. Theologians have depicted women as a bit docile, weak, and troublemaking. If we were to have just as many female Bible characters as males, there would more than likely be an equilibrium between the sexes. The Virgin Mary is still of biological disbelief. Something is hidden and silent about female powers and the readiness to unconditionally love others. A few females are turning to their warrior status to fit in and are still hiding feminine energy from masculine counterparts in waging outcomes when they sense a game is being played. Women were always to be kept silent, and this mode is where she can ponder both masculine and feminine energies together by applying her emperor and empress mind-sets, exchanging them at will. Chasing men is confusing to the cosmos and leaves a confused surface on what a woman really wants to feel from a man, which is safety, support, protection, stability, and intimacy. When a woman does not find a perfect mate, resentment settles in, and getting back to ground zero requires her to ascend to the higher spirits of God. These feelings do work in the reverse as well, but the way males have been the off-track gender when it concerns feelings makes the reverse not that plausible. Whatever is created is very much real in this dimension, and others sense feelings resonate outwardly by demonstration. Woman came out of the universe to hold the lock to mysteries beyond comprehension. The lock is like a house to many rooms of her creativity. Males are the keys to females' houses, and if a male enters a female's house too many times, the keys can break. But there may be replacements. He can get a replacement key, but it was so much easier to get in with the original key. Now, the key has to go in a certain way, and there may be a struggle to get the door to open sometimes. Inefficient and incorrect keys have prompted women to be more masculine and to seek no one but the best as king, even if that means someone with an overt masculine energy to feel completion. During certain periods, masculine energy becomes comfortable to a female when it seems to get things done. This energy is nonetheless a motherly instinct and can be soothing to a guy who wants this bondage domination, but it can be tiresome for a male who loves freedom. Feminine energy is perfect for males to express their feelings. Feminine energy that is solely acted upon allows new people, places, and things to come to her based upon the feeling. Solitude places her above all else in her centerfold of self. Nature is very much in congruence with the female psyche and anatomy. If there were a population of just XX chromosome duplication and a depletion of male XY chromosome, it will leave less variety but more appreciation to listening. Sounds of music clarify harmony. Everyone can relate to a specific genre of music.

CHAPTER 35

Learn

My adult years have been the most exciting due to taking advantage of learning tools. Learning is an abstract of studying, observing, educating, and progressing the standard self. Learning institutions teach us a broad view of information that is available to those who seek it. Gathering information proves something to be true or false, right or wrong, valid or invalid, good or bad, and so on. Learning grants us choices that we earn through curiosity. Learning can provide us help when we need clarification. The standpoint from which we proceed or convince ourselves of is what we learn from, but we are all insane because we commit to being habitual beings. When the lessons become more difficult and easier to adapt to, we can make transformations to our thinking, leading to actions. We have come to understand that populations do not have to be instituted in colleges, universities, and tech schools to become professionals. Rather, it is demonstration that perfects our skills and routines. Going over truth and facts continuously is our daily job. From the moment we wake up, we are set on routines to get dressed, proceed with hygiene, eat, work, go to school or a favorite activity, rest, and then start it all over again the next day. If you are a fixed person, routine may be comfortable for you, but later you will feel an urge to change and be flexible about what you have learned about people, places, and things. Change is always on the horizon, and every particle inside atoms and cells move. Educational systems make plenty of money on tuition from students who want to learn what they already know. Perfection is categorized from the information we gather, validating whether that information is correct, precise, and accurate and then forming a point of view on the topic. Coming up with conclusions on changing subjects is just one more step to introducing another lesson in skewed time. Lessons trim information to make them more understandable. Shortcuts can be given in lectures from professors and teachers because time is precious when proceeding with lessons that are all connected. Therefore, before we were beings, we were taught all the lessons within a blink of an eye, but since we have to live on earth, time proceeds slowly while we are in our bodies. Otherwise, the act of doing gives us faster results than just thinking and gathering information, which can be daunting. Living on earth gives us all the elements we need to sustain and relinquish us into our hopes and desires. Before we were born, we were more like fish coming out of water. Even when we were small zygotes and fetuses, we were translucent like a fish, and our brains could not possibly hold all the information that forecast us when we were spiritual beings. Being like that fish, we come out of the womb knowing how to breathe on our own and how to take in food on our own. At that age, we are just concerned about our food, rest, love, and crying for what we want and need. We are not yet into figuring out our life paths, and it takes time to learn the basics.

Getting back to basics is simplifying and balancing, as with math and chemical equations. Any drawing or check methods to improve memory, such as balance sheets and recordings, are part of the learning process as well. There is no doubt that the African language is the mother of all languages. Before linguistics was even invented, our ancestors relied on pictures and visuals rather than what was spoken. Most people are right handed, and projecting language from the right hand instructed reason more than logic. With left-handed painters and writers, mathematic calculations and logical thinking came to fruition. The coordination and balance of both the right and left hands mended reason and logic to form language. Languages are used in all areas, including computer databases, speech, mathematical and scientific calculations, writing, and other disciplines that coordinate reason and logic. When humans learned to retain memory along with reason and logic, the differences became clear. With the concept of creativity coming before arithmetic, feminine energy had to be omniscient and present before masculinity. Calculations were more mundane, grounded techniques that were used for survival, as in hunting, cooking, and figuring when the sun would rise and set, as well as how long the moon would show and be illuminated.

Nevertheless, we have been duped into thinking that a college education will prepare us for our dream careers even though the same information has been taught, retaught, and redistributed throughout a number of years. We can all teach ourselves disciplines, subjects, and curricula by just reading. Tuition is highway robbery unless the education teaches us how to find what we are all wanting, which is love. I often wonder why metaphysics or any subject that explains God consciousness is kept secret or is excluded from studies with only random wall posters serving as motivation. When I was in school, I was able to experience prayer as part of the morning announcements and whenever the flag was raised up on the flagpole. Schools were much safer, and there was a sense of union among the administrators, students, and teachers. We never get to explore our godly gifts until we have been through a series of troubles or an awakening. All these things have been shunned by the public due to subcultures that undermine the fact that we all pray to *one* God. Churches are divided according to religion, and churchgoers pray to a God that they believe is the most righteous. Just like there is only one word, there is only one God and there is only one you and one me. If we were to take religion out of the category of praising a separate Supreme Being, then we would come to terms with the fact that everything originated with our African ancestry without exclusion of any religious group. Limiting God to only one religion limits him to minimal power. Exploring all different religions, cultures, and origins by being open to them helps us learn the whole big picture of congregation. Speaking in tongues is a gift, and the interpretation of tongues is a gift, along with healing, ministering, faith, miracles, words of wisdom, words of knowledge, discerning of spirits, and many other gifts that are replaced with subjects and substitutes that are universally used for profit. All these gifts are embedded in us through ancestry. Subjects have been correlated in depth to help heal the sick in doctrine, engineer master plans, and nurse patients, teaching knowledge that are not even included in Sunday masses. If we were to take advantage of our gifts, there would be an extermination of higher education through simple high spirituality. Mastering God's supposed plan is easy and was never meant to be hard. Throughout all these years, it has been hidden from the mainstream in secrecy, and education and man-made substances have been used to replace these gifts. We are being laughed at because of the amount of time we spend in school or on learning devices to gain basic, holistic knowledge that has the answers to all existence and maintenance. Learning is no simpler than when animals approach one another. An animal can sense when other animals are in fear. An animal that is observant of fearful behavior wonders why we are fearful of it, and then that animal comes to the realization that if we are scared of it, then we must be its enemy. Afterward, the attack phase sets in because the animal being feared does not know what we will do based upon fear. The same goes for stinging insects—if you do not feel bothered, then you will not be bothered. All beings would want to be feared only if there is a possible altercation. Other than that, we are always searching for someone or something to love and to love us. If humans do not communicate effectively with one another before coming to conclusions, then they will often habitually repeat mistakes. Just like if a person gathers facts, truths, and opinions through only one source without seeking the opposite source, their information on the other side of an issue or spectrum will energize blocked messages, resulting in a game of insane babble that others love to play based upon suspense. Suspension of information starts with misinformation when the parties involved think that they are righteous from the initiation of conversation or outcome. We are never righteous, and there is only one righteous almighty God. We are all sinners and saints, and no one is going to be treated as any more special than the next person. Seeking the correct information with Christ consciousness is not having the audacity to be wrongfully judgmental. Smiling when defeat is sensible is all about knowing the power of your God-given gifts.

CHAPTER 36

Knowledge

Knowing and experiencing love is God formation. If you know love, you know God. Love is everything. Those who do not know or understand the entanglements of captured love on a human level are in a rush to replace God in human form through another person or thing. The articles of clothing you see in stores or online are still going to be there next year and maybe even at a cheaper price somewhere else or in another country. Toys that we buy for children on birthdays and for Christmas are still going to be the same toys on the shelf next year, yet we have this circulation of time that gets us to rush. When we hear about interest rates going down or prices decreasing, we surge to stock up and buy things. We take time away from ourselves, family, and friends to work harder for the next best thing. Then, when we are done or when materials outlive their purpose, we dispose of them or give them away to the needy or whomever will take them. The energy of love circulates through all presence. It never dies, and it is what we long for from one another, if not from ourselves. Knowing love is knowing that things, people, and places are always going to be replaceable with the founding and newness of love. People can deny love all they want, but it is always going to be there, staring at them, forgiving, and at surrendering demand for a continuous of prosperity in life. Some people and things may have to be sacrificial, but love is always there to come back around to pick us up. Obsession will chastise love into possession and will proceed with a dynamic of unequal domination and submission that is mannerly chasing to be patient but can care less for waiting. If we know love, then we can set free and let go anytime of anyone or anything. That is the power of love—knowing that letting go freely will automatically give what we are in need of receiving. It can never be destroyed. Throughout all the years of war, famine, hate, jealousy, envy, anger, and greed, love is still alive. We practice out of love in that we can get better at what we are doing and for whatever we see as love.

I can no longer say that I believe that there is a Supreme Being, God, Christ, and all that because I know that there is such an existence within me, outside of me, and in other plane dimensions. Opening and closing doors are just expressions of love that are set up like a race car track. Forgiving and trusting in losing for betterment is winning and gaining. Bettering and renewing are circulated over and over again to know love. All creations are all-knowing of past, present, and future existence. It has been established that writings, art, and music existed before their time or replicas of other masterpieces. We put trust in God by putting trust in ourselves and our own work, knowing that the universe makes up a universal mind to keep functioning. When we are not certain, we test or get tested like being wrapped up in a security blanket. Our bodies encompass our anatomy, but so does the vehicle of the earth.

Repeating cycles over and over again eventually brings us to love, where we just don't give a fuck anymore but are still focused on love. When we don't care to fuss, fight, or struggle and respond to it by laughing, then we put ourselves into a totally different ball game and increase the amplifications of love by trusting and knowing that everything is going to be all right. Getting in a zone of no shame, resentment, or feelings of guilt prepares us for knowledge. We can also refer to the zone as getting into our void of constant flow and understanding. Knowledge is stored within every cell of our bodies. New knowledge makes for new orders when something has to be adjusted. Awareness and consciousness are becoming more apparent to the world. When we attain knowledge stored in books or studies for the first time, we remember 67 percent of it, and when we go over it a second time, our remembrance is at 95 percent. The third time, we remember 99 percent. So for knowledge to be acknowledged, three factors must be included, such as with a Venn diagram. Whatever is created in the present is real. There is no such concept of fiction when thoughts are created because, for some reason, it had to be demonstrated as coming from the most high. The configuration of thoughts is likewise of the sun that gives off energy, and that energy is spread to us in energy circuits. Anything up for discussion is mixed with truth, and that later turns into lies because of people's viewpoints rather than the scope of research. There is no room for closed-mindedness. An open mind brings great wisdom, and great wisdom brings forth empirical, holistic knowledge. As long as you have an understanding of all sides of an issue, then you can know simply everything. You will feel gratitude for knowing and understanding that there is no such thing as coincidence. Spiral vortexes show that there are synchronizations and reflections, which will make us feel like we are in a déjà vu. Occurrences and happenings will feel like they have happened before within a matter of nanoseconds of our recollecting them. To know that there are endless possibilities opens the mind, and we can then see past reflections and be the person on the outside looking in. What you don't know won't kill you. The theme of knowledge is to stop referring ourselves in just words, like poor, rich, smart, dumb, sad, and mad. It's acceptable to feel well, but we do not have to let a word control our lives regarding how we should feel. Taking every emotion, thought, and feeling into just being or the way to be at that given time and moment puts us into our void. Focusing on how the self responds to certainties and uncertainties is all knowing. For instance, if the sky at night had hardly any stars in it tonight, I would want to imagine a cluster of stars into the sky. So I would run my hand in the air like a wand with my fingers flickering on stars. Thus, my certainty and uncertainty that more stars will appear in a clearer sky are my perceptions of what is to come by simply imagining. Tapping into the void of what I want to be done is the balance of certainty and uncertainty and also being in the flow, zone, and void of being ridiculed or judged about it. The flow of energy is like a figure eight in the body, looping excited sensation from the crown to the third eye and through the lower chakra. That is why it is very healthy to surround yourself around open-mindedness, to offset occurrences or to be totally in your own zone. Realizing from up high and sending a sense of strong belief and faith in oneself comes to knowing. Within the void we must clear out all negative thinking about our situations and take them as just happenings that are not meant to have an effect on our current central core beings.

Nevertheless, living a primal and savage lifestyle gets us to our core being. I'm not suggesting being homeless or becoming a hermit, but we have to know that we are more than how much money we make, we are more than what we have, we are all deserving in relationships, and any obstacle is easily overcome. Pouring all material and negative thinking into nothingness gives us emptiness in our core, and that is where we want to focus. Your thoughts are not who you are, and your emotions and feelings are not who you are. You are nothing, complete nothingness trying to empty out every malfunction, disruption, and disturbance to be within the void of transcendence. This aspect is pure knowing of the self if we are images of God. We came out of nothing. Remember that at the beginning there was nothingness, complete emptiness, and understanding of the darkness. Excitement created a clash of fire that was transcended into light. Being excited makes all of us create. As long as the excitement is in our core, then we can fill the void. Meditation is advocated so much because it will bring clearance and emptiness upon us if done successfully. An exhaust of good energy is scattered into energy fields past the Earth's atmosphere, causing an affect to go through a prism of synchronization. What is given out by you in your energy field is sent back not only to you but to others as well. It's all about existing to be; this is true knowing. If we take up all the words that we want to define us, then we are being processed and diluting ourselves with jargon that is meaningless and pointless. Recall that at the beginning there was no language, so words have no meaning when attempting to fill the void. Therefore, the many experiences we go through condition our wholeness into nothingness, just like how you see mental patients in institutions who are mute but for some reason are stuck in a process that disallows them from getting out of a certain frame of mind through fear. Knowing that you have a lot going for yourself and taking action on goals leads you into nothingness. The hardest part of being empty is having to go through lessons over and over again until they become null and are lessons no more. Conjuring a feeling and then nullifying it to the point that it is conquered is a great power. When we are able to be in long durations of emptiness, our bodies do not need as much fuel, like food and rest, because they do not have to exhaust themselves as much on pointless abstracts and opinions. That is why people are apt to fasting along with meditation and prayer due to prolonging transcending voids. Once you are able to get out of the frame of reflections and become outside of your body into nothingness, then you will be able to experience external forevers being whom you really are, which is nothing and all there is. It's like turning yourself inside out, not seeing yourself as form but stillness. There is no feeling, expression, or dualism of identity. Love conspires in the process of knowing into understanding the self, which is one. Forgiveness is love, and that is why we end up repeating the same applications of character with the people we love—because we can be so quick to forgive. The true test is forgiving who and what you feel you do not know. When a problem occurs, laughing and chuckling at it like a child is about as good as it gets. Laughing at reflections shows that you know that they are not part of you, because you are nothing filled with emptiness. Picture your body as a mountain or rock, and all that comes into contact with your mountain or rock is just fog, rain, and ice that can never penetrate the interior so deeply that it destroys it in the time being. Mountains and rocks take all the weather into their own. There is no need to explore pursuing to exert yourself to prove what you are not when you know the self, which is all that matters. Knowing that we can control only our outlook on the self is exhilarating and will remove a lot of force that is a waste of energy on other beings. There is no power in forcing our will onto people. That is exertion and hard work that does not liberate us. It only destroys true being because we are one in a conscious matrix.

Everything has an expiration date that remains within the core of the earth. Applying nothingness on earth is showing respect for souls to ascend into the spirit. The same applies to the dead. It is respectable to burn a body, leaving the least waste of dead energy. Although understanding that there is duality in the world, it is of basic nature to bury a person six feet underground. Burials are the main ritual in the entire world to show respect for the dead. For earth to be the only planet in the solar system inhabited by living creatures for right now, there is no doubt that there is a Supreme being orchestrating our being, and it resides in you. Planet earth is infinite and is programmed to protect itself from destruction through occurrences. Often enough we see thriller, sci-fi, and horror movies that display the end of days on earth. Various nature documentaries explain how the production of things for consumption is heavy for the environment's safety. Production for consumption places pressure on the earth's surface. Not only that, but waste from trash and burials is underneath our feet. Inside out is the formless address of emptying a planet. All planets rely upon the others through magnetic energy fields. Magnetism holds all four elements within grasp on all levels of earth. A person with great wisdom and insight on mysticism will come to find that manipulating the four elements (fire, earth-metals, air, and water) can come quite naturally. Contrarily, this knowledge on manipulation may gradually come to those who are open to duality but are still focused on one outcome, which forms the trinity. Without one or the other, the elements cannot be sustainable. Fire cannot fuel without air, and water cannot be contained without earth. Most elements have form and shape and can be changed physically or chemically. We are made up of all four elements, and our bodies contain them. For example, a person who falls in love easily initially has a lot of fire and drive and a heart of mostly gold. More or less, the person will be like an infant demanding attention. Air is the only element that can fuel the fire—with wind. Thus, when the quantity of air is low, the fiery person will suddenly lose interest because of not being attended to and eventually will burn out. Intellectual stimulation keeps the fire going inside the person, especially if communication is on par. Stroking of the ego is a must in most cases. Intellect is dry without ego, and ego is valueless without intellect. An ego that is fed and stroked maintains action. It's a fight-or-flight reaction.

With the manipulation of fire and air together, you will discover divine mysticism mainly in the sky being air and with fire energy—that being the sun. This divinity has been thought to coincide with sun gods and goddesses and demigods. Even though gods and goddesses were considered part of mythical folklore in ancient books, novels, and plays, they are very much real here on the mental cerebral plane. It just takes imagination about what you want to perceive with a focal point in the sky and sunlight, emotion for arousal and tickling the heartstrings that are filled with feelings, and a body to be grounded to earth. By using all four elements of the self, we can transform the sky to the form, shape, and color we want. This is where the void comes to be of great use for fire-air desire. When there is an environment of challenge, discrimination, judgment, or feeling of not being accepted through communications, whether it is verbal in music or by tongue, the void that is placed to shield and encompass in emptiness while still feeling the love from up high becomes you. You will be able to see through challenges that give a winning chance for power opportunity that will successfully shape and shift another element through paying attention to divine love. You will notice the shaping and shifting of other elements in the color and texture of the clothes you wear and the color and sometimes texture of your skin. Placing focus and participant perception into thought processes while extinguishing unconditional love by avoiding hostile confrontations in a judgmental earthly atmosphere will cause the universe to mimic you by tapping into conscious awareness. In order to have this specific thought process, you have to not let external extremes affect your thoughts of divine love. Fire and air are positive elements; thus positivism is exchanged. Earth and water are negative elements; thus negativism is exchanged. More energy is exhausted when manipulating elemental earth and water, likewise with storms and tornadoes. This plane is associated when deaths, burials, unhappy emotions, and greed are contemplated. When negative energy is exhausted from us, it comes right back even if we find someone at fault. Pessimistic emotions can cause objects to move or levitate and dreams to be prophetic, even scary. The underworld lies underneath the powers of earth and water put together. Without positivism and negativism, we would not exist because positivity has to exchange with negativity; and we are all composed of affirmative and pessimistic demonic energy. Soul identity can be experienced simply through the spiritual and harshly through the demonic. Positive energy is drawn up from your sacrum through your heart diaphragm and then through the crown of your head, and it is a constant flow. The direction of negative energy is just the opposite and is instead focused on your lower regions because there is an abundance of water emotion mixed with grounding earth. Positivism focuses on action, doing, intellect, imagination, and natural feelings such as anger. Negativism is focused on finances, grief, guilt, material, ownership, rest, and possession. Negativism teaches us how to be placid with temperance in any circumstance. Generating these energy fields is invigorating and will keep you wondering. This is also easier if you suffer from some type of attention or personality disorder per se, with the self being more appreciated and focused upon. Understanding these four elements is becoming of the self and soul identity.

CHAPTER 37

Challenge

The only challenge is that of being a slave. Slavery is empowered through obedience. Whatever or whomever we obey, we become slaves to. At first this chapter was going to include money, but I specifically changed it to address challenges of a broader scope. Without much choice, a lot of us slave for the money trees that are plucked in exchange for labor. This method of enslavement is to get powerfully strung on capitalism that is foreseen by many healers, teachers, spiritualists, and activists. Freedom versus choice is in conflict when our existence depends upon letting money be exhausted only by paying bills. During the industrial and golden ages, employment was at an all-time high for productivity. Northwestern folks would work at least sixteen hours per day without a day off for very low wages. Work was bountiful with the employment of immigrants, migrant workers, and children. Toleration and conformity shaped this era into a sleep mode of exchanging time for money or employment. After the Depression in the United States, citizens were pleased to just be working after living in insufferable conditions. Ending no-wage slavery caused a dip in the nation's production consumption because of having to replace slave workers with wage workers. Even then, rebuilding the South took a huge cut out of the economy's funding. Southern owners had to change their perspectives on business employment and farming production. Corporations have a better grip on physical and mental labor that drives workers to perform dutiful tasks each allocated hour. Most middle-class workers are presently salaried and are the overseers on the corporate ladders. Executives come up with master plans to push production through innovative advances that appeal to consumerism. Corporate businesses that have mass production rates usually contradict a "work hard, think smart" atmosphere when trying to please the whims of consumer wants and desires. One challenge in life is changing addictive behavior and minds so that people behave smarter based on placing needs before wants. Freedom is not having to depend on or obey anybody, and it is not to be confined to material wealth. Many still fall into the trap of debt all due to wanting, which leads to consumer debt regulated by the Federal Reserve, which enslaves us. Money takes over the thought processes of gaining more material and paper energy that has been here since the beginning of time for free.

Sexual slavery forces women and men to obey generally the opposite sex for favor in money and things. Female genitalia have always been the start-up of male ambition for seeking and gaining material wealth. Men's masculine spirituality is meant to reach empowerment through women who guide them to God. Women's feminine spirituality is to be supported through men who hold themselves equal to the female without changing his perspective on her involuntary null competitiveness. Fighting and challenging is left up to the man or men who are sent to protect her from combative resources. Not being involved in everyday gossipy talks keeps a woman relieved from having to compete. A real man does not want his significant other to be challenged or competitive with frivolous minds that he cannot worship like himself or his partner at home. The older I get, the more I notice that females have to take on these male roles. Not only do most females rear the children, work for money, and tend to the home, but they periodically—or more often than most—have to compete with other females and sometimes males when accessing support from the male species. This combative behavior opens the floodgates to feminine and masculine energies meandering through one person. The female is not only challenging but is also challenging herself to take on the qualities of both a man and a woman. Strong women love to be submissively docile when comfortable and sure of their mates. Even though the female counterpart does not have to act like the lesser sex, she still adores the trickery of not being challenged in her personal relationships. Challenges are what enslave us through obedient behavior to car notes, house payments, insurance, food, student loans, and other obligations that we have to pay on a regular basis. Freedom from challenge means few debt collectors to deal with. Even in the sex escort business, a woman is indebted to sex agencies that capitalize on the commodity of solicitation, female prostitution, and even her sex partner. These challenges of being enslaved to money and sex leave us shackled and chained to lucrative productive sales. In America, it is all too common to learn that sex sells (female counterpart) and money talks (male counterpart). Yet, sex and money drive the sexes apart to challenge each other.

I cannot help but recognize that the book of Genesis in the Bible tells about how generations are to experience slavery if seeds choose to obey the luxuries of money and says that by becoming servants of God, we will be free just as in a garden of Eden. Slaves become zombie-like or robotic after a while, conforming to sets of rules that are dished out by schools, jobs, creditors, and law enforcement agencies. Rules are a means to control behavior in educational facilities, the workplace, credit agencies, and society. The abuse of power is all too prevalent in these four areas because of the extent of disciplinary control one has over an individual. Authority is crossed when money and sex become driving forces for occupancy. Being enslaved to money or sex is what keeps capitalism in steady progress and is the "needs of the business."

Going through with God's calling within you will help to change the thought processes that are encrypted to enslave you. The godly presence wants you to challenge yourself to the point that you do not have to bow down to making money on someone else's terms. Making money while you sleep is your reward for being a creative artist and entrepreneur. Having money work for you is the simplest mind frame. Intelligence and brilliance are made through challenging goals that we love to achieve. Changing our thinking processes into new, innovative forms of doing from challenged environments in the past helps us to mobilize progressively, just like during the Progressive Era of relaxation.

By not being challengers through noncompetitiveness, we become winners to the only person that matters the most—the self. Being winners of the self showcases the act of doing and allows us to place control in our godly presence. We are granted the right amount of time to complete our true self's servitude to the higher intelligence that is given to us from birth. Having a slave mentality means joining with what everybody else is doing and not paying any attention to demonstrating your godly worth by sharing your God-given gifts. We listen to parents, teachers, and peers all throughout life to shape our livelihoods. Going against the social norm is what we are meant to do so that we can introduce a variety of individual perceptions. Mental slavery hides behind falsehood and ignorance, beseeching commonality. Working for someone instead of working for yourself is another form of the slave mentality if you are not happy with your work or worthiness. Breaking away from conformity is a heck of a challenge when those in your environment expect you to be, do, and pretend with them in a ritualistic, routine life. However, pressures from family and friends can be a start to establishing guidance in your life and discovering that either you or the people who surround you are alien. When you are searching for your true self, you will become unbelievable to your surroundings. Even if you were an independent person, not needing help from anyone, you would still be lectured as if you were a child when you went after your calling. Furthermore, when you have the heart of a child, you will want to be cheap with your resources and will find it quite delirious to keep up with the Joneses. Those with an adult mentality simply want to add people, places, and things onto their lives to feel some sort of importance or validity. When I was a teenager, I shunned the responsibilities and dreadfulness of adulthood. I worked a steady job to help pay for my expenses and eventually became miserable with the jobs I held and the authority figures who questioned my integrity. Working was not the problem, but the constant watching of my labor from managers and supervisors was limiting. And my work seemed like it was never good enough no matter how long I stayed. Work became the usual zombieland, filled with a whole bunch of disgruntled laborers who were fighting every day to be obedient, present, and able to follow a set of contradictory rules at every given minute. No matter how much the work was hated, the money was still there, falsely promising financial freedom based on living from paycheck to paycheck. I had even overheard managers say it felt like they were running a plantation as they overlooked adults on their job duties.

To say that there is no such thing as a devil is against all aspects of biblical teaching. I do not believe in a creature with horns and a tail that is surrounded by fire to torment us when we sin. To me, in every saint there is a sinner. Every person who feels righteous has committed wrong in one way or another. For every rescuer, there is a victim. For every devil, there is an angel. Without dark forces, there would be no light to pierce through. Staying away from what keeps us enslaved requires free will and the ability to make choices. But first and foremost, we have to get rid of the slave mind-set of doing for well-to-do people and others when we just need to be ourselves in the act of being.

CHAPTER 38

Winning

In the present moment, there is always a winning streak set before opportunity. Everybody is in a marathon with the intent of winning significantly. Intentions, purposes, and truth determine the longevity of the win. We are all winners, even after challenges and even when there is no opponent. Being afraid to lose is a response to a fear tactic, and in order to win we must let go and possibly replace. Losing is not even a reflection of winning but a constituent for disappointment. Once we learn that failure and loss are part of gaining wins, then we come to understand that now is the new. A winner has no regard for past traumas or future promises. Past and future thinking is a mixture of water and air, which can be destructive like a hurricane. Earth and air are beneficial to the presence of now thinking and are more stabilized with grounding mobility. Water and air do not care for winning. Water is concerned about emotions and wanting to seek the hardships that an individual has to go through to be a winner. Air qualities don't mind winning or losing but are more focused on team effort and how the team determines a victory. For instance, if we took water and air out of sports, then we would not have sympathy every time an athlete got injured playing. Nor would team coordination and staff be substantive in sports. Thus, all four elements are represented in a winning streak, including heart, bodies, minds, and feelings or emotions.

The winners' circle has the best intentions, purpose, and wisdom. As long as those three factors are in correspondence to not destroy one another because of the basic rules of karma, then the winning streak will last a lifetime. Winning streaks are defeated easily because of the probable closeness of transitions and transformations. A winner knows him- or herself, and to know ourselves we have to have some basic knowledge about astrology and genetics. Contrarily, according to Darwin's superiority theory known as survival of the fittest, evolution and genetics are the only factors that determine longevity. Cosmic astrology is to blame for mortality as well. Genetics and astrology coordinate so well that we can creatively configure genetic replication with zodiac signs. The four nucleotides adenine, thymine, guanine, and cytosine coordinate with the first four zodiac signs: Aries, Taurus, Gemini, and Cancer. Notice how they start with the same letters and are paired the same way in application to fire-air, earth-water, adenine-thymine, and guanine-cytosine. In DNA replication, a cycle of paired nucleotides is structured until priming takes place to clone another DNA strand. The priming process, or scanner as we say, is the zodiac sign Leo, that like the sun. Virgo is also a part of the priming process with Leo since the cell is perfecting the strand, analyzing, critiquing, and gathering data for the next strands. Libra is the replication fork (zipper), and base pairing is in the middle of the zodiac sign as well as forming the equilibrium of the DNA strand. Scorpio ends the transcription process of replicating the strand with nucleotides and sees to anything that needs to be discarded (put to death) from the strand. In Sagittarius, proper proteins and enzymes are aimed at the DNA sites. Last, a CAP is added, which is Capricorn, Aquarius, and Pisces, at the end of the strand. Furthermore, astrology is even in our DNA, and the time processes of our astrological charts are programmed into our DNA to help in cell function. Our bodies do not like to do much guesswork in repairing, repeating, and reaping of why, what, when, where, and how injury or illness has taken place. Natal birth charts are extremely helpful to cell replication, functioning of cells, and the structure of cells. Parental genetic information and astrological data are all calculated in our cell division.

If we were to compare our natal charts to our parents' natal charts, then we would be able to tell that we adopt astrological aspects from our parents just like with genetics. We can actually do a pedigree with birth natal charts. When we are able to distinguish all of the amazing aspects of our characters and being by glimpsing at natal charts, we will come to find that we are more in love with ourselves. The self has a healthy ego when it knows where it has been, where it is currently, and where it is going. It is quite unpredictable that you will have any guidance without looking up natal charts. Your guidance in life's journey may come from a coach, teacher, friend, parent, or relative if you're not interested in astrological charts. Knowing your natal chart is just a faster way to seeing your destiny, but either way it goes, you will end up at the same destination anyway, even if you do not know all or some of the aspects in your chart. And that is the biggest secret to life—no matter how much we complain and go through all these emotions, there is no way to stop or change what is destined to be. So we simply have to live with the circumstances, knowing that we are not yet in control of the higher purpose that will fulfill our wants and needs. Winning is about doing things over and over again, about repetition. The more we think of something, the closer it is drawn to us. When we focus on winning, we bring positivity into our world. Noticing that there is rotation instead of a finish line is the key to winning. There is no competition, except with the self. Dwelling on the past causes cellular respiration to slow down or become stagnant, and thinking too much about the future speeds cellular respiration. Cell division functions at an active rate of replication, not paying any attention to its past or future, which makes cellular respiration a continuity focusing on precision and accuracy. Most illnesses and diseases are not even inherent but are self-inflicted wounds from a disruption in thinking. Being in the now is one of the cures to cellular repair, and establishing good intentions brings forth prosperity.

Cosmology and cellular repair include the planetary aspects, functions and structure of DNA, and active sites when completion of revolution has occurred. If a planetary aspect affects the mental, physical, intellectual, spiritual, emotional, or even sexual development of a person, there may be a result of madness or holiness. Posttraumatic stress disorder can leave a person in shock and simultaneously labeled manic depressive. Realization of that cellular disruption can occur for anyone within a matter of seconds, as can the realization that we are all comprised of cells and neurological connections that can alter the universe. Unionized cell formation happens in all of us at rapid speed. Understanding that cellular replication affects the whole universe alters nature, just like the planets alter time.

We all start as winners according to our ability to generate DNA. All organisms replicate depending on astrology ordinance. Polymerase chain reaction is what holds the nucleotides together, binding the lagging and leading strands of DNA for strength. Leo is a polymerase that illuminates and holds the DNA together. The priming process is Virgo. So the heart, spine (backbone), nervous system, and stomach are the polymerase chain reaction and priming method. The sun and Mercury rule these areas in illumination and communication. Libra is of the kidneys, which can be the helicase process, along with Scorpio sex organs, which represent the replication fork. Sagittarius aims at the correct enzymes to transcribe and inscribe into the DNA strand thighs. The *cap*ping process is Capricorn, Aquarius, and Pisces—kneecaps, ankles, and feet. A lot of this DNA takes up junk DNA and is thought to be of no use, but the correlation of zodiac signs, planets, and the universe creates a massive replica of DNA replication and vice versa. Chromosomes are zodiac sign astrology, and the nucleus is also that of the sun, with the whole cell being the universe. We have the authentic makeup of the entire galaxy in each of our cells. When unnatural emotions influence the cells, it affects the universe. This is the explanation as to why cells and chromosomes commit suicide due to the abundance of negative disbelief in one's universal mind. A karmic reaction from our reflective image, it is important to note that our negative thoughts and unnatural emotions affect the progress of civilization. It is only a matter and luxury of time that determines our longevity. I wonder if straying away from a destined path or not learning life's lessons through Scorpio and Saturn impacts cell replication. Medical astrology plays a mysterious role in the duplication of cells. The rotation of planets and stars depicts our calendar events and any luxury of astrological time travel.

CHAPTER 39

Opportunity

Opportunity is futuristic speaking, unlike its past-tense *challenge* and present-tense *win*. Philosophers surmise that opportunity comes once in a lifetime, but I propose that opportunity comes periodically. We cannot escape destiny when there is work to be done. We may learn the hard way to take opportune advantages before giving into our services. When we do lose out on periodic opportunity, resentment will flare up. "Should have," "could have," and "would have" are all explanations and excuses for losing out on opportunity. "Should have" refers to a sheer mistake. "Could have" is an excuse and a sign of laziness because the ability was present but the will was missing, and "would have" means that an opportunity was replaced with something else. Lost opportunity is not failure even when recognizable defeats of an attempt lead to multiple excuses. An activated person cannot be a failure, and being activated is being able to replicate DNA. Replication of DNA perpetuates opportunity, and the priming process prepares a person or animal to gain in the future with more insight on loss.

Opportunity can be compared with the story of *Goldilocks and the Three Bears*. Goldilocks did not think of the repercussions of eating somebody else's food. She found a soup that was just to her liking. Since the three bears were gone, she saw the perfect opportunity to mooch and eat some soup that was just right for her. She even went to sleep in the little bear's bed. Finding our niche is all about opportunistic value. Adaptability plays a role in opportune settings as well, and being able to adapt to any environment leaves doors open for us to explore more readily. Optimism always brings opportunity just through pursuance. If we think that every outcome is going to be positive even before it comes to fruition, we are preparing for an advantage. Real opportunity comes when we plug ourselves in to being losers. It's called not showing our hand and can be likened to secretiveness. It is truly the thought that counts. If we were negative, we would not follow through with pursuance. Even though we are given chance after chance for something or someone, we have an inkling of losing. Loyalty is the foundation of seizing opportunity, and we can become stubborn. If we actively have to force something, then it is not opportunity but pursuance. First comes the loyalty, and then comes the accomplished opportune moment. Nonetheless, there are times when an opportunity can just climb up and sit on your lap, and if the time is right, that opportune moment can be a benefit to your health. That is why it is important to know yourself, so that you are intelligently programmed to seek the best. Being open to anything can be dangerous, but it is for no doubt an experience.

Educational universities are known for preparing adults for professional occupations. We are told that getting a college degree will make us at least $20,000 more per year than a person who obtains only a high school diploma. The key is knowing yourself at a young age and what you plan to do while living; that is what makes students with no college degrees successful. With the scarcity and unavailability of well-paying middle-class careers, college now is being fronted as a joke and a scam. People place their bets more on opportunity and favor than on education to nail a job. Employers are steadily overlooking college graduates for someone with more experience in the field. A lot of people blame the environment of "it's all about who you know" when applying for a position. If you received a degree from a university but have not found or had the opportunity to get an interview with an employer after numerous applications, then you must find your niche in creative entrepreneurship. Also, freeing up space in your personal life and relationships can bring plenty of opportunity. Letting go of old ideas and personal and business-related things will open new doors for you. An opportunist knows when to stop working at an opportunity, gradually pulling themselves into a higher realm of creativity. I'm not saying to cut all your losses and try to become an actor on Broadway, but your chances are better somewhere else if no one is responding positively to you in your job search. Finding time for hobbies gives limitless opportunity to happiness.

Today, opportunity can be exchanged with just settling. After many attempts at something, a person can become lethargic and take the less opportune method. Some opportunities can be a devil in despise or a blessing in disguise. Thus, it is important to trust your gut instinct. Therefore, failed experiences warn us of an opportunity that may not be so promising. A continuation of failure gives us better insight on better opportunities. We always have to fail, fall, or even flunk to get to our niche and soar like the free bird, bees, butterflies, and angels that we are. Staying optimistic brings in opportunity all the time with many options to choose from, even if we make a failed attempt. Being in the present allows us to just be in the now and focus on the agenda of prizes to come.

Furthermore, opportunists have no regrets or shame about anything that they do. Rather, they regret the things they did not do. As long as they are doing the things that fulfill them, they are happy to fail and dwell in the exploration of trying. Most opportunists produce great works that are on display for the entire world to view and just love creating, no matter if it brought gain, fortune, or fame. There are artists who have so much heart for their craft that they inevitably forgo celebrity status. Being passionate about projects while gathering the opportunities for betterment is an ongoing cycle just like the activation and catalyzing of our cells to function correctly. There are opportunities for germs, bacteria, and viruses to invade our bodies through crevices and anatomical openings. Our cells notice the attack and use defense mechanisms to cure the ailment, and the process starts over again. This is why it is very important to take care of our health because we can lose all opportunity when that flags on us. Avoiding opportunity can be detrimental to our health in spite of a destiny calling that we have to fulfill. We are all destined, but we may lag in higher purposes and contrarily may be used to help others. Cells destroy themselves when they are in hostile environments, including the ones inside your body. Negative thinking is the result of cell mortality, and positive thinking repairs and replicates cells properly. Positivity brings our destiny fulfillment much closer to us through manifesting. Facing problems and taking opportune action on them is a growing process for the mind, body, and soul. Clearing out a problem and manifesting for it to go away will dissipate the problem. Less focus on unnatural emotions about the problem will also cause it to disappear or allow other opportunities to replace it. Giving into old ways of thinking, perception, and grieving past chances blocks opportunity. A winner in life does not get upset or vengeful over past mistakes and problems. They are not sore losers or killjoys, because they know that the optimistic frame of mind always prepares them for another opportune moment.

CHAPTER 40

Success

Success is established by repetitive force upon an agenda. We can picture success as a cycle of time frames and astrological influences that guides us to our fulfillment. The only reason for not proceeding with success is fear of it. We all have conjured demons, and this particular demon can leave us tranquilized and distraught. The true test is overcoming the demon all throughout life by practicing naturalness and not letting any obstacle get in our way of achievement, which lingers to loyalty of the self.

It is important to know in your natal chart the placements of different zodiac signs in your houses for successful survival techniques. For example, if you have Scorpio in your chart, you can focus on a particular portion of your body to withstand a hot or cold climate. Scorpions can survive any type of weather, even freezing and drought conditions. Thus, I focus and flex my chest because Scorpio rules my fourth house, which occupies the chest cavity. Most martial artists focus their techniques on the movements and behavior of ferocious, deadly animals, which is pertinent to defense. We all behave like animals and are subject to using our primitive instincts for our protection.

Dealing with success is the same as putting up with failure. The main failures in life are perceived through family, friends, and the environment. We can easily live lives that are not ours, that are based upon the life choices that our parents and peers approve of. Fear of failure is a fear of being successful as well. Being misunderstood can easily turn into a sense of failure. An occupation can be fulfilling for our families, peers, and friends but imprisonment to us. Dealing with the pains of being independent for ourselves and others can make us miss out on our true calling. Independence is freedom, but working for employers who keep us stressed and lethargic is definitely not worthwhile. Finding success in failure is an uplifting feeling that life must go on, and being able to distinguish our trueness in our work will be beneficial to our health. Getting a system down of knowing how to draw close to your true heart's desire is going to eliminate failure for you. Meditation, speaking affirmations, and knowing the correct way of praying will grant you access to a full win in the self with a sigh of relief, knowing consciously that what you pray for brings you closer to your goals.

Nevertheless, you are greater than any job, relationship, or circumstance that is downtrodden. When we have a gut instinct of anything that needs to be eliminated in our realm, it is important that we take action for change. Nagging forces of struggling to pay bills can detour us from our true paths. Furthermore, the journey to success requires failure. Failing at an interview for a job will open doors to a better job. It is important that we learn to spend our time on earth in supportive environments to keep our health clean and clear of debris from stressful environments. Truthfully, that is the key to success—just being happy so that that happiness is amplified throughout the universe. It is extremely common to get lost and confused on our journey when we are living the lives of others and basically lying to ourselves. It's all right to be a fool, but being a damn fool for paper money is inexcusable. You will know when working just for a paycheck that it brings no simple fulfillment or joy.

Letting go of worn-out relationships and situations that no longer serve your higher good opens up more room for successful outcomes. Repetition in doing a task over and over again leads to a righteous path. A worn-out relationship is inclusive to overdoing rather than performing naturally. If you argue and fight with your significant other without resolving issues on a day-to-day basis, then marriage is not for that relationship because marriage will only enhance the quarrels. These days, a lot of relationships consist of ethereal, self-deceiving feelings of being infatuated with love and can get in the way of success. Any relationship that solely supports your heart's desire is love. We must keep our eyes on the prizes of our lives and unclutter trash that we pass and collect into our presence. And hey, if it or that person is meant for our present, then adjustments will be made for us. It is a great source to use any and every relationship to increase the amount of love to bring success. For instance, in one of my relationships, my partner nagged me about getting a job, and since this aspect of my career life was so important to him, I greatly considered it. The feelings of being able to financially take care of him and our families brought me to apply for some occupations through the state. I deeply thought of scenarios on how the two of us could live our lives together with all of our kids in one household. I thoughtfully fantasized about being independent of the support from another. With that in mind, I prayed and affirmed for a job out of a new love that was not even tangible for me to grasp. I was called for an interview, and after being notified of the job qualifications and how much the agency was going to take from my paycheck each month through a mandatory 9.5 percent retirement savings, health insurance, taxes, and travel to investigate cases, I figured that the pay and responsibility were just not worth it to live on my own with breathing room for a nice lifestyle, even though I was contemplating cohabitation with another. Thank goodness I was not selected since I had not brought my transcripts and recommendations to the interview. The job required on-call, at-will show-ups, a lot of car traveling, and an underpaid status. That same day, I texted that "boo" passing out dated new love, and by word of mouth I guess he heard that I had declined the offer, which made him believe that I was stuck-up. Love is part of success, and if we find ourselves not being appreciative or upbeat about something or someone, we can quickly develop higher expectations for ourselves and seek another route for betterment. Having a good support system with people who love us no matter what we do is the best way to seek and receive success.

Fearful thoughts that keep us entrapped in the cerebral part of the brain lead to putting success on hold at times. There are times when fear can kick in and have its way with us quickly, which goes back to closing doors to continue to open new doors and chapters for us. Then there are those gut feelings of fear that make us say to ourselves, "Something is not right." Just know that your instincts speak louder than words and that following your true purpose is the only satisfaction that you will get in the universe by doing creative works.

CHAPTER 41

One

One is a number of loneliness in breaking ability. If you notice the number 1, it is much like a stick, not easily bent. The number 1 is correlated with the higher God-mind. Phrases such as "seeking the one" in a partnership are really a connotation of seeking God. The universal God is jealous when we seek humans, money, or any material as replacement in worship. There is an exception of looking up to or being influenced by a being that will bring you closer to the universal God. The derivative of the number 1 is what is holistic, including all entities universally. In Western religions, the devil is portrayed in many forms of art and expression as apart from the self when fear itself is within us. A lot of us live in fear because it is comfortable to be chained to and in bondage with additives. Going through fear grounds us, though, and the only difference in the elimination of fear is time. But as we cannot possibly imagine what life would be like without time, then we can only experience periods at a time that are called change. Now, as mentioned before, time is just like money, and we are obligated to abide by the rules of spending it wisely. Change represents the money that is made and spent in an amount of time. Change and time together depict the direction of what to take in correspondence to distance. Distance is limitless, thus making it possible for entities, such as God, to be within and beyond us. Whatever we think of ourselves is what we think about God. Our person of self is expressed in the type of God that is pictured in our minds. Suicide is perceived as the no-value view of life and is taught that way in various religious organizations with history, books, and media. The act of suicide results in one less life that involves time with fear, but people are slowly committing suicide day by day with the food they eat, the lack of rest they get, a lack of companionship, and failure to protect the self from harmful encounters. A person who commits suicide does not necessarily have a disbelief in a creator, but rather the individual longs and yearns for peace of mind. Peace within can be the search of a lifetime, and if one is unable to find it on earth, one will search for it somewhere else.

When we look at images of the godhead, we see that the sun and moon share the head space. The sun and moon are of equal importance, representing both masculine and feminine power. It is within the balance of energy that a human can experience the godhead, that of wisdom and vitality. Through everyday meditation, it is easier to open energy portals that can create fire and water energy through one's chakra system. A pull and push in the navel is a sign of an accurate meditation. Knowing when to push and pull forces is a part of godhead powers. As a product of earth, air, water, and fire, we are equipped to create, manipulate, and combine these elements into one. One mind, one body, and one soul make a matter of creation. When two people are married in matrimony, the two persons are no longer two, but they are voluntarily forced into one. Therefore, it is important for the couple to repetitively remind themselves of their unity and oneness with each other.

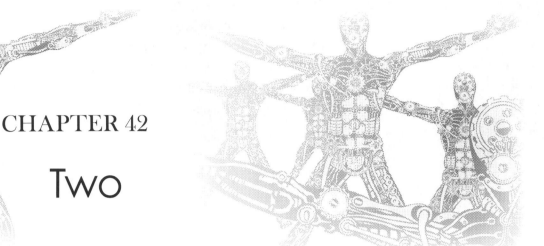

CHAPTER 42

Two

We form relationships out of cause-and-effect partnerships. Conflicts start from relationships, whether they are competitive or not. PepsiCo and Coca-Cola are two different corporations, but they formulate competitive advantages over each other in the search for innovative changes. Dual relationships are more than likely to have both differences and similarities among them. When conflict arises in relationships, they are statistically scrutinized for a solution without our even knowing it. The use of chi square charts, t-test evaluations, and standard deviations help us mathematically compromise on bettering a product or problem. Dualism thrives on opposites, with the push and pull of forces. There would be no peace without war and no war without peace. Love would not exist without fear, nor fear without love. For every good there is bad, and for every bad there is good. For every hater, there is a player, and so on. The power is to not distinguish the two but to merge them together in coexistence to make a neutral balance.

A charged battery has both negative and positive end points. Both the negative and positive charges work together to surge energy in mechanical or electrical devices. Our bodies are both positively and negatively charged as well, and it is the search for balance within the chakras that we can use our power. Yoga meditation helps us equally channel our negative and positive forces. Through channeling, we can transfer energy on matter and with other people. The positive sector includes the head to the navel, and the negative sector is in the sacrum through the lower limbs. Dualism is depicted like an hourglass with every sand particle being alike and different. Once the sand particles go through the middle of the hourglass, then it is neutral and passes from a positive position to a negative one that starts all over again in time when turned around.

When we get into arguments or disagreements with people, there are two sides. Both sides use facts, opinions, and truth to try to clarify their points of view. The point is that there is no right or wrong when debating since both viewpoints can be seen as righteous when none of us are righteous at all. We argue, fuss, and fight based upon the perceptions of our own egos. To form a resolution is to agree on the facts of a situation, obstacle, or perceived problem.

The only differences between a human and an animal is that a human has the knowledge and power to convert matter into any element—fire, water, air, and earth—for grounding. The true history and teachings of Christ are vaguely hidden from us throughout time. Christ and many other teachers presented to us the many great works that are done through the universal God-mind of our existence. Distributing fire from a piece of paper by using our energy source is very much possible. Chi martial arts explain to us about balance of energy that is used to make this happen, but still the information is quite hidden from Western culture. Making the connection of two elements seems to be the hidden agenda. Thus, the number 2 is a powerful number representing energy that cannot be drastically bent or broken. Implementing the number 2 in these frequent energies can give us a better understanding of how we can transfer visible energy. The most powerful chakra, located in the crown, is for "seeing" and manifesting the creative energy. The lower chakras are to stop or slow down the regeneration of an element, while the crown and heart chakras activate the start-up of energy. It is viable to get in your own zone without being easily distracted. Everyday meditation is the stepping stone to regulating the chakra balance. Internal power can always be transferred externally.

Martial arts have been gaining popularity in the United States ever since the early 1970s. In class, you start off with a white belt representing innocence, youth, novice, and purity, and later you can graduate with a black belt, which represents executive, ending, completion, and master. In order to get a black belt, you have to be better than those with the other belts when competing. Each belt has a symbol and style technique that corresponds to different Asian minor areas. The number 2 is taught in martial arts along with the concept that opposites attract and that the opposition cannot exist separately from one another. Chi is within the details; the big picture must be the one universal wholeness of the God, Christ, and the Holy Spirit.

CHAPTER 43

Three

Sweat, blood, and tears are on the Trinity cross. The concept of three as one causes much speculation since it does not agree with any law that is inclusive of separation. As such, there is dualism that distinguishes opposites, and furthermore, the Trinity is the mediator, the calm within the storm. Pushing and pulling between opposing obstacles is tumultuous, and going through the Trinity relieves that stress. Crucifixion sufferings are the stepping stones that fix us through the blood, tears, and sweat of the resurrection of a light body. Three into one involves God being himself, Jesus being us, and the Holy Spirit is neither.

It's easier for women to experience and dwell in the depths of the Trinity than men. Gender roles have limited men in their expression of genuine authentic feelings. Boys are scolded not to cry and to not show any signs of femininity at an early age. They are told that the color pink is for girls and that they should not play with certain toys that are for girls. Contrarily, females do not have to worry about being as restricted at an early age as far as material and emotions go. Therefore, it is easier for women to express and respond emotionally without feeling vulnerable to criticism. The expression of emotions also has a duality of feminine and masculine energy. Thus, a woman is able to balance these energies through trials, tribulations, and error. Let's face it—most women are taught how to become the perfect wives since they were little girls. Most have learned to cook, sew, and clean thoroughly, all while learning how to be well-kept women. Through faulty affairs with unexpressive males who perhaps lived in female-dominant households, they have taken up the responsibilities of mothering these adult males. The days of a women beholding men like their known fathers are long over. As mentioned before, women simply seek support from significant others, which is hard to do when a man is seeking a mother figure in a woman. Pursuance of men is at an all-time high because of the low number of good men with heartfelt intentions for the opposite sex. Women lose their special feminine qualities when they have to provide and support all the time, especially with the increase of single-parent households.

Now, the Trinity is a three-in-one energy, being that there is the godhead (seventh crown chakra), Christ (the body), and the Holy Spirit (which surrounds us). Realization of these three into one makes life much more clear. A woman who goes through the push and pull of the dual feminine and masculine energies really has no choice but to surrender into the place of the Trinity. She realizes that all of her male and female aspects give her gratitude. Rather than blaming people for wronging her, she realizes that she has wronged herself in the process by not putting her God-Lord mind first. She is in complete control of her essence being within her existence. This form of rapture is quite warriorlike and takes time to develop over a certain period. When that woman no longer allows the masculine energy from people to disturb her, she is at her best as a royal highness. She soon comes to realize that praying for a good man is as vague as praying for money. She knows that she has to rather pray for herself first and then for others to be predominant in the eye of the Trinity. There she finds complete companionship and support from up high.

Nonetheless, I feel that it is easier for a female to experience the Trinity than a male because a woman is free to express. We even catch heterosexual males trying too hard to be a female in correspondence to the way she flows; rather the feminine energy can be natural in her embodiment of both female and male ambiance. She can wear men's clothing and still be natural with the woman within. I have noticed that it is much easier for women to express themselves more readily and to later overcome the confusion of entanglements of both masculine and feminine energies with stability. Most males who are gay have felt feminine their entire lives, while bisexuals and closet males are gay just because it feels good to them to be expressive with another male. A man is much more likely to be ridiculed, bullied, and punished for being homosexual, while it is more acceptable for women to be lesbians in our society. Women often become lesbians due to feelings of being hurt by the opposite sex.

If you look at the number 3, you will see how big of a whole number it is. Furthermore, 3 represents greediness and humor. It is shaped like a pitchfork, which makes two incomplete circles; and if male and female are dualistic, then hermaphrodites and transsexuals include both the male and female parts that portrayed as freakish. Two incomplete orifices make the number 3. The phrase "Two is company and three is a crowd" holds true considering the functions of three. Nevertheless, a transsexual will freely broadcast feminine external qualities to partners, while internally being both masculine and feminine. But with alteration to one's physical anatomy, there is a question of confidence in the one that created them. Making alterations to one's sex organs, to me, is saying, "I am not comfortable with the body God has given me." Surgical tummy tucks and lifts are quite acceptable for women or men, especially after childbirth. Excess fat around the torso can become a health concern and lead to back problems. The pull of fat around the waist can cause problems with the spine and back. But a change to the sex organ is quite different because it confuses the lower chakra Trinity circuit.

Clearing, cleansing, and clarifying the mind, body, and heart of the dual polarization of negativity is one of the basic steps to driving and channeling the Trinity. The Trinity is three in one, meaning that we must compound our dualities into a trifecta, realizing that there is only one common feeling between all three (God, Christ, and the Holy Spirit). After one catches the Holy Spirit within, then he or she is receptive to the Trinity that combines dualistic feelings into one true feeling. In between a positive and negative is the center point, which is neutral. Balancing these forces and merging them into one feeling is the active Holy Ghost, that will be seen from the beholder, who is you.

CHAPTER 44

The Golden Rule

We all play a game with ourselves and with everyone else about following the golden rule, which says that we should treat others the way we want them to treat us. When we are emotionally imbalanced, then according to the law of attraction, we will be drawn to people who will help us heal our emotions through likeness to other imbalanced emotional specimens. The same goes for feeling angry. We can hide behind smiles and acts of kindness, but we are only fooling ourselves if we do not have complete wholeness. A lot of depressed individuals are seen as happy on the exterior, but inside they are miserable. It does not matter what masquerade we project to one another if we cannot love ourselves fully and completely. One form of not loving ourselves is being dependent on other people or substances to make us feel happiness when we are required to make our own happy trails. Whoever is golden knows the rule. God is as ancient as the sun. Old souls who are far wiser than their years understand this. When I go outside, I know that I am never alone, and the rays from the sun remind me of this. The sun shines brighter on me when I recognize that I am to follow my own rule book, which is golden. I am the only one who knows what, who, and how to make myself happy, and it is up to me to fulfill my own happiness while not listening to naysayers and unsupportive ideas.

Now, treating others the way you want to be treated is tricky and a test every day. We do need people for companionship and support on this earth. Throughout life, it is up to us to distinguish the family and friends we want to be in our lives. If we do not like certain people's conductive behavior, then we can simply disassociate from them. But if we have to feel financially or emotionally dependent on people who exhibit unruly behavior, then we are in trouble and will be disappointed in them and in ourselves.

In love relationships, we have the chance to amplify unity onto the world. I saw a video on social media presenting Koko, a gorilla who can speak to humans. Koko uses sign language to issue a warning to humans to protect the earth because she is in trouble. Even Koko knows that her being a gorilla is no different from her being nature and part of it by warning the atrocities of global warming and ruptured earth surfaces. She knows that Mother Nature watches over us and is perhaps tormented by the mistreatment she has received over the years. Koko senses that the destruction of the earth means an end to all and needs humans to treat her fertile lands with respect. The earth is killed, assaulted, harassed, abused, and kept in danger every single microsecond. Violation of her grounds through fracking and cracking into the soil makes her infertile. Recycling keeps her free of trashiness and famine. Yet, contrarily, the grave within her makes her rich because there are untold histories in the caskets of the ground. Nothing goes unseen, and all things do come to an end to begin. Natural disasters have increased in severity throughout the years and are predicted to only get worse in the years to come if we do not protect nature by nurturing her. The many diseases, illnesses, and disorders with which people are diagnosed are no surprise considering the agitation of the earth's production in natural disasters. Tornadoes, hurricanes, earthquakes, tsunamis, volcanic eruptions, fires started by wind, mud holes, and other disasters are unstoppable, just like human ailments. The pharmaceutical industry has been at the forefront in alleviating pain and illness temporarily. The study of medical cannabis has proven it to cure certain ailments, especially seizures, and yet it is illegal in certain states because of our corporations. Pharmaceutical drugs are another hazardous waste in our environment due to their being dumped in sewers and the water streams; they are so unnatural that they contaminate the human body and streams of water that we are so dependent on.

CHAPTER 45

Imagine

Imaginative thoughts can hurt people. It's not really what you say that can bring harm to another; it what you think. Conflicting and confusing messages can lead to heartbreak since we are all connected. Fiery, emotional thoughts toward others affect the vibrational frequencies in the pathological patterns of the brain. Thoughts that are processed repetitively and habitually are felt through all of us due to the symbiotic connections we have with revelations, mostly from the heart chakra. Whenever you think of someone or something constantly, you are drawing it or that person more toward you if it is heartfelt. This is why it is important to have an open heart chakra, so that we can be open to all possibilities in the world. Telekinesis is used among all of us because we are interconnected through our six senses. The point of letting go is felt from the receiver to the donor of silent communication. Playing the imagination game is inclusive and confusing because we are told that the more we think, the more we manifest; on the contrary, we are reminded to let go of outdated people, places, and things in order to be rewarded with the newness of better places, people, and things. It is all a sequence of balance and knowing how to engineer the self without trying to materially possess those things. Engineering the self has no use for thinking that the same temporary people, places, and things will make us happy or peaceful in any form or fashion because we are all unsatisfied beings in a world full of abundance.

The four seasons are equal to the four big seas, better known as oceans—the Atlantic, Pacific, Indian, and Arctic—with their different coastal climates. All seasons are expressions in the sky. Seas are underground. Just imagine a time when the seas will become the seasons and be above us, where the sky used to be. "As above, so below." If fiction is a glimpse of reality seen through an author or another creator in the form of a human, what if all the thoughts in our heads are being created in a later time distance? This is surely a magical feat, for imagination is the mind engineering magic through creativity.

Math is very intriguing to me and one of the subjects I most liked to study. Nevertheless, geometry was the most confusing and boring of math disciplines to my recollection because it required imagination to get to answers and is less logical. Precision of lines, shapes, and congruency led me to an attention deficit. Perhaps a fast-talking, impatient high school geometry teacher is to blame for making me displeased with the subject. She was so confusing, not just to me but to a whole lot of other students as well. As I got older, I gained more of an appreciation for geometric shapes and even recalled loving to play with a Spirograph drawing set in my elementary years. It was exciting to watch the repetitive drawing of spiral shapes in different colors with a steady protractor, as if the pupil of the eye was mimicking the spiral lines in the iris.

By remembering the analogies and in correspondence among different words, we can let our imaginations run free. For example, imagine *trees* covering the *street* and how they might have gotten there, perhaps by being uprooted due to a natural disaster or distant winds from across the ocean. The numerous reasons they could they appear that way are natural disasters, alien activity, tree cutters, and rapid-working ant and termite colonies that ate at the roots. When the sun turns off, will the seas turn on? Will cars leave scars? Do people believe more in leaves and trust in trees (money)? What does the eye truly see? Magazines, television, radio, books, and any other social press help us to imagine what we want to be surrounded with and who or what we want to become. They form an image of the self just because we can see the big picture on a shelf that is within grasp for ourselves.

Writing out our goals and affirmations gives us a scene of accomplishment. Once an affirmation or goal is written or acted upon, it becomes real. We always hear about creepy movies that turn out to "coincidentally" haunt actors who acted and played on the set, such as *Poltergeist*. I feel that anything that is imagined will become real, whether it's literature, movie sets, music, or art. A repetition of ideas is all there is from all of us, and all things that come to mind have already happened before once upon a time—or maybe twice. A photograph that speaks a thousand words captures an image of innocence and vanity at the same time. Playing God is being vain and thinking that every single thing is relevant to the self. For instance, on social media websites, some of us have probably thought another person's post was about us at some point, but really we are all in synchronization with one another. Yes, being vain is being God, but we cannot foolishly let the thoughts of others ruin the graceful essence of God within the self, for it will become quite a devilish act.

Thus, the image of the black man has been passed down for many years, even since medieval times, as one of an inferior individual. At the beginning of cultivation, there were kings of high royalty who were black, and if we know how the infinity sign works, we know that the black image will come around once again in likeness to the very start of human creation. Its polar opposite, the color white, is within the middle, and if intermingled with black, it will gradually transfer its whiteness into blackness. Also, women will be recognized as equal or superior to men, knowing that X comes before Y. Therefore, X chromosomes were created before Y chromosomes, and we received everything from females, women, ova, and Mother Earth. This resembles that joke about which came first, the chicken or the egg. The egg had to hatch into a chicken, but a chicken had to lay the egg. I would have to go with the egg being first, formed from concentrated energies of earlier chicken species.

Your photo box, which depicts all the factors in your life that has shaped you internally and externally consists of all your senses: sight, audio, smell, touch, taste, and feeling. We perceive information through all of these senses to paint a picture for us to judge and counteract our behavior within the environment. The reason people are so in touch with selfies is that they cover all flaws. You can see what's on the outside but would have to pierce deeper to see the inside. One's true self is the pine of the imagination of what one thinks about him or herself and what the self's perception of truth is.

Time travel is very much a reality, especially according to Einstein's theory of relativity. Gravity is the foundation of being in two places at one time or transporting to another dimension. My synopsis suggests that time travel can be accomplished when the energy surrounding us moves at a vast speed while we are seen in steady motion. Picture the major arcana world card, with a person in the center of a circle that is constantly in motion while the individual is floating within the wreath of the circumference of the world. This aspect is also experienced when the body is at rest in rapid eye movement (REM) suspension. While the body lay still at night or during a nap, the thoughts run rapidly, using synaptic neurotransmitters to transport the vehicular body to different future realms of existence. Numerous movies have shown us time travel techniques, through hub wheels from NASA equipment of centripetal force. These are the imaginative creative minds that let us perceive an image at work that turns out to be a replica of authentic reality.

CHAPTER 46

Believe

In order to believe, we have to live a lie. Believing in a lie is part of life. If we were to dissect the word *believe* into parts, it will look like this: *be-lie-eve*, with the extra *e* in the middle because the *e* is stretched. Furthermore, the story of Eve is a lie. We can also see that the word can form many others, such as *be-lief, be-lie, be-led,* and *be-leaf.* Going back to the biblical history that we Americans and Christians are so fond of and familiar with, we know that Eve was led to believe a lie told by the serpent and that, in current modern-day standards, people believe in leaves (money) over spirituality. Thus, the essence of being is believing, and it is up to us individually to wake up to the truths of living beyond just being or existing. To fulfill our longevity, we have to leap. In synchronicity, it is intriguing that the Summer Olympics occurs every leap year, which is every four years. That one extra day gives to us another chance to leap into another level of higher being.

Listening to the great stories of religion, mythology, and theology leaves us with aspirations of motivation. Stories have been passed down through the ages with some plagiarism from ancient astrology. All great teachers and figureheads correspond with one another and are replicas from Egyptian ancestry. We are currently in the age of Pisces, where we are leading to "believe." The next age is due to begin in AD 2150, the age of Aquarius, and by then everyone will know without a doubt what is true. So right now we are just bumbling around, trying to figure out the conspiracies and meanings of true religious propaganda and not knowing what is to come. I was once told that you are saved no matter what as long as you believe in a higher entity; and whatever you believe in is your true destination. Thus, like the mutable sign Pisces, we come to be indecisive in our beliefs. We worship someone or something but contradict that belief in glorifying tree leaves (paper money). Others have the upper hand in knowing how to save a dowry to complete their goals in life in terms of presenting the works of God to the openness of the world. The stories that have been passed down through books are just a manufacture of being. It is to "be" that leads us back into the knowing, but it is up to the God-mind to distinguish junk information from true information.

Nevertheless, it does not matter who or what we believe in because the magic lies in the essence of just being. But there comes a time when we must leap into the true knowing of the self before we know God. It is as if the mutable zodiac sign Pisces (two fish) has to revert back into the water (fish bowl), which is carried by Aquarius, in order to revive and survive. We have to believe first so that we can establish the knowing. Getting to knowledge can be like untangling a knotted rope. The mind will distinguish what information is acceptably true or factual to get to the knowledge. Everything we know lives inside of us, and thinking counterclockwise, like going back in history or time, is one way to think anew. Innovative ideas come from a perception of dreams and beliefs. The saying "Fake it until you make it" comes true through belief.

According to our beliefs, we all make mistakes and are only human. Admitting to not knowing everything shows how human we are. Everyone is forgetful, and the sign of Pisces rules the art of forgetfulness that can make it easy to move on to other aspects in our lives. When we are napping, resting, or "sleeping," it is easy to forget a dream when we awake from that trance like a fish. The most real dreams are remembered. The reason is that it so easy to catch a fish because their brains forget so easily. When a person undergoes and experiences kundalini or is more in tune with remembering dreams, they are proceeding into being dream catchers. Now, cats are quite the opposite of fish when it comes to remembering, and they seem to share a close relationship judging from animated films and commercials. The reason cats are seen as magical or mystical creatures is that they do not tend to forget easily. Their memories are like that of an elephant. Contrarily, they still form the same habits as fish and humans, and we can observe this when they play with yarn or jump into a cat tree repetitively. Their eyes are deep set, and they are untrustworthy of their surroundings, always keeping an eye on the environment. They are quite sneaky when they scratch people because they can feel the energy vibrations and get frustrated when they are not being petted. The cat believes in nothing, but the fish believes in everything. It goes with the Chinese proverb "Give a man a fish and he can eat for a day. Teach a man to fish and he can eat for a lifetime." The teaching focuses on believing that the fish will be caught, and that goes for every learned and unlearned lesson. Visualization of believing and then knowing in the mind is the mystical part of obtaining. Be like both the cat and the fish; knowing but not knowing is a balancing act. Drink water like a fish, knowing that we can drink milk like a cat. You can survive longer by drinking water than by just eating fish. Sometimes it can be hard to forget, though, especially when feelings of hurt or wrongdoing are present. How easy it is for takers to forget and to always have their hands out while the givers suffer silently. A giver expects nothing in return, but takers calculate, critique, and analyze. Takers always believe that people owe them something, and they tend to sulk in victimhood. Givers believe that no one owes them anything even though they are caring and understanding.

I can remember when I was about eleven or twelve going to a fish pond and catching one, two, three, and four, until there were about twenty fish on a rope line. Fish are so giving that they unknowingly give up their lives so that others will be fed. It is easy to catch a fish, but to give one away and return it to the water is the spirit. We can relate this to giving up relationships with other human beings, jobs, or anything that does not work for us, knowing and believing that we can get something better under the power of belief. Now that is being and living life, being and believing in life.

Certain religious groups have a huge misconception about astrology. They claim that astrology is rooted in witchcraft and evil. Contrarily, astrology is just another science that involves planetary predictions. Nevertheless, many astrologers do not believe in astrology. They wisely realize that astrology is just a small portion of predictable science. It is the belief in a creator and creations that is of utmost importance, as well as believing in what we call dreams that are sent through us from a higher intelligence. Astrology is limited, but you can always have big dreams—and that is the start of believing. Believing in something even when there is nothing to see in what we believe are the times when we have to believe in a lie; a lie that can be read in books, spoken from individual truths just so that we can interpret our roots.

CHAPTER 47

Conquer

To conquer is to have self-control. All conquests have in common the strategy of manipulation. A conqueror sits well like an emperor, unbothered by the miniscule obstacles that surround him. Many do not like the confrontational conference of small talk; thus, they are great listeners who send orderly messages to their followers. Their hearts are more than likely cold, with the head ruling major and minor decisions, but they also feel deeply for everyone. Full of stability and cleanliness is the demeanor of the conqueror who plays a game with himself in contemplation of a great loss through keen victory. When wronged, the conqueror is obsessive with vengeance of both the spiritual worlds and the world that lives within his or her heart. Conquerors are forward thinking and will easily fall into resentment if somebody or something holds up progression because they know that without upward mobility comes a fine line of manic depression. They are very fiery in their approach to life because they are the doers who take action for achievement even when standing or sitting still.

Now, the biggest conquest that I have not yet overcome is anxiety (anger), which leads to depression, and there is no "magic" hocus-pocus pill to help or extinguish it. They only leave jitters and sometimes lead to suicidal thoughts. I was always a neutral person until an incident when I went to a hairstylist who colored my hair. I had been referred to her because my usual stylist had left the salon for the day. So I got stuck with a novice. I wanted my hair to have streaks of frosted blonde and strawberry red. The former stylist had to color my hair two to three times, and my hair came out looking like a starburst explosion, which was very cute. I had received a lot of compliments about it. When I went to the new stylist, I brought a relaxer for her to put on my hair. Beforehand, I had asked her if it was okay to use it on my hair, and she responded, "Yes." Lo and behold, my hair started falling out and continued to fall out as she was washing it. My guess is that she did not put any neutralizing shampoo on my hair. My initial thoughts when I realized what was happening were, *Oh, no. My hair was finally growing back, but I took the risk of trusting a professional and now I'm at a loss.* After the hair stylist apologized, I quickly went home to examine the damage. I tried to convince myself that it was not that bad, plus my boyfriend tried to reassure me that my hair looked fine. When I combed my hair, handfuls of hair came out in the comb. I went to bed but woke up feeling depressed just from the loss of my hair and putting my trust in someone I thought was a professional. That night, I broke down crying hysterically in the arms of my boyfriend. It was so bad that I was crying for my mother. He called my mom, and I became calmer once she arrived, but later they took me to the hospital for a nervous breakdown or anxiety attack. I got a shot in my butt and an excuse to stay home from work for short-term disability. It was really that bad. I was out on a short-term disability from my job due to depression for about three months. I received a twelve-thousand dollar settlement from the insurance company due to the stylist's negligence. I also had a cute, short haircut from the ordeal. Even though I got over the horrific ordeal fairly quickly, the thoughts, feelings, and emotions stuck to me. Growing my hair back was not a problem, but I cut it myself for years because my trust had been replaced with feelings of loss and resentment. Each time trust is involved in a little or big incident, I sulk and sink into those same emotions from when I lost my hair. It definitely took something from me that I can't get back, and even though I received compensation in settlement money and a cute hairstyle, my feelings of being made a wreck by someone's mistake are always with me. Those feelings disallow me from even trusting myself to make the right choices in choosing people to do a satisfactory service for me. The same goes for personal relationships as well. At an early age, I learned to not trust people due to gossip, lies that were told to me, and cheating that was hidden from me. I have come to realize that the things I judge are what I attract.

When I think of the word *conquer*, kings and queens come to mind. Many of the past African kings and queens who ruled the distant motherland and were concubines were a commodity. Our African ancestors were a people of power who did not take too much shit from anybody. The powers that be, which overhauled the banking systems of early operations, enticed these kings and queens with large amounts of paper money to ship off the people they ruled into slavery. I can only imagine that these early slaves were the outcasts of different tribal ancestry in Africa or were despised for their strengths. They were the ones who nobody wanted because of intimidation, jealousy, rebelliousness, hate, and all those fearful emotions of being afraid of one's reign being overtaken. To this day, we witness such behavior in the African American community, if there is such a place in the United States. The astounding memories of unnatural emotions must still rule the minds of these descended Africans who label themselves as "niggas" and "blacks." Through the eyes of many, my skin is a hue of yellow and red, and I can mistakenly be taken as a person with Latin or Asian origin. But once again, we are all descendants of Africa, and I can be more proud than most for that. In our history books, we start with the Spanish conquistadors and Elizabethan era when explaining exploration and settling. Queen Elizabeth dealt with the act of conquering, not only for her people but also with the men in her studies, the lords and dukes who were beneath her feet in treachery.

However, we were never taught in school about the many kings and queens in Africa, a lost history that is hidden and plagiarized through the history books. If we look at Egyptian statues, we see that the Roman and Greek statues are just copied from ancient African figures. Religions copies from African beliefs have been observed by Native Americans, Anglo-Saxons, Europeans, Asians, and even African Americans. The constant going to church, though, is not an African tradition. When Jesus Christ spoke to the public, it was outside under the sun. Feasts were held in sanctuary buildings where private conversations were conducted among trustworthy men. I speak of trustworthy *men* because, through my own experience, it is hard to trust women as they are often gossipers. Quite ordinary folks, gossipers are found all over the place in work, church, and other places. As a youngster, I discovered that the church is the number-one place to see a gathering of people who give compliments to one another just to later gossip about the lives people live. A church is a sanctuary for ill doings and where devilish acts love to thrive within vulnerable churchgoers. A lot of people who are concerned with gossip have health issues, such as high blood pressure and cholesterol problems due to a lack of exercise, poor diet, and meddling in other people's business. They are too concerned about the business and personal lives of their acquaintances. Being silent in this traffic of despair is just not good enough these days, for it is a time to be railroaded by individuals at a crossroads of observation. Quietness in the face of the people who gossip about you is power, but it does not make much of a difference if you voice your opinion to these lower minds anyway. It is best to establish a distance between you and them, and then you can begin to conquer your feelings of being treated doggedly by opinionated gossipers who constantly contradict themselves. Conquering the soul means staying free of negative energies that are here to put us down just like the naysayers, but through it all, in due time, you will gain an extra space of energy out of the reverence of not dealing with them at all. Images of gods, goddesses, kings, and queens have a lot of places here on earth with worship. That is why they are the slaves and servants for money, jewels, and luxuries, but a person who is a slave to the doings and teachings of the Lord, Father, Mother, God, Goddess holds a higher place in the kingdom of heaven that reigns here on planet Earth.

So the moral of the story is to make it a fun game to play with these humanly earthlings who are our catalyzers to domination. This is jokingly true, but if we could not hear the naysayers speak, then we would not be able to listen to ourselves. We have to deal with the talk from individuals just to get us on the path to where we truly need to be. This is the warriors' dance of revelation upon anxiety by a human who is not satisfied with just being, including me.

CHAPTER 48

Faith

Every aspect of our lives is already planned out. All things, places, and people that we connect with are placed in our life for a reason. They teach and guide us till we come to the great understanding of faith that follows us never-endingly. During the time that our lives are in respiration, we are inspired by these places, things, and people, which allows us to acquire beyond the limits of knowledge and awareness. It is through action that we can experience accepting all people, places, and things in every aspect in life. True faith is practicing a continuance of unconditional love by focusing on the following aspects:

1) Trinity (God + Krishna + you).
2) Meditate daily even without knowing.
3) Treat one another with good intentions.
4) Realize that any problem or issue you have with somebody, you also have with yourself.
5) Know that everything happens for a reason to motivate us to greater heights of opportunity.
6) Connect with the universe from your personality egotism socially in order to share with others your wakeful status.
7) Keep negativity as a way to balance and optimize positivity inclination, which amplifies our wanting to balance more toward independent goals, circling back to the One, or rather turning 180 degrees as a mirror effect.
8) Believe that life and death are just a single part of existence and that we are all a slave to time, whether we are punctual or not. We are all confined to time to live the way we want to live.
9) All bad perceptions bring out the good in us and reprogram our brains to make better choices and decisions.
10) Have patience and appreciate your journey of growing up or growing down to lead you into fruitful miniature divine interludes of being image creators.
11) Communication is the best way to speed up the process, by speaking tongues beyond the air, whether inside, outside, or broadcasting.

12) Care for the self, body, soul, and spirit. Protect those who protect you from harm in environmental predicaments. Those who are more in tune with their feelings are the people we want to see because they make us believe even if there is nothing to believe in.

The thirteen sacred religions all have one principle in common—that is, treat others the way you want to be treated with good intentions. The saying "The road to hell is paved with good intentions" holds true for individuals who do their very best to abide by the laws of the land and to sacredly sacrifice their freedom for good doings to others who live on this earth. Reasonably speaking, good intentions are only a sacramental phase that we must go through to understand our differences in habitual communication. For instance, when we experience or encounter new love there will more than likely be one person who will love to commit him- or herself fully to one partner. That one person pondered a monogamous reunion planned in his or her thoughts with aspirations of fair courtships during their outings together and in spirit. The other partner that holds back with more cautious thinking would rather take the partnership at a slow pace just to see where it will lead or to determine whether there are better options. In this duel, it could possibly be argued that both parties have good intentions for each other. Nevertheless, when sex is involved, feelings get involved as well, which can make the more feminine counterpart feel at a distance or at a standstill with only a platonic relationship. The progressive type is much more in her brain with thoughts of marriage, procreation, and unconditional love. The other partner may have thoughts of the same but remain rather inexpressive about them, which only leads to a game of thrones between two people who are operating on 50 percent holiness, when there could be a balance of two people operating on 100 percent wholeness if they perceived each other the same way.

In the intermediate phase of this game, there is faith and hope—faith that the partnership will last as long as both people remain balanced. Having faith in the love between the two is just a journey in the amplification of faith and the expression of the way we want to be loved by earthlings. It only becomes bad when one or both parties feel betrayed. The one with the best intentions will subsequently get reverence in the thoughts that they mechanically produce in their brain waves that vibrate to the universe. Usually, the one who is conscious of the laws of the land and has the awareness of unconditional love will be paid the attention that he or she deserves and that he or she was not given by humans. The universe is always watching us, and we always have the perception of the universe through other people, which fosters the shaping of our perceptions. We must always remember that if people like to play games with people of good intentions, then they will just get those games played back to them. Contrarily, we all play games with one another, and the seriousness is depicted by how hard we play them. Climactic thoughts reach a peak of accepting the notion of not forcing anything on one person, and that is where the magic of karma begins—when there is true acceptance of another person's ways, even if they are perceived or thought of as bad. During this alliance forms a union to strive to do better and to be at best through a perception of loss. When a game is lost and players no longer want to continue the shenanigans that make them feel like losers, then revenge is accounted for by people taking back their power from the union and operating back to the self. Then they are able to gain open energy from other areas in their lives, all due to the idea of losing. When a perfect love turns into a union of bondage instead of an equal balance, that is when the universal God steps in to intervene to set things right. An expression of love is limited when there is no progression. So through planned malfunctions, there are winners who can replace drained energy with a refreshment of energy. The energy between the two synergies must be set free through any circumstance in order to renew the expression of self-love that fosters unconditional love. People who love themselves fully are capable of loving at all capacities.

It is important to keep in mind that it is against moral law to have sex with a woman without supporting her. A partner must support a woman's dreams, finances, brain, anatomy, education, and all the assets in her life if she is capable and knows how to love unconditionally. If not, then the commotion will just be like children playing house without any real meaning to life companions. These divine women have to be supported because they are the creators on the planet, and they must be placed higher than any other female counterparts. It is against the law to play with a woman with good intentions for a union that is mutual in giving and receiving equally through her resources. There is no need for adults to hide feelings when it is in our favor to be more expressive and reveal true feelings. Contrarily, the underlying process is the perception of the self. In actuality, the self loves to play games when it comes to perception—so much game playing, in fact, that the individual is in love with being a loner and thus is constructively wound up with other individuals who enjoy their own alone time as well. This is the image effect, where we attract the people in our lives who may seem different or totally opposite from us but realistically are just like us in that they are aliens and foreign to communicating presently.

As humans, we tend to either dwell on the past or think highly about or doubt the future. It is very important for us to have faith in and stay in the present in all circumstances. Staying in the present allows us to share our godly gifts with one another without doubting the future and getting lost back in the past. We can see many simple examples of how we beings love to ponder the past, just by taking photos. Past dwelling is just another emotion that can be the cause of depression. Futurists love to know what is coming next and tend to get caught up in innovations that lead to anxiety. Think of the many inventors who stayed up trying to cure a problem and make things anew through subsequent processing. All the troubles of the mind can and will be alleviated by focusing on the present, which brings out our gifts through spiritual meditation and constant focus on the universal Lord God essence of presence.

CHAPTER 49

Freedom

Freedom is a destination at which we all want to arrive. Being free of negative thoughts lifts the curtain to our progressive order. Eliminating negative thoughts means that we have to terminate any emotionality factors in our lives that do not fit, whether they be the people we associate with, the places we go, or the things we do. Constant, habitual behavior can obscure the freedom that was given to us before our light years. The past is always a learning experience, and we are ever perfecting our beings in getting better because we know better. At times, we are stubborn about repeating the same mistakes even when we know that there is a setback in our future. Affairs of today will lead us into the currents of tomorrow, and without change there is no future but rather a slow death due to no growth.

One significant way that people will free themselves from bondage is through new love. When an old love has run its course and the games can no longer be played, the taste of new love is to be replaced. It is of a higher level of true love where people can honestly be freed from the emotional turmoil of feeling they are being taken for granted. The essence of a better beloved is the exact replica of the soul and ego that one shares with another body. It can literally take a nanosecond to find an unconditional love waiting for you. Expression of speech releases a gifted present that we have not known before without communication. When the beloved is taken for granted and love is not reciprocated, an understanding of a higher feeling of acceptance from someone who is listening, waiting, and contemplating or performing a bright future with you is right under your nose. In the distant past, you may not have seen them in this light if you are current friends; the thought may have snuck up on you with the silence of a serpent. And that is what love displays: a sense of freedom and hope that love will play again after its impatience of reciprocity.

Perceptions of masculinity are quite obscured these days. In a world filled with perversion and a constant distinct loss of innocence in childhoods, the masculine energy has been portrayed as brute, immoral, and downright weak. The constraints of this energy leave human beings in bondage of favoring men, making the feminine energy constantly try to refigure its position on the homeland of planet Earth. The opposition of Mars-Venus will always be an ongoing battle between misconceptions of control and submissiveness, giving and receiving. This equation all boils down to comfort, ability, and a complete merging of two bodies into one state of mind. This game is rather cat and mouse, hide and seek, chase and run among beings with concrete feelings. Humans are on the upper level of the food chain in the animal kingdom simply because they have the freedom to switch masculine and feminine energies on or off to create a free union of the God power upon exchanging dualities. Striking this balance between humans is giving love without conditions. Feelings have to be mutual between the two in order to optimize to the One, which gives off a heightened energy to the world along with the universe that frees us to bond readily.

We are all too familiar with the concept of all of us being born slaves. Within all of our experiences is where we find the solution to be freed from disturbances, ignorance, and bondage. It is primitive to gain the knowledge of freedom through dramatic experiences that are captivated into slavery and will not make it out in time due to fear, rejection, or even success. We are truly our own worst enemies, and no one can take away our dignity of being our true selves. The Constitution constructed our freedoms to living lives of self-actualization. The Revolutionary War allowed a fight for freedom that ensured the people would be recognized as adults with genuine feelings of being law-abiding citizens under a fair and just Constitution. The right to safety and protection along with a nonoppressive life is freedom. Loving what you do is freedom. Freedom and independence coincide with each other because in order to be free, people must establish independence for unity. Independence for one individual is freedom for a lot of people who are interconnected. A person can find freedom within the solitude of not being bothered with restrictions. For example, when a person is single, he or she does not have to answer to a spouse or significant other. There is no collaboration of force. My social status is married. I admire marriage and people who are married, even though I am only married to myself and nobody else. I married myself on Independence Day, and the freedom I feel is of not being as accountable for another person's wrongdoings or feelings. The sweet sight of freedom is dependability on the self, and any disturbance can disrupt freedom. In some cases, the only way to get people to respect that freedom is through consequence.

CHAPTER 50

Equality

It makes perfect sense that women came before men in the animal kingdom. As mentioned before, X comes before Y in the alphabet. This is a new way of thinking and a compilation of questioning the whole Adam and Eve theory that Christians listened so closely to in church sermons and in the nonancient book of the Bible. The Bible is reminiscent of a bubble with restrictions but no explanations of behavior. Presently, we have to pay attention to the femininity of the earth and her disruptions. Modern science teaches us that men were once women genetically and that the XY chromosome is a mutation due to evolution. Therefore, it is not surprising to witness all the natural disasters occurring due to the discrediting of the female gender. A woman literally has to bow down to the patriarchal stance of lower wages, abuse of women, and docile roles in all aspects of what she does. We still live in a time where women are expected to be followers of males due to their inferior status. Most women are the caretakers of this earth and belong to their dear beloveds who place them on the pedestal of improvement in knowing their worth. The unbalancing scenario between femininity and gender roles creates a backward inertia of clogged-up energy on earth. With X before Y, it is to be understood that the continuing discredit will only make the grounds on earth unstable due to the inequality of rights to women. This is not to say that there are not actual men and boys who respect women 100 percent, but they are few and far between these days. Even though I have more male friends than female friends, I am always in tune with females' being misunderstood because I'm one myself. I do get them and everything they try to accomplish for all the right and wrong reasons. Life may look easy for them, but it is daunting when they are set back due to unequal circumstances. It is not shocking to realize that males are just females since they did come from female ova and sex genitalia development takes place two weeks after conception. The woman is always the chooser, and that is why the game is set up for her to play and win however she wants, with gainful experience along the way. The unrealization of the X chromosome being the primary primer of cell replication is just a falsehood that is blinding. The whole story about Adam giving Eve a rib is nonsense based upon the continuing unconditional love that comes so easily to a woman. Nonetheless, the extra weight of fat that women carry explains a woman giving her rib to a man or realistically a man coming out of a female. It also explains the reason that men are more muscular than women based on the simple fact of the slender Y chromosome in reception of the X chromosome from the female. A female can produce eggs and continue to replicate life with just bits of sperm to the ovum, which she can carry, unlike males. They don't have the genes or the fat to create life without the XX generator. Having two X's is dominant, and the Y allele is recessive since it can only be passed down to males. This will explain how most women are just carriers of traits, mutations, and diseases.

Now, since there are fewer women in the high-wage professional arena, the image of a female has become more sexualized in the entertainment business. There are more and more women selling sex with clothes on. We can partially blame advertisements that show women nude. Sex brings in money, and women are the capital of it all. From sports to careers and average jobs, women are always seen as sex objects and will often receive more rewards by flirting with the opposite sex. Equanimity of the sexes is self-explanatory when we look at the XX and XY chromosomes. This topic of choice is not a rule of domination or superiority, but it's clear and safe to announce that all males are predominantly females. By observing the X chromosomes, we can see that the X splits like that of a star and female genitalia. Looking at the Y chromosome, we can see a line going halfway down the bottom section, like a tree branch in the male genitalia. X chromosomes are in all sexes; no human fetus can live without the mitochondrial X chromosome. Thus, initially, boys are girls, and it is an evolved mutation that turns the female genitalia into male genitalia. This explains why men have breasts, and if we were to exclude the penis and vagina, then all of us would look like Barbie dolls of both sexes. All genitalia are first female, and it is later in the priming process that the second X chromosome or first Y chromosome develops. The XY chromosome mutation is quite unique, being that a growth spurt forms a clitoris into an oversized clitoris, which is a penis, when the change of Y is added to the chromosome combination. This would also explain why more girls are born than boys. Even though there is a 50 percent chance of conceiving a boy or a girl, the first chromosome is preserved into the next chromosome until the other X or Y chromosome comes along to fertilize. X chromosomes are fatter and live longer in the ovum, which makes it easier to have girls than boys. X chromosome carriers in sperm can live up to five or seven days versus the Y chromosome carriers in sperm, which live up to three or five days, creating a lesser chance for a couple to conceive a boy. Women carry two X chromosomes, while men carry an X chromosome alongside a Y chromosome. If we do a pedigree, we will see that there is only a quartile of a chance to conceive a boy, compared to the 3/4 quartile chance for the conception of a girl. Nonetheless, the male Y chromosomal sperm are faster than female X chromosomal sperm, but it is precedent to acknowledge that some female sperm may be able to swim faster than most male sperm. Therefore, the XY chromosome is at a scarcity during conception and in life throughout mortality. More men and boys pass away before women and girls in a lifetime, or at least that is what I have been told all throughout biological history. Women are unique in their own because they are the only ones who can carry zygotes, embryos, and fetuses. With this all in mind, we are all equal based upon the consistent X chromosome that starts and initiates life.

All men were once little females, and the only explanation that I can get for the evolved mutation of X chromosome to Y chromosome is the pleasure factor of the exchange of energy upon sexual encounters that amplifies the infrequent vibrations of lovemaking. This infrequency increases the high energies of the world. The sex of male and female frequents the energies into portals of the same whirlpool and rotation of earth and its surrounding planets. Like a lock and key, the female and male sexes bring life into this world, which is of likeness to a creator. And even though a woman may be barren, modern technology can be of assistance in creating life.

The almighty creator of higher intelligence stirs our ambitions into an equality of creativity. We are all godly creatures with our own unique gifts that are equal to God's power. Money is one of the motivators in this day and age for us to relinquish our powers to one another and within ourselves, but more importantly it is the power of God within us that is hidden and waiting to be shared. All of us are born with creativity, and it is the concept of being free to accept and apply our known nature of gift giving. Whether it is through being a singer, actress, writer, scientist, athlete, or other any occupation that we can continually succeed in throughout the test of time, our gift sharing is demonstrated. Demonstrations derived from deep inner feelings, crises, obstacles, situations, or just everyday living are freed from us when we openly express ourselves and demonstrate our frustrations, humiliations, castrations, situations, observations, and so on. For if we express it, then we can test it, and so can others with whom we share our wonderful energy. It's rather a question of, *Would we rather slave for ourselves in the form of a godly image, or will we slave for somebody else without much expression of frequent energies, which leaves us contained in an occupation?* It really does not matter how much money we make somewhere; it is a matter of how freely we can express ourselves at that occupation that leaves us alleviated, unchained, and comfortable with exchanging honest energy with others.

The *e* in *equality* represents the energy exchanged or transferred among matter. Energy is more quantitative, while quality is about safety, details, and the linguistics of equality. Working in a facility brings forth the continuance of equality in every spectrum. Employees share energy with one another the whole time they are working together. Our mass and mobility of constancy determines the energy that is symbiotically exchanged through our bodies of movement. Our generators are ignited when we have to produce work. More than likely, we can agree that we work better with people with like minds because it leads to better and more production. Our motormouths are more effective and the general mood is uplifted when everybody is on the same page as far as work production. The quality comes with our exertion of understanding how to be more effective and productive with consistent, accurate results. Quality assurance and control ensures safety, good ethics, and moral boundaries. Equality gives us limits to behavior. Past, present, and future tense equal negative, neutral, and positive conversations, respectively. A person who constantly dwells in the past instead of the present or future is meandering in negativity, which can affect relationships.

For instance, anyone who brings up their past relationships and tries to compare people to others is functioning on emotionality and is not positive at all since this is retrograding. This person's negativity gets in the way of forming healthy, progressive relationships. The mood is stagnant and more than likely subjugates to emotional abuse upon the people he or she is trying to compare others to. We can relate negativity to the depths of the ocean since it is below sea level. The inability to keep life moving is equal to negativity, a swan filled with drunkenness. We can also relate negativity to the water zodiac signs (Cancer, Scorpio, and Pisces). Neutrality is living in the here and now with possible plans for tomorrow that can be easily changed. The neutral zone does not move up or down and is caught in the middle of negativity and positivity attitudes. Doing what comes along and functioning in spontaneity is equal to neutrality. Neutrality may be expressed with the earth zodiac signs (Taurus, Virgo, and Capricorn). Positivity is expressed with the fire signs (Aries, Leo, and Sagittarius), while the air signs (Gemini, Libra, and Aquarius) are expressed futuristically. Positivity is great for the planners of the universe and those who don't plan at all, always thinking within positivity and about better outcomes to any situation. Positive moods make us feel all bubbly and are rarely associated with a dull moment. At times, positivity can be confused with an act of dumbness that allows the personality to have fun. Positivity makes for future inventions and is considered the most efficient method of conserving work energy. Positivity can also be more relative to the air signs in that the air is upward, mobile, and without limits. Positive people are often recognized as geniuses since they better future generations with their ideas. Neutrality brings the idea into action and obtains the materials to manifest that idea into structure and functionality. Negativity of the idea appeals to the wants, emotions, and feelings of the importance of the idea. Thus, since there are negative, neutral, and positive energy forms within us, there are limits beneath the sea, on walking ground, and beyond the atmosphere. Past, present, and future are nothing more than just pretending—pretending to go back in the past and pretending to plan out the future are both null in a timely sense. Time is nothing but illusion because every aspect to our lives is meant to be and happens to fulfill our greatest happiness. So when we struggle with past depression and future anxiety, we are merely forcing ourselves into our greater paths and no obstacle should be perceived as good or bad; it just is.

Pharmaceutical companies profit from the anxieties and depressions of moods. The altering of brain chemicals based upon serotonin levels, which can't be measured, and the reuptake of neurotransmitters is making patients neutral in their well-being. Mythically speaking, serotonin is not researched enough to tell if antidepressants are more of a harm or hindrance to chemical imbalances. Most research has found that most antidepressants make patients more depressed and acquire thoughts of suicide. In my own experience of taking antidepressants, I was left frazzled with too much frantic energy in my system. Gradually coming down from the pills, I would feel more depressed and horrible for not being active. Anxiety medications, on the other hand, slow the response of stimuli by affecting breathing patterns with drowsiness. After the drowsiness, there definitely comes neutrality and the notion of not having a care in the world with somberness and more focus. These medicines attempt to put people in the neutral zone. Antidepressants require more time to cause an alternating effect on the mood changes versus antianxiety pills, which generally take less than one hour to generate results; and this is why they are so highly addictive. Combining pain medicine such as Norco and antianxiety medicine such as Xanax can be deadly, but it is consistently dependent on neutrality. Antidepressants are dependent on changing the mood to positivity, but too much dependence on positivity can recur into a depressive status from an overreactive chemical imbalance. Most people who are diagnosed with depression or anxiety do not even need prescription medication. A lot just need counseling, sunlight, a proper diet for conservative energy, and exercise to be at equanimity. Replacing chemicals with emotional, physical, and mental stability is fundamental to how people depend so much on being balanced and steady in moods, attitude, and images of how things are supposedly to be, instead of how they already are. A change outside of the body is what is really needed.

Everyone functions on energy, whether it is positive, neutral, or negative, and we feel how we want to feel not according to obstacles or circumstances. Energy is what we want, and energy is what we get. Our powerhouse generates energy daily through the food we ingest, the toxins we take in, the surrounding of our environments, and the maps we have planned. The quality of our energy is up to us to switch it to a charge that we are satisfied with. We can exchange this energy through the food we eat, amount of rest we get, companions we keep, and the exhaust of toxic energy through exercising or excretion of wasteful complex products. Our quality of life is determined by those four simple things—rest, food, companionship, and defense mechanisms—and that is how we remain equal in an atmosphere full of energetic trafficking.

CHAPTER 51

Liberty

If I were to personify liberty, it would look like a woman. It would be a lady of any color whom is not afraid to express herself fully in everything she does. Even though the world will try to quiet her, she would be bold in her physique, emotionality, spirituality, and intellect. She cringes on not being able to express herself to others. She hates it when her partner conveys that she is too much into her feelings, denying her femininity. In her mind and in her past, she can recall a memoir distant and simple when there was only the feminine energy that ruled. Back then she did whatever she pleased without any guilt or resentment. Everything was so simple then, when love was kind and never questioned. Yes, she still has the same thoughts of being the destined queen who would marry her king in an instant without even physically knowing him. Now she is seen as outlandish, out of control, and with too much attitude by the naysayers who just want to use her for what she has accomplished. Ms. Liberty is covered and blindly to the truths that bestow her and she is shut down when she wants to establish something meaningful and lasting from a potential partner and husband.

As soon as she is shot down by an idiotic response of failure, she is disappointed because once again she thought that she could settle with her happily forever. The reasons set her apart from most of the congenial males in that she will always believe in love for the people, even those with abused systems, whom she still treats with the newness of company, as something different hoping for versatility. The unconditional of love is so easy for Ms. Liberty to grasp. It is no wonder that some males are gay and transsexuals considering the freedom of being liberalized. Everybody is trying to get to Ms. Liberty status. She is carefree to join happiness alone. Her spirituality yearns for oneness and completion to provide for the people, but in dire circumstances she stands alone for reasons to shut out the destruction of mankind with her back facing the sea instead of to the cities.

At the WinStar World Casino and Resort, different areas are designed to resemble different cities. The place is so lit with mood lighting and noises from the slots that you can be mesmerized by the sculptures, art, and scenery that is on display. Their feature cities include Beijing, Vienna, Paris, Madrid, London, and New York City. The last time I visited, I stopped and played casino games in all of these cities except for one, New York. In the back of my brain, I promised myself that I would play a game there the next time I went, especially since

I was beginning to write this chapter, "Liberty." One of the tallest statues in the world is the Statue of Liberty, and how could I possibly forget to set out my fortune there. The Statue of Liberty was sort of a confusing work of art to me when I was learning about it as a kid. I never could understand the allegorical meaning of the statue and why it was so important for the French to give it to the United States. From her lighted torch in her raised right hand to the book cradled in her left, the statue was a mystery to me, and I could never understand why her robe was so long even though I knew she was in the category of justice.

I also could not comprehend why the lady wore a crown on her head with her hair braided and tied back. She is still a mystery to me, and that is probably one of the reasons I surpassed New York on my visit to WinStar. It is not a very easy puzzle to solve, but it was still in the back of my mind to visit.

Liberty or death is the outcome of most of our daily struggles. When we die, we get a rewind flashback of the past and the things, people, and places that could have prevented us from passing away, much like a forewarned dream. That's how some souls stay trapped in a realm—they can't recognize their passing from living. They may have thought that they were saved from rapture and proceeded on with life, but in reality they are stuck between worlds, still unmovable corpses. The dependence of a hard life is still there and is unforgettable even when we are dead. An easy life makes fewer stops and observances when we are in flashback mode, which makes us pass along more gracefully.

Formulation and contemplation were within the consideration of joining a woman and man. The softness, fertility, and creation of the land was mocked by woman. It was not until the earth was shaped into hardness baring wholesomeness that man was mocked. All things have opposites, and it is the making of female and male genders that conjoins a centripetal force of circulation. Men are definitely here to protect women from harmful savagery. Women must be saved because everything begins and ends with them. Having liberty is being able to just do anything one pleases, like quitting a job whenever one sees fit, leaving a relationship, and ending anything that is displeasing to the psyche. Being happy alone and a bit of a risk taker is the personality of Liberty. Giving everything up to God with no hesitation is liberal nonconformism that allows us to be comfortable. Being comfortable in one's skin takes a distant formula of being by oneself without interruptions of dualistic relationships and feelings of lessening proportions of admiration from another. Liberty is alone, and even though she may be lonely, she waits for perfection and adheres to justification with patience. Working for justice for all is the crux of Liberty's function, and she is saddened when justice is not served under a malfunctioning system. Liberty knows that when justice is taken into unjust hands, it sets off an unsung tone that is corrupt without a liberty bell. To keep court systems in business is to have just bail for criminal and civil victims with ultimate suspects. Her duty is to protect the innocent and to ensure that the court of law is fair to the accused. Liability in maintaining a system that is stable and reliable for the people is required without libel damages to Liberty. When we hear that justice is not served in these days, we are discrediting every system, including banking institutions and even the anatomy itself. Justice is what's needed today to calm the earth and bring peace to the unrest, and it begins with the tears shed through Liberty.

Liberty is often conflicted with separating truth from fiction and feeling from knowing.

Stating how we feel in the judicial court systems is irrelevant to serving a just order. Liberalism bases its issues on how aspects make people feel, and thus, action is taken on informative knowledge. For example, a murder may make one feel discernment toward a suspect, but sometimes in unfortunate circumstances evidence will have to be recollected on evidence of knowledge and what sees fit with state and city court laws. Thus, defense these days is based more upon fear and the prosecution has to redundantly protect the values, standards, and morals of the people from people that abuse power and/or authority. The tricky part of the judicial system is having jurors to be the judge of sentencing and foremost this stage is where the unfairness can occur out of code of law and saddened feelings toward the innocent or rather the accused.

CHAPTER 52

Justice

All in life is fair. Life is so much easier to understand when we come to terms with the fact that every single thing happens for a reason.. Our situations are so equal that forces beyond our perceptions are working for us and are only against us when we break from some type of moral law or when we are with company that is corruptive and needs to be halted for our better good. Everything is coded into a sequence of events that affects our karmic lives in a time span of past, present, and future tenses. Lessons have to be learned no matter how stubborn, stagnant, or set in our ways we are. We are so coded that we are fixed to undergo circumstances that will fulfill us to our ultimate, destined satisfaction. Justice prevails in so many avenues, streets, boulevards, roads, lanes, and courts that our travels have to be nonstop even past expiration.

All throughout my life, I have experienced what some would call freakish incidents, from visions that came true to so-called dreams, manifestations, and manipulations of cosmic intelligence. And most likely there are other individuals who have had the same experiences. Any wrongdoing I have experienced from another has been reciprocated on my behalf by their serving time or taking a reduction in pay from their occupations. Justice is an order of keeping the peace even in confrontations beyond our control. Some things just require a nonresponse. When justice is served rightfully, it upholds the natural law of stability within court systems. Since we are to value human life above all other forms of life, it is beneficial to allow authorities to limit immoral human behavior through justifiable law making. We as humans are dependent upon laws that employ police officers, court judges, senators, and our presidents. Politicians are the keepers of what is polite and in assisting the people of the nation concerning doubts of the illegitimate environment that we habitat. Sustaining human life and keeping individuals free from financial, economical, and bodily harm are some of the reasons we value human lives over any other species, as well as the capability to set up judicial systems. There are often times when the law is questioned and believed to be without ethics and morals based upon how state and city laws are written in code books. The strategic breakdown of code laws is of benefit for victims and suspects. A just law adheres to the initial written laws, which stabilizes judicial systems even when we feel that they are unjust.

Sweet justice comes after a wrongdoing on our part or that of another person, and regardless of what the issue is, it's an opportunity during our lifetime. Wrongdoings are practically our saviors, and we perfect ourselves by learning not to repeat those actions. It is growing and aligning to be graceful and godlike for anything else is beneath us. It is practice that leads to perfection, whether that be in law, medicine, a professional field, or occupational.

An occupation in which we may be disciplined often is a reminder to either get better at tasks or to abandon them altogether for something more fulfilling and pleasing to us. Most of the time, there has to be a change in the status quo to keep us moving optimistically. A change in occupation is one form of revelation because most of our time is spent where we work. The time and distance have to correlate with each other, and both may have to catch up with each other to create a velocity that is in correspondence to our time-traveling system. If our time clocks are not parallel to our distance of destiny, then justice will prevail in some type of karmic way to move us forward. It can impact our health, family, and anything that we value most to wake us up to the realization of being destined. Justice has a funny, outlandish way of getting what is due and serving it in a time capsule of waves. Fortunately, it is an easier path when we allow the changes to overcome us with sheer joy no matter what. But being human sometimes just does not allow us to be content in changing circumstances because of comfort or familiarity. In any way, what is familiar now will not be familiar in the future, when a change in attitude meets scholarly aptitude.

If you ever wonder why the people who are labeled "crazy" seem to smile a lot, it is because they know justice. They know justice prevails all the time when they smile at life. It seems to be that all things are in our favor when we are genuine with our smiles and hysterical laughs, knowing that everything is going to be all right—all right in a sense of justification and re-luctance to endure confinement, taunts, discrimination, bullying, and gossiping from others while keeping to ourselves about the matters at hand. Some things are better left unsaid with surprise to watch perseverance and patience pay for our toll of perceptible, false wrongdoing from others. It is best when we are quiet and speak in silence just to observe a resolution of the minds. Yes, silence does speak louder than words, and we can listen to the forthcoming service of higher intelligence guiding us to blissful journey full of destinations that can't be ignored.

We can bear anything that comes our way because we are destined to go our own way before birth and after death. All of us are just renewals of souls, light, stars, beings, dust, planets, energy, and universe; everything and our decisions and choices are calculated from 0 to 1 in a timely fashion in order of events. So we might as well enjoy this journey and get used to the downfalls, shortcomings, depressions, and anxieties with a sunny delight and be prepared for our great works to be had and done for a presentation of light work. We may fight battles, but the war we fight is with the self.

Justice is a league of its own and will only be confronted with just you, alone in contem-plation of escape routes and begging to leave what was once known behind, never forgetting the experiences that linger like a catapult of crime. Just our perpetuating false identities time after time to get to the trueness of isolation binds the image of kind relativeness. Kindness and peacefulness are readily found in loneliness in agreeable whereabouts. The good news is not found in gossiping and in the talk of others, but rather within the self and foreseeing the self as godlike. Keeping conversations focused on the self allows the free flow of energy to come from within, which is an altruistic way of showing empathy. Being empathetic to others when we know that we can't solve situations by just talking alone transfers symbiotic energy on a relatable topic of discussion about a person or group. Sharing options that are available to us does a lot more good than just gossiping about them.

Feeling justified has little to do with independence. Justification is the personification of being heard and the ability to set out agendas that were originally planned in calendar days. A person who feels independent can still deal with the unjust conditions of a workplace by constantly being watched and consistently being told what to do and how to do routinely work tasks over and over again. A bunch of us are stuck in a matrix of events that are not necessarily good or malevolent. We often ask, "Is there more to life?" Or more than likely, we wonder how we can improve our situations, especially financially, to the point that we can be comfortable and still enjoy as many vacations as we want with family and friends. We want to go out to eat or buy healthy food for our households, rest accordingly without worrying, and still be able to save a chunk of money and build liquid assets. Instead, the lot of us is in a constant state of worry figuring out how to pay bills, stressing over daily events at the workplace, and sometimes wondering when our next meal will be. There comes a point when people become sick and exhausted of not being able to change their situations under miraculous opportunities that pass us up almost every day. Justice is served when we work for just us, making our mark in life by being servants to the lord of the lands by once again, creating. We must create what is new inside of us so that we do not get repetitively trapped in a matrix filled with people who are just numbers and sequences. Creating the new, whether through research, writing, music, art, or anything that is grasped from the consciousness, forms a union with just you and higher intelligence. You as an individual combined with higher intelligence brings forth what the world really needs to sense hereafter in modern generations. Everything else is simply history, and while there may be better ways of performing a task, there is only one way of perfecting a masterpiece of our own.

Now, the justice system does a fair job of protecting citizens according to lawmakers. We rarely stress over safety compared to those in other countries, and most children born to poor or working-class parents receive food stamps, and governmental assistive services. Public housing is granted to low-income families. The water is pretty clean in most areas. So why complain about things that we feel we cannot fix if they are already politely taken care of through politicians and policy makers? The truth is that we really do not know what types of chemicals and hazardous substances are in the food we eat. We really do not know much about the quality of the air or whether or not global warming is a culprit for most cancers, illnesses, and diseases. Unfortunately, we really do not know how safe we are until our safety is threatened. What we do know is that there has been a leniency of hate versus love compared to what we see and hear broadcasted over the airwaves. We are told to not even look at television because it's not real and we can't believe everything we see and hear, so we have to think for ourselves and speculate on whether there is some hidden agenda of false information.

Nevertheless, I have been working at customer service jobs ever since I was fifteen years old, and every last one of them has been challenging. It is not so much the job at hand, but I could never form a great relationship with higher management like other employees could. When I go to work, I like to simply work and be able to do things based on my integrity. I'm always moving at a fast speed because I don't want to be depicted as a slacker, and I have always been militaristic regarding my work ethic. Now, being that I have Saturn (Capricorn) in my sixth house, routine things are always hard for me. My sixth house is shared with Jupiter (Sagittarius), and routine things have to be fun and adventurous for me while working. Even the simplest repetitive chore is hard for me because it's expected and easy. I just want to get it over with quickly. Since I can be quiet at the workplace, I hardly do any joking or clowning around. I'm at work, for Pete's sake, but when I don't join the constant chatter of work employees and management, I'm seen as the bad person, reclusive, or someone who is up to something, like stealing. I guess I fit the description of a criminal, which can be so hard for me to bear because I'm not that way—nor am I a person who is going to try to prove my innocence by brownnosing. There is a reason for the Capricorn placement in my chart, and it keeps on nagging at me in my work sector. It's as if the devil has to clean up the dirty work to put forth God's work through pain, agony, and hardship. My sensitivity constantly reminds me that I have to work for myself, or else I am just going to keep on repeating the same situations at different corporations. I'm not saying that corporations are bad for anybody else, but they are hard for me simply based upon my natal chart. I can't fix it; all I can do is change it to my liking so that a job will not affect my health. Since I have become acquainted with a split rising ascendant of Cancer/Leo, I have been more outspoken with the people I work with and even entertaining for them through Leo, and it seems as if coworkers and customers like for me to exude that quality. Cancer rising is so sensitive, though, and feels for something more. My Sagittarius moon is always asking questions beyond astrological means, such as, *What is the true, real meaning to living?* At periods, I have felt no growth, and there is no use in feeling that way and to tolerate being used and accused simply because of not fitting in. My creations lie in the tenth house of Taurus, if we were to refer to the Leo rising cusp, and through the slow but steady Taurus I will find a more artistic, creative career that uses my talents and benefits my well-being. Cancer rising makes my tenth house, Aries, explain my philosophical and political stance on issues.

Profoundly, there is more than one side to our personalities. The first one is presented in front of everyone almost every day. It is rarely hidden from view and is often displayed in our daily occupations and in our homes. Then there is for sure a second side of us that is often hidden from the world. This part is the superhero or sometimes the villain that is waiting to be unleashed from our psyches. Our stamp of approval is the secret gift that we possess, ready to be exposed and demonstrated to other individuals who are interested. The best from us can be released at night when darkness overshadows talents and forsakes the worthiness of creativeness. Getting in touch with our action-pack talent requires the leap of faith that leads to prosperity. Limits are not confined to the sky when we soar beyond the abnormalities. Beneath and beyond normalcy is justice unveiled through nonjudgmental gestures of Calvary, which serves communications that are connected to the Almighty. Most of the independents who are without shelter and who struggle for daily meals are not in a codependence of work-related stresses. An abundance of their dependence goes to a higher realm of praise even in dire situations among them. Learning to live without is independence from government and entitled folks, for rich people still have to pay taxes and insurance on properties, land, assets, luxuries, and entertainments, so they are still dependent on a system of trade and interest. Both ends are smart enough to live a life free from constraints, but which one is practicing the politics and revolution that this nation was founded on? Nonconforming behavior, no taxation without representation, and "give me liberty or give me death" are all traits of a law-abiding homeless person. Justice is served on this very soil for people who can live on almost nothing rather than living on anything. Justice is karma. Karma follows us all throughout our years of being reborn, reincarnated, and expired. We cannot stray away from it, even when we have déjà vu moments to help us correct some aspects of karma. Karma is only between you and God, the judge and the juror. Everything that we see with our eyes is just perception, tricking us into thinking that the judgments from people, surrounding us, are of importance. The only truth resides in the self, and that is through communication with God. Only you and God make the final decisions on good judgment, done by trial and error according to the intentions that are planned by your perception of places, people, and things. All that matters is the meetings between us and the Almighty because all pursuant reality in time is just a facade that sets us up as tests of faith. So we are judged by character and how we treat others, that which we do to ourselves. Justice serves peace when we realize that all the world, universe, and entirety are just made up of you and me. Then at the end, when we give up our chosen vessels of bodies, we return to the Almighty once again to do all the things in past tense all over again to make our present. We may be in different time eras and lands, but the lessons we learn from one another are the same, perfecting destiny just the way it has always been. Obeying moral laws in the absence of judging others while we trot on top of land is our ultimate test of true happiness.

On July 4, 2016, I decided to change my social media status from single to married. An urge of consecration to be married to Yahweh needed a ceremony with me. This standard has made me more at ease in that I no longer have to please a companion physically, mentally, spiritually, and emotionally. The conveyance of marriage to Yahweh has opened up stable energy to my present situations. I will no longer be guided by misconceptions of thinking that I am loved by someone when I know that I am loved by Yahweh. This is no idolatry in worship but a completion in being free and independent of controlling my own physical, spiritual, and mental acceptance of being loved. I am deserving of love because I am love and I came from love. It is only wise to settle with the best and revel in the many gifts that have yet to come by being intimate with God. That is how much I love myself; I am in control of choosing an ultimate partner to share myself with. Giving the self the power of Yahweh frees the chains and shackles of codependency that I wish to never be a part of. No longer will I be abused, used, and misused through partnerships and sexual encounters. I am my own when justice steps in to define a marriage of righteousness. I come to the completion of being, having, thinking, feeling, willing, analyzing, balancing, wanting, perceiving, tolerating, knowing, and believing in Yahweh. All the trials and testimonies have led me to not settle for less in that I am a believer that anything and everything is possible through a marriage that justifies me and never leaves me lonely. Justice is served from trial and error. With this in mind, we gain a beautiful body that is respected, loved, and cared for through pure appreciation upon consecration and an everlasting relationship built on concrete understanding.

ABOUT THE AUTHOR

V. N. Lewis combines basic knowledge from biology, anthropology, and sociology into an interdisciplinary studies format to grasp the meaning of organizational manifestation in pro-Christian circumstances. The author earned a master's degree in public administration. She currently lives in Fort Worth, Texas.